ITINERARY 15

PORTS OF THE FAR EAST WITH INDONESIA

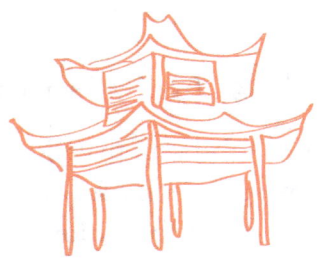

SHERRY HUTT

Copyright © 2021 by Sherry Hutt

All rights reserved. No part of this book may be reproduced or transmitted in any form or by any means, electronic or mechanical, including photocopying, recording, or by any information storage and retrieval system without the written permission of the author, except where permitted by law.

Bound: ISBN: 978-1-942153-24-5

Epub: ISBN: 978-1-942153-25-2

TABLE OF CONTENTS

Preface 5
Acknowledgements 9
Introduction - Travel the Blend of History in the Far East 11
Map of Itinerary XV – Ports of the Far East,
including Indonesia 14
Timeline 15
Russia – Petropavlovsk - Vitus Bering in the Arctic 17

Japan
    Edo-Tokyo: Capital of Emperors 31
    Culture as Art in Japan 45
    Shogun, Samurai and Ninja 67
    Hiroshima & Nagasaki – The Bomb and Modern Japan 85
    Kabuki, Noh, Doll and Comedy Theater 97
    Aomori - Ancient Jomon 111
    Hakodate – Battle for the Empire 125
    Yokohama Meets Commodore Perry 133

Korea - Jeju and Busan - Ancient Ways and
Modern Adaptations 143

China
    Blended History China-Korea-Japan 157
    Beijing - Forbidden and Inviting City 179
    Shanghai - Home of Old and New China 199
    Hong Kong - High Rises and Street Markets 219

TAIWAN – CROSS CURRENTS OF CULTURE 235
PHILIPPINES
    Steel Butterfly and Sainted Madonna 251
    Manila Galleons to Modern Tigress 267
BRUNEI – SULTANS OF BRUNEI AND RAJAH OF SARAWAK 285
INDONESIA
    Java Ancient and Modern 297
    Bali – Rose of the Winds 313
    Going to Battle with Dragons in Komodo 329
    Creating Unity out of Diversity in Indonesia 337
INDEX 351

PREFACE

Cruise through History is a collection of short stories grouped by the sequence of popular cruise itineraries, rather than by country, or period of history. As stories move from port to port, they randomly move through time. Stories are all true. They introduce the traveler to history and culture of a port through a long-ago, or not so long-ago, resident, whose exploits left a castle, palace, or lovely site to explore on a cruise shore excursion.

The host character for each port is chosen for inspiring actions and visible sites today. Some names are familiar, presented with depth to their personality. Other characters will be new friends, too long unrecognized. Stories offer a twist to school-age history of place, putting travels in fascinating context for the short-term visitor. Travel is an opportunity for events of one's life to give rich meaning to stories of fact for which fiction is no rival.

No apology is made for the choice of subjects. They were chosen arbitrarily, on whim of the author, accumulated from past travels, for your enjoyment. Readers share the fun. No attempt is made for political correctness or a chamber of commerce gloss to stories.

Knowledge of history teaches us a great deal about ourselves and the human condition, but only if it is honest and fairly told. The quest for "real" draws adults to travel often.

Praise is due to historians and scholars who delve into source data to ponder minute details of history. Such information is mined here, with attribution, for lively details. History is a public good. The more it is enjoyed, the more it is valued.

Apology is due to those who hoped to foster disciplined scholarship in the author. This is reading for an out-of-the classroom experience. Footnotes give due credit to scholars and remind the reader that stories are true. Presence of source notes is not to feign an academic appearance. Editorial sidebars and fun bits are in footnotes.

When there are gaps in facts, or mysteries remain, they are not supplemented by fiction. Rather, stories relate the known as a guide to the unknown. Readers draw their own conclusions, daydream through gaps, and enjoy the reason so much popular fiction and movies are drawn from historical facts.

Stories are offered to give historical context to sites visited as cruise destinations. In these stories, meet characters who walked the same streets in the past, that visitors walk today. Go beyond castle ruins to envision people who built them and lived there.

Stories in Cruise through History itineraries inspire cruise travelers to rise out of deck chairs to investigate a destination with honesty and irreverence, or the potential traveler to rise from the sofa and embark on a Cruise through History. There is no stigma of a school assignment. Earn an "E" for enjoyment.

Itineraries in the Cruise through History series available and forthcoming:

1. **London to Rome - 2014**
2. **Rome to Venice – 2014**
3. **Ports of the Eastern Mediterranean - 2019**
4. **Ports of the Black Sea - 2019**
5. **Ports of Arabia to the Atlantic, across the Southern Mediterranean - 2021**
6. Ports of the Atlantic Coast of North America, with Cuba and Bermuda – coming 2021
7. Ports of the Pacific Coast of North America, with Hawaii – coming 2021
8. **Mexico, Central America, and the Caribbean Islands – 2015**
9. **Ports of South America –2017**
10. **Ports of the British Isles - 2020**
11. **Ports of the Baltic Sea – 2018**
12. **Ports of the North Sea - 2020**

13. Ports of Africa, India and Southeast Asia – coming 2021

14. **Ports of the South Pacific - Australia, New Zealand, and Polynesia – 2020**

15. **Ports of the Far East, with Indonesia – 2021**

    Cruise through History – Shakespeare as Travel Writer – coming 2021

Find all the story books at cruisethroughhistory.com.

Author with Friendly Samurai

ACKNOWLEDGEMENTS

Writing travel stories began as therapy from the world of Washington, D.C. Thanks are due to the Summer Citizens program at Utah State University, Logan, and to the several cruise lines, book clubs and community associations that have given me opportunities to share stories with their guests and students.

Much appreciated are those who help produce the series, including Digby and Rose, publisher, art director, and publicist. Diana Verkamp created the CTH logo. Elizabeth Herrgott at Feast Studios creates CTH videos featuring CTH stories.

These stories would not be possible without the treasure trove of material in libraries and used bookshops. I am indebted to the Battery Park Book Exchange, Asheville NC, the Lanier Library, Tryon, NC, and the Library of Congress. In this increasingly paperless world, bookstores and libraries provide solace and an opportunity to revive our humanity.

Much appreciation is due to those who apply their skill to preservation and protection of heritage resources in the United States and around the world. Greatest thanks go to my husband, Guy Rouse, who has lugged my camera equipment all over the world for over thirty years. So many good times, so many photos, have all become the fabric of memory and inspiration for stories.

All photos and art are property of Cruise through History, unless otherwise noted, and all rights are reserved. No use may be made of the photos, art and text, the construction of history in stories, without prior permission of the author.

INTRODUCTION

Travel the Blend of History in the Far East

Enter Itinerary XV in Cruise through History at the northern divide of east and west at the Bering Strait and sail south through the Far East to the Wallace Line, dividing Asia from the South Pacific at the eastern edge of Indonesia. Along port stops meet cultures known to each other through trade for thousands of years, yet thought exotic to westerners until the mid-nineteenth century. Meet real kings, queens, emperors, rajah and presidents, building nations ancient and modern, and mythical Righteous Princes and Queens of the Southern Ocean. In this Itinerary Dragons are real and endangered.

Begin the Itinerary in the developing cruise port of Petropavlovsk, made possible by a Dane, Vitus Bering, at the insistence of Peter the Great. A museum and monument to contributions of a foreigner are small in this Russian outpost. Bering's story is a chilling tribute to his skill, when he gave his life to map the northern reach of the world.

In Japan, history is a celebration of culture expressed in art forms of haiku, raiku, bonsai and ikebana, evoking Zen balance in the Wabi Sabi of life. Enter Japanese theater in Kabuki, Noh and Doll theater. Visit Tokyo, begun as Edo by Shogun, Samurai and Ninja, until an emperor reasserted authority and built a modern nation. Visit the stunning site of ancient Jomon people in Aomori; cherry blossom covered grounds of historic castles; the fort of the last Shogun in Hakodate; the last Samurai; and the opening of Japan to the world in Yokohama, at the insistence of Commodore Perry. In Hiroshima and Nagasaki view the Bomb and Modern Japan from the perspective of Japanese people today.

Korea, caught through history between China and Japan, built its own culture from Ancient Ways to Modern Adaptations. In Busan and Jeju visit a modern tiger economy and an island preserve of natural vegetation and people with a comic sense of humor. Dive deep into history and culture with mermaids of Jeju.

In China discover the root of blended history of Asia, in the beginnings of writing, currency, drama and art. Visit Beijing, the Forbidden and Inviting City and Shanghai, the Home of Old and New China. View the recent history of Hong Kong from rocks on a beach to High Rises and Street Markets.

Taiwan sits at the Cross Currents of Culture. Geography placed indigenous cultures, varied and independent, under rule by the Dutch, Japan, China and the exiled Republic of China. The story in Taiwan is a continuing search for identity in a tumultuous history.

In the Philippines learn of two wars known to Filipinos and not taught in the United States. Enjoy travails of election battles of two female presidents, the Steel Butterfly and the Sainted Madonna. Sail on Manila Galleons to Acapulco, beginning trade connections between old and new world, upon which a Modern Tigress economy is built.

Brunei's story begins with a rogue adventurer, muse for Joseph Conrad's *Lord Jim*. The little-known British Rajah of Sarawak fought headhunters of Borneo. In Brunei today, the wealthiest monarch in the world enjoys the small domain that fended off giant nations.

This Itinerary moves due south to include eastern islands of Indonesia in Java, Bali and Komodo. Java, Ancient and Modern is central to the story of Indonesia, with its wealth of ancient temples to ancestors, large Buddhist temples, cities built by Dutch in the colonial era and a modern powerhouse economy. In Bali, Balinese Aga maintain their compass Rose of the Winds in a sea of Islam and ancient rice cultivation, amid artist colonies and beach resorts thick with tourists. The Indonesian government battles to preserve Dragons in Komodo as it seeks to Create Unity out of Diversity in Indonesia.

As in all Itineraries in Cruise through History, stories enhance enjoyment of places visited on port stops through the perspective of locals. The travel experience begins and ends with meeting new characters without bias or judgment. Read, enjoy and learn from travel!

CTH

14 | Cruise Through History – Itinerary XV Ports of the Far East, with Indonesia

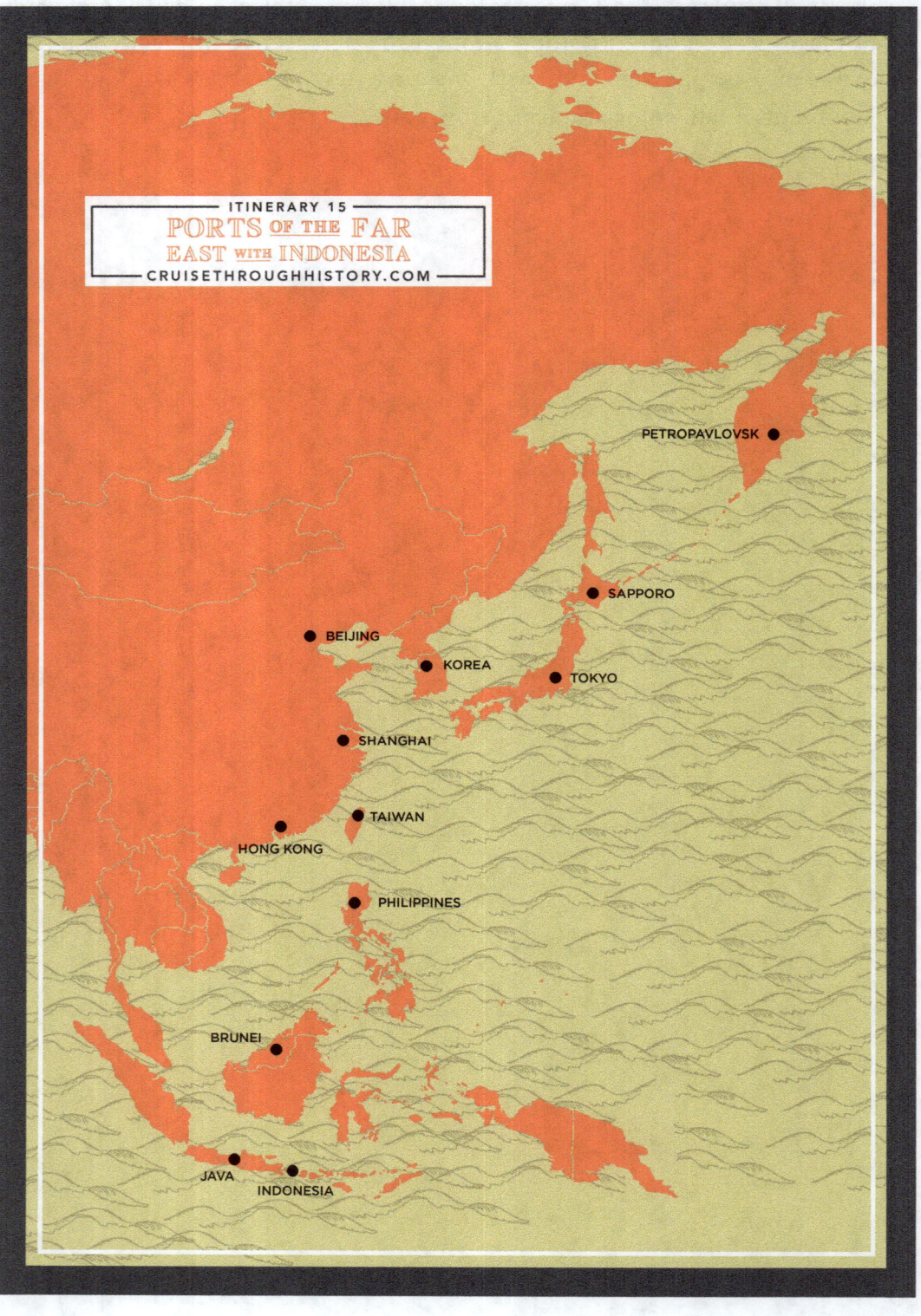

Cruise Through History
ITINERARY XV
Timeline | cruisethroughhistory.com

Ancient Era

Aomori Jomon
Java Ancient

Early Trade Era

Culture Japan
Theater Japan
Blend China
Beijing
Manila Galleons
Bali Rose

Colonial Era
17th to 19th Century

Petropavlovsk
Edo-Tokyo
Shogun Samurai
Hakodate Battle
Yokohama & Perry
Hong Kong
Taiwan
Sultan Brunei

Recent History
20th c

Hiroshima & Nagasaki
Jeju & Busan
Shanghai
Butterfly & Madonna
Komodo Dragons
Unity Indonesia

Bering Museum Petropavlovsk

Monument to Bering in Petropavlovsk

Bering's Ship St. Peter

At the insistence of Empress Anna, Bering had Russian subordinate officers, who held control over navigational decisions. Sea councils, a committee of officers, voted on the route, as it went along, causing delay in reaching land in Alaska and on return causing a stop on Bering Island, the final resting place of Bering and the *St. Peter*.

Sailing with Bering was his physician and ship's naturalist, German theology student, Georg Wilhelm Steller. Steller's diary, published after his death at age thirty-seven in 1746, casts him as a petulant academic, who felt unappreciated by veteran seamen. Steller shared Bering's cabin, yet the two rarely spoke. Though initially critical of Bering, the naturalist appreciated Bering's navigational skills.

Bering charted a route enabling arrival of *St. Peter* in Avacha ahead of the *St. Paul*. His decisions were countermanded by the Sea Council, to a fatal result. The crew enjoyed holding power over their captain, the Dane, who considered himself a Russian noble. Steller was the target of their jokes, when he wanted time on shore to collect specimen.

When it was clear to all that the Sea Council made poor decisions, prolonging the voyage and subjecting the crew to illness, including dreaded scurvy, Steller was the voyage savior. Acerbic plants, collected by Steller and fed to the crew, cured them of scurvy. He became the chief cook of nutritious meals. The Steller sea cow, a sea mammal, caught to feed the crew, and Stellar jay, spotted in North America, were named for him.

Petropavlovsk to Alaska 250 Years

On the outbound sailing, Bering took the *St. Peter* south of the Aleutians and east to the Gulf of Alaska. He turned north to Kayak Island, where Russians made the first landing of Europeans on Alaskan turf, on July 20, 1741. A few days prior, rains stopped and clouds cleared, bringing St. Elias mountain range in view. The scenery was breathtaking.

Steller wanted to find natives, who left campfires still warm when they absconded upon arrival of the Russian ship. Bering was anxious to fill water barrels and head home. The Sea Council voted to follow the Aleutian coast westward. Storms, avoided in the open sea, pounded the vessel and made the crew regret their decision.

Part of Bering lore is that he shipwrecked on the island named for him and died of scurvy. Actually, the Sea Council voted to land, erroneously thinking they were on Kamchatka. Bering calculated the ship was not near the mainland. Charting new territory in open sea was a skill Bering sharpened over his career. He was correct. If the ship continued west a few more days, port was ahead. Bering was outvoted.

The *St. Peter* crashed on approach to land. Storms pushed the ship inland, where it was covered by sand by October 1741. At the time, Chirikov on *St. Paul* reached home port.

Bering did not die of scurvy. Steller cured Bering of scurvy, as he did many of the crew. Bering died of heart failure, on December 8, 1741. At age sixty, having weathered many days at sea, Bering was not a fit outdoorsman, living without shelter on a beach. He died, half buried in sand, attempting to keep warm. Many of the crew died slowly and painfully.

In spring 1742, Steller roused surviving crew to build a small ship from remnants of the *St. Peter*. Survivors arrived in Avacha on August 25, 1742. Anna was no longer empress. Ruler of Russia was Elizabeth, Peter's daughter. She had no interest in foreign captains.

Success of Bering was cast into shadows. His log was edited and published by Russians. Sea Council improvident decisions were attributed to Bering. Russia published maps of the expedition, keeping presence of fur seals in Alaska a state secret. A monopoly in fur trade was lucrative for the Russian treasury. That is another story, in another itinerary, in Alaska's Russian history.

Post-Script to Bering in the Twenty-First Century Across the Pacific Arctic

Arctic Passage was a priority for Russia at the beginning of the twentieth century. Russia was at war with Japan in 1905. In the Battle of Tsushima Strait, every Russian ship in the engagement was lost. The Trans-Siberian

Railway proved an insufficient means to send troops and supplies to the western frontier. For the next eighty-six years, until dissolution of the Soviet Union, there was a focus upon northern transit of the Arctic to the Pacific.

The last Russian monarch, Nicholas II, capitalized on advances in ice-breaker technology on two ships sailing from Murmansk in 1909, which reached the Bering Strait in 1910. The feat was repeated in 1914, leaving from the Pechora River Delta into the Kara Sea and arriving in the Pacific in 1914. The route was not sufficiently reliable for regular use.

Stalin made mastery of a Northeast Passage a priority. In 1932, he created the Central Administration of a North Sea Route. That year, the first single season voyage for any vessel, from any country, was the Soviet icebreaker Sibirakov. The following year the super-ship *Chelyuskin*, captained by Vlad Voronin, tried to repeat the feat. The ship anticipated a light ice year and was surprised by a sudden onset of ice at the Barents Sea. Trapped in ice, the ship floated to the Bering Strait. The current dragged the ship back north, where it sunk. Captain Voronin planned ahead. All crew and officers evacuated successfully. They were sufficiently provisioned until all were rescued by plane.

During the Soviet Era, sailors mastered a route of ten days from Murmansk to the Bering Strait, sometimes two or three times in a single season, over several years. Weather along the passage was always difficult to gauge. The voyage never became routine.

In 2010, China sent four ships across a northern route to the Bering Strait. Two years later, Chinese vessels, avoiding a route through the turbulent Suez Canal, employed the route. In one year, forty-six ships traversed the Northeast Passage.

Small luxury cruise ships, of an expedition class, competed with Spartan icebreakers for guest travel in 2016. Staterooms are pricy as the season is limited. Travel across the Pacific Arctic affords guests amazing views and unique bragging rights.

Petropavlovsk Kamchatka Today

Visitor Center Petropavlovsk

Today cruise ships port at Petropavlovsk on the Kamchatka peninsula, typically on cruise itineraries leaving Japan, or Vancouver, and transiting the Pacific Ocean. The port has increased attractions for cruise guests, with a craft booth village, built of logs, in the architecture of early Orthodox Russia. Land tours offer spectacular scenery.

Bering's monument in Petropavlovsk is obscure. It is only visible when climbing beyond the street. The statue to Lenin is prominent, as expected. Petropavlovsk is a small city, with little traffic, and few tall buildings to block views of surrounding mountains.

Bering, a Dane who served Russia, still has a stigma from days of Empress Elizabeth and her distain for accomplishments of non-Russians. People of Kamchatka remember Bering fondly. The museum to his accomplishments is small, yet interesting. It tells the story of exploration during a Siberian winter. Cruise travelers are beneficiaries of efforts of Bering, Cook and Vancouver, who made the north Pacific part of the known world.

Travelers Love Petropavlovsk

Red Lacquer Temple Entrance in Tokyo

JAPAN
Edo - Tokyo Capital of Emperors

In 700 CE, Japanese scholars compiled a definitive record of Japan, then burned all prior books. *Chronicles of Japan* begin with ancient mariners, from whom the first emperor of Japan emerged. One hundred and twenty-five emperors ruled Japan, all of one dynasty.

From the ninth to the twelfth century, emperors lived in a grand palace in Kyoto. Lulled by peace or shielded from controversies of warring lords, power ebbed from emperor to advisors, until advisors were rulers, known as shogun. Lords of powerful families jousted for control as shogun.

Ascendency of the eighty-second emperor in 1183, while a young child, coincided with a decisive battle between clans for control of Japan. Yoritomo, leader of the prevailing Minamoto clan, became the first shogun. While the emperor remained sequestered in Kyoto, Yoritomo built his power center in Kamakura, a fishing village, in the midst of family estates. For almost seven hundred years shogun ruled Japan.

The final family of shogun was the Tokugawa clan. Tokugawa era, from 1603 to 1867, is regarded as a time of peace, prosperity and enjoyment of the arts. Success of the shogunate was dependent upon isolation of the country from contact beyond its borders. Tokugawa capital, on the east coast, to catch the rising sun, protected from China and Korea, was Edo, the bay.

In 1868, an emperor of Japan rose and wrested control of the country from powerful shogun. He seized the palace, moved his imperial court from Kyoto to Edo and changed the name of the capital to Tokyo. Resurgence of the Meiji emperor as ruler is known as the Meiji Restoration. His reign was the beginning of modern Japan.

The story of Tokyo begins at its historic center, the great walled palace of the last shogun and resurgent emperor. Temples, shrines and theater of the Edo period remain as places of special reverence. Around the Imperial Palace are edifices of the new Tokyo.

Emperor Meiji recognized that Tokyo was the centerpiece of a new Japan. Design of the capital was informed by street plans of great cities of London, Paris and Berlin. The new city accommodated business and manufacturing. As a nation of cultural abundance, historic buildings were preserved and a national museum founded. Hotels, public transportation and parks were part of the plan. Emperor Meiji envisioned the world coming to Tokyo.

Edo - Capital of Tokugawa Shogunate

Tokyo Edo Castle

Goddess of Mercy at Senso-ji

The height of Tokugawa clan rule of Japan, and the height of isolation, came when Ieyasu Tokugawa was shogun in 1603. Ieyasu moved the shogunate to Edo. Edo developed as the political and cultural capital of Japan.

Ieyasu was a veteran of shogun politics and intra-clan competition. His father was murdered when Ieyasu was five. He claimed descendancy from a son of emperor Minamoto, deemed excess and demoted to noble Samurai.[1] When appointed shogun by the eighty-seventh emperor, Go-Yosei, he ruled as he might have done had his rights to the throne not been removed. Two years later he retired.

Ieyasu was not the first shogun to *retire* in a few years. His was an active retirement, ensuring control of a successor and deferring leadership in battle to a younger shogun, while directing all political decisions from the safety of a fortress. Avoiding power vacuums, when a young shogun died in battle, kept Tokugawa shogun in control for two hundred and fifty years.

To establish connections in his adopted home of Edo, Ieyasu paid his respects at Senso-ji Temple, the oldest Buddhist temple in Edo. Temple legend holds that seventh century fishermen caught the golden image of the goddess of mercy in their net and dedicated the temple as a shrine. Ieyasu astutely made the goddess protector of the Tokugawa clan[2].

Free of daily details of governance, Ieyasu focused attention on building Edo Castle. He financed construction by pressing lesser lords for contributions. Each lord gave generously, with the hope they, or their progeny, would occupy the castle. In 1616, Ieyasu died, at age seventy-three, and was entombed in a Shinto shrine in Nikko.[3] He did not see the castle burn in 1657. The rebuilt Imperial Palace greets visitors today.

Shogun Naosuke ascended in 1858, the year a United States warship sailed into Edo bay and demanded the shogun open Japan to trade, on penalty of cannon fire. He entered into the Harris Treaty, a trade agreement between

---

[1] Sons of the emperor deemed excess in the ninth century as a cost saving measure became Samurai.
[2] See the goddess statue in the garden next to Senso-ji.
[3] Take a train from Tokyo to access Nikko and climb several sections of a staircase to reach the tomb.

Japan and the United States, believing it was time to open Japan to the world. Aging samurai disagreed. Naosuke was murdered in 1860, as he entered the gate at Edo Castle, on the spot where visitors pass today.

Tokugawa in Yanaka Cemetery

Shogun continued to rule in Edo, though their glory days descended. The last shogun was Tokugawa Yoshinobu, who resigned in 1867. He is buried in Yanaka Cemetery, the resting place of fifteen Tokugawa shogun. Today an obscure path to the cemetery from the train station winds through nineteenth century, Tokugawa era, neighborhoods of wealthy Edo residents, ending in a large cemetery of classic Edo era monuments. Locals come to pay respects to founders of the city, at the end of the shogunate era.

Tokyo - Capital of Meiji Emperor

Emperor Meiji was born the year before Commodore Matthew Perry arrived in Edo bay and demanded trade rights from Japan. He was emperor of Japan at age fifteen. His preparation to rule consisted of education in classical poetry. It was assumed the shogun would run the country.

National Diet Tokyo

Outside Kyoto Palace there was widespread rebellion against the shogun, for allowing foreigners into the country. At the same time, people were displeased with feudal life. Feudalism was preserved by shogun in Japan, long after Europe entered the industrial age.

Meiji entered Edo as a victor in battle. He immediately took possession of Edo Castle, which burned in 1873, and from which he built an Imperial Palace. Meiji built initially of wood. Later buildings were built of brick. Wooden bridges were replaced with stone.

Meiji Palace was built in traditional Japanese style. Rooms were separated by rice paper screens. Floors were compressed rice straw board, imitating wood. Gentle curving roof lines had wood shingles. In later years, shingles were replaced with copper plate.

Adjacent to the Imperial Palace, neo-classical style buildings of government administration were built. The Privy Council, predecessor to a parliament, was first housed in the Imperial Household Ministry, the government inventory and property maintenance bureau. When a parliament was initiated by Emperor Meiji it was known as the National Diet. First sessions of the Diet were held for decades, in temporary space.

It took fifty years for the Diet to agree on a style for its home. At issue was whether the building should be of classic Japanese or neoclassical western design. German architect Hermann Ende submitted plans for a neoclassical building, which were refused. Ende's design for the Ministry of Justice were executed in 1895. The building is vaguely German, with a French roof and Moorish columns. When a commission for the Diet Building was awarded in 1920, Fukuzo Watanabe's winning entry was similar to the Ende design.

Akasaka Palace

On the avenue behind the palace compound is one of the prettiest settings in the city, the former Akasaka Palace. The palace was built for the crown prince in 1909. Today it is the State Guest House for visiting dignitaries. Akasaka Palace is a National Treasure of Japan.

Unfortunately, during World War II and firebombing in Tokyo, many of the large and beautiful Meiji era buildings were lost. New residences for the royal family and administrative offices were built in the west gardens. The remainder of original Edo era palace site is preserved as gardens. The palace wall and moat built by shogun remain.

When Emperor Meiji took control of Japan, a cadre of nobles drafted a 1868 Charter Oath. The Oath defined royal reign and established principles upon which modern Japan was built.[4] By 1888, the Oath was written into a constitution.

The Oath contained five points. First, the emperor established an assembly to pass recommendations to the emperor. Second, all classes of people were enfranchised to participate in the assembly. Third, people were granted freedom of movement and choice of profession and employment. Fourth, in the Shinto tradition of melding the law of nature with human endeavor, justice and fairness replaced arbitrary punishment. Finally, knowledge of world affairs was afforded Japanese. The emperor granted travel stipends and sent people to various countries to bring home accumulated wisdom of the world.

Unlike China, then in the midst of a cultural revolution, respect for the past continued in Japan. Shinto and Buddhist practice continued. Secular knowledge grew.

Emperor Meiji was popular with most of the population. He was well received in New York and London. Samurai were among those displaced. The emperor had no use for a mercenary army. Military of Japan were professional soldiers, in snappy western uniforms. Spending on military increased and pleasure palaces of nobility were private obligations.

The royal government appropriated land from feudal lords, which was given to nobles. Some traditional power-families of the shogunate became nobles. Later, in 1947, as part of post-World War II changes, family-based, hereditary peerages were abolished.[5]

Change-resistant Samurai rebelled. In the twentieth century, Samurai swords were no match for German weapons. Traditional dress was relegated to ritual ceremony. Samurai joining the new army needed a haircut. Carrying swords in Tokyo was banned.

---

[4] In 1945, after admission of defeat, Emperor Hirohito adopted the Charter Oath for rebuilding Japan.
[5] See generally, Jonathan Clements, A Brief History of Japan, Tuttle, Tokyo, 2017, p. 186.

The modern economic marvel of Japan began in the late nineteenth century. Mitsui Bank was founded in 1876. In 1870, Mitsubishi was a shipping company, which expanded into coal mining to supply its steamships. People free to relocate to cities became a fresh supply of labor. Living standards increased, including for impoverished Samurai.

Modern Tokyo

Modern Tokyo Across Palace Moat

So much of the appearance of central Tokyo today was planned under Emperor Meiji, that it is appropriate to extend his story into the modern era. Emperor Meiji saw that foreign businessmen wanted a western style luxury hotel, when conducting business in Tokyo. In 1890, the Imperial Hotel was built so close to the palace grounds that parts of the Edo era wall and moat abutted hotel property. The hotel was aptly named the Imperial Hotel. Twenty-one largely Japanese investors backed the project, including the royal household. The hotel opened in 1890. Unfortunately, during a visit by Edward, Prince of Wales, in 1922, the hotel was destroyed by fire.

A second Imperial Hotel was begun in 1923, utilizing designs of Frank Lloyd Wright. Wright designed an annex to the Imperial Hotel, replacing a section lost to fire in 1906. While working on the 1922 annex, a 6.8 level earthquake occurred, causing chimneys to crash around the architect. It did not diminish Wright's enthusiasm for Japan. His Tokyo project was so damaged, that it was later demolished. Parts of the entry hall, which could be salvaged, are incorporated into the Museum of Meiji Restoration in Nagoya. In 1970, a third Imperial Hotel opened on the site. It is seventeen stories, in keeping with the growing volume of visitors coming to Tokyo.

An investor in the first Imperial Hotel was Shibusawa Eiichi. Ten years older than Emperor Meiji, Shibusawa was born into a modest farming family. Educated at home, he reached out to scholars to complete his education. As a young man, he worked as an assistant to an aspiring shogun. He so distinguished himself in the area of finance, that he was afforded opportunities to travel and deepen knowledge of international finance.

Shibusawa[6] was one of the young talents poised to launch business ventures, until he was enlisted to the Ministry of Finance for the new Meiji government. He aided the government in designing national financial policies. Shibusawa left the government in 1873, becoming president of the First National Bank of Japan.[7] As bank president, he aided growth of Japanese institutions, such that Shibusawa is credited as the father of Japanese capitalism. In true Shinto/Buddhist fashion, he believed that good business was grounded on principles of good ethics, invoking harmony in business dealings.

As a philanthropist, Shibusawa afforded higher education to women. He died in 1931, at age ninety-one. Look for his picture on Japanese currency in 2024, as exemplary of Japanese business talent, contribution to the economy and Shinto ethics.

---

[6] Shibusawa was made a noble. Shibusawa is the family surname.
[7] Dai-ichi Kangyp Bank.

Visiting Tokyo Today

Tokyo Imperial Garden

Today the Imperial Palace, in the center of Tokyo, sits on one-half square mile of some of the most expensive real estate in the world. Meticulously maintained, the approach to the palace, across the moat, is a walk back in time, despite being in the middle of a busy traffic circle. Enter through the gate, where the shogun was struck down and meander through gardens. One of the few buildings open to the public is the Museum of Imperial Collections. On view is a rotating display of treasures from the household collection.

Just as Emperor Meiji desired, the Tokyo underground train is efficient and user friendly for visitors. Stations are numbered and lines are coded by color, so reading Japanese is not necessary. Once in a station, there is no confusion about which exit to take among many options. Just look at pictures above the exit halls and walk out the exit displaying a picture of the site you wish to visit. Trains are clean, frequent and inexpensive.

Imperial Palace is walking distance from Tokyo Station. There are fifteen exits to the station. Imperial Palace is on the west side and tony Ginza shopping district is on the east side of the station. Further north, a few stops on the local train, is Ueno Park, home of the Tokyo National Museum and a park promenade. Immediately to the west of Ueno, is the older Yanaka district of little shops and restaurants. Behind the train station in Ueno, over the bridge, across the train tracks, and through a neighborhood is the cemetery.

Senso-ji Temple Tokyo

Back on the Ginza (gold) local train line, travel two stops to Senso-ji Temple. Tucked in a dense shopping district, it is not difficult to find the temple. Just follow the mass of people. Despite destruction of Senso-ji in bombing during World War II, it has been rebuilt with attention to every historic detail. Breathe the incense with locals.

The best place in Tokyo to experience the transition of Edo to Tokyo is at the Edo-Tokyo Museum.[8] Walk through a mock old city street and admire scale models of the Imperial Palace. Then have lunch at the top of the museum and try a snack plate of local treats.

---

8 Take the purple line to Edo-Tokyo Museum from the fish market, Tokyo midtown Roppongi shopping district, or the Meiji Shrine.

For the best view of Tokyo, let the elevator stewardesses escort you up the Tokyo Tower. A little bit of Paris in Tokyo, it resembles the Eifel Tower. At the top are observation decks. At the bottom is more shopping. For even more shopping, wander Roppongi or the Ginza district. Feel like a local where young businesspeople shop.

Real estate in Tokyo is at a premium. Modern Tokyo is a vertical city. Some of the best restaurants are on upper floors of buildings with retail outlets on lower floors. Emperor Meiji's legacy to Tokyo is your invitation to enjoy the city that welcomes foreigners.

Tokyo Tower

Buddha Japan

CULTURE AS ART IN JAPAN

Culture in Japan is expressed in art. Culturally and commercially connected to mainland China and Korea, until the twelfth century, when shogun, powerful rulers-in-fact of Japan, closed the island empire from contact with outside influences, Japanese people in seclusion polished knowledge and skills to high art forms. Unique Japanese culture developed, in an aura of humility, simplicity and restraint. Nothing is mundane.

Japanese Historic Shrine

In Japan, papermaking, received from China in the fifth century, became origami. Poetry and calligraphy, Chinese imports, in Japan became haiku verse, written in calligraphy, a performance art. Pottery skills and gardening became raiku, ikebana and bonsai.

To understand the importance of Feng Shuí and meaning in stark rock gardens of Japan, it is necessary to start with the philosophy with which Japanese are imbued. The spiritual core of Japan is in Shinto, an ingrained practice of humans interacting with mysteries of nature, that is spiritual, although not a religion. Spirits in rocks and trees are regarded, yet they are not gods. Shinto was joined by Buddhism in the twelfth century. Buddhism is a path to individual enlightenment, not in conflict with Shinto regard for the environment. Japanese built temples to the Buddha and maintained Shinto shrines.

Buddhism practiced in Japan is Zen. Zen Buddhist monks teach that to seek enlightenment one must first unlearn preconceived notions of life. They coach lifeways of simplicity. Unlike western world Hellenistic ideas of permanence, grandeur and symmetry to achieve perfection, in Zen there is humility in imperfection and transience of life. The Japanese concept of Wabi Sabi accepts impermanence of fleeting beauty, such as the bloom of a single flower, the cycle of natural life and the pleasing flow of the moment.

In Japan, the Way of Zen is in *dó*. Do is the way. Boshido is the way of samurai and the ritual of war. Shodo is the way of the brush, seen in quick strokes of Japanese painting and calligraphy. Kado is the way of flower arranging. Kyudo and judo or aikido are the way of archery and martial arts. Simplicity is not easy to achieve. In each dó is a ritual polished to a tradition.

Personification of perfection in Japan is attempted through geisha. The institution of geisha was corrupted in the twentieth century, in the World War II years and contact with Allied military, when geisha were portrayed as courtesans. The notion is illustrative of western thinking. To Japanese, geisha are unattainable women, just as perfection is sought and rarely achieved.

In this brief look at the culture of Japan, through Japanese art, the scene is set with a modest understanding of Zen, Shinto and Wabi Sabi. Perfection sought by geisha and the Way of Tea is seen in streets of Kyoto, where geisha in kimono, performing traditional music and dance, serve tea in centuries old ceremonial fashion. This story seeks context for enjoying Japanese calligraphy, ikebana, raiku, haiku, origami, bonsai and rock gardens. In a solitary rock garden concepts merge and allow contemplation.

Philosophy of Existence

Zen of Katsurahama Beach Kochi

Chinese emperors were enamored with their immortality. If they were godlike, might they be immortal. Buddhism came to China from India, in the fifth century. Buddhist monks carried the message that human life is physical and bounded, whereas there is a path to spiritual immortality. Chinese nobles were pleased. Buddhism flourished.[9]

Fifth century Chinese were not devoid of philosophy when Buddhism arrived. In the ying and yang of Chinese life, Confucius provided an ethical code of social order, which was highly structured. Taoism was life force in a natural

---
[9] Buddhism did not flourish in India, where its egalitarian concepts conflicted with India's social strata.

flow, like water. By fusing Tao with Buddhism and Confucius, Chinese gave the world Zen, The Way of an ordered life.

When Zen Buddhism came to Japan, a few centuries later, it meshed with Shinto beliefs. Shinto has no doctrines. Personal purification is in harmony with nature. Immersion in water is the experience of purification. Well-being of nature is linked to spiritual well-being of people. Famine, earthquake and violent storms, indications that not all is well in nature, gave cause for people to doubt their leaders and toppled dynasties.[10]

Shinto Shrine of Single Rock

---

[10] For a deeper understanding of the relevance of Shinto in the modern world, see, Motohisa Yamakage, The Essence of Shinto, Kodansha USA, New York, 2006.

Zen and Shinto exist in a harmonious duet in Japan. Zen is introspective and Shinto explains forces of nature. Prior to introduction of Buddhism, Japanese revered memory of their ancestors in temples. Reverence evolved to Buddhist temples in the names of ancestors. Shinto observance is found in the natural environment. Cross a red lacquer bridge to a Shinto shrine, where a saying carved on a rock evokes regard for life.

Emperor Meiji Shrine

Shinto Shrine to Ancestors in Tokyo

Zen essence is seen in an uncluttered room. Shinto shrines are built of wood and are stark in decoration. Emperor Meiji, the great farsighted emperor, who regained the royal throne and opened ways to freedom for the people, is highly revered. His shrine in Tokyo is a simple wooden structure of open courtyards. Spirits of the royal couple are here, not their bodies. All may enter the shrine and give respect, as well as request positive life forces. Message boards are filled with wishes for good life.

Wabi-Sabi is an extension of Zen, that is a practical effect of Japanese cosmology, not a separate doctrine. Wabi is liberation from the material world and Sabi is recognition of the transience of life in which nothing is left unchanged. Focus is not on the certain death of a flower, rather, on enjoyment of its purity, color and fragrance in fleeting moments of its existence. Tea bowls gain patina with use. Humans become wise with age.

Geisha – Personification of Perfection in a Kimono

In Kimono Leaving Good Wishes at Senso-ji

Traditional dress for men and women has been kimono, since the style came to Japan from China in the seventh century.[11] The robe is wrapped right over left, unless dressing a corpse, which is in reverse. A wide sash, an obi, is tied around the waist of a man and full mid-section of a woman. Obi ties hold the middle of an obi. Ties are plain twine or silk.

In fashion of the Edo period, the early to mid-seventeenth century, sleeves had elongated pockets. A fan was stored in the pocket. Secret messages were conveyed in long pockets.

Women did not wear lavish jewelry in early Japan. In the eighteenth and nineteenth century, when Edo became Tokyo and swords were no longer seen in the streets, sword-makers used their skills to create ornate obi-domes, small ornaments worn front and center on the obi cord. A modest woman would say the jewel held the obi in place.

Men often wore their kimono open, exposing an under shirt and their long, lose, pleated pants. Women wore undergarments, then a full-length under-dress, over which was a long, pink or red dress. The kimono was the topcoat, tied with elaborate obi knots.

An under-collar or neckline liner added color to an ensemble. It also protected kimono from wear. A change of collar was an inexpensive means to make fashions look new. Sometimes collars were embroidered a bit each year on each side, working toward the center at the back. When ends of embroidery met, it was ready for the wearer's wedding.

Kimono were made of muslin, linen, cotton, or silk. Creative weaving techniques produced puckered cotton and silk, textured linen and a silk linen of fine weave used in the finest tailor-made suits today. Dyed threads created stripes, never plaids. Twisted threads made strong cloth. Women peddlers wore heavy muslin, dyed indigo. The blue with white design became a classic working women's dress.

---

[11] Enjoy the colorful book by Keiki Nitanai, Kimono Design, Tuttle Publishing, Tokyo, 2013. Also, see layers of kimono dressing in: John Gallagher, Geisha, PRC publishing, London, 2003.

When woven of undyed threads, kimono fabric was dyed. An assembled kimono became canvass for the kimono stylist, who drew designs directly on cloth. An army of kimono painters filled in the design with color. Expensive kimono, usually for weddings, had designs executed in embroidery. A finely made kimono today may cost $10,000. It is a work of art, to be worn on special occasions, carefully hung and preserved over time.

Nobles, people with leisure time and distance from soil, wore silk kimono with colorful designs. Kimono designs followed seasons. Kimono worn in the spring featured spring blooming flowers, such as the plum blossom. Although depicting cherry blossoms is popular today, for centuries the dominant flower seen in kimono was the plum blossom.

Also popular for spring designs were peacocks, feathers, parrots and flower bouquets. Summer designs were stripes, flower baskets, seagulls, blades of grass, insects and waves on the beach. In autumn, designs seen were maple leaves turning color, fruit and nuts. In winter, colors were subdued, in heavier fabrics and designs were of toys, embroidered handballs or drums, lions, turtles and the winter heron or duck.

Kimono were canvass for display of contemporary events and commemorations. Kimono were made showing arrival of American and European ships, popular Gosho dolls, in real form made of ceramic covered with layers of paper and painted, and the Wheel of Genji. Tales of Genji, the tenth century novel by a noblewoman and her handmaiden, were widely printed and popularly read. Scenes from the book appeared on kimono, just as scenes from popular movies appear on t-shirts today. Landscapes of the four seasons appeared on kimono, including a day at the beach in summer, or a snow-covered landscape in winter. Water scenes were always popular.

In traditional life, up until the mid-twentieth century, women wore kimono when they left the house, to entertain at home and for formal wear. Today, women wear kimono for celebrations. Most often seen at heritage sites are ladies in rented kimono for fun.

On formal occasions, men and women wear black kimono. Look for family crests on kimono. For descendants of high-ranking nobility, crests appear five times on kimono.

As Samurai found less interest in hosting a tea ceremony, women stepped forward. These women were geisha. Just as The Way of Tea was executed in a ritual to exhibit perfection in manners, geisha were trained to be perfection in a hostess.[12]

---

[12] The plural of geisha is geisha. Plural of kimono is kimono.

Being Geisha for a Day

Geisha are not courtesans. For centuries, married men expected geisha to serve at special teas and meals, perform at ceremonies and be present at court, representing perfection in style. Geisha represent unattainable perfection beyond nature.[13]

Traditional geisha begin training at age fourteen. They spend years learning to dress with various obi styles, apply white make-up and black hair, with proper ornaments. They are schooled in classic literature, poetry, music and dance. It is a rigorous course of study. There are few geisha today. Although many girls enter the course, few complete. There were few male geisha, who undertook private study at considerable expense.

---

[13] Arthur Golden wrote *Memoirs of a Geisha* in 1997, after interviewing a real geisha. The book was stunning fiction. The geisha upon whom the story is based wrote her response, *Geisha: A Life*. Golden's geisha was a courtesan in love, popular with westerners. The response sold better in Japan.

A geisha in training is known as a Maiko. Maiko are distinguished by bright kimono, long dramatic hair ornaments and the telling dip at the back of the neck of the kimono, exposing several inches of neck and upper back. An exposed neck was sensuous in the seventeenth century. Maiko wear straw platform sandals, that are several inches high.

The house mother sells the virginity of the Maiko, when she is ready to become a woman geisha. This is the only sexual transaction of a geisha. In the sale, the house mother recoups geisha training costs. There is no ongoing relationship of a patron and a Maiko.

Geisha parties are expensive gatherings, where geisha serve tea in formal ceremonies and engage in knowledgeable conversation with guests. Modern geisha scan news outlets on a smart phone prior to a tea ceremony. In geisha parties, geisha are expected to perform traditional music and dance, and serve heated sake. Geisha perform at festivals, tourist events and government functions. They earn barely enough to support themselves and the necessary seasonal wardrobe of expensive kimono.

The geisha industry employs geisha, Maiko, house mothers and staffs. It also employs wig makers, kimono painters and make-up artists. Geisha are performance artists. Like the theater, costumes and continual maintenance of skills are required. In return, successful geisha have a career for life. There is no age limit to being a geisha.

The Way of Tea

The great tea master for Samurai, Sen no Rikyu, was born into a family of fish sellers.[14] He left home to become a Zen monk. Over the years, Sen became a style guru and expert in tea ceremony. Tea ceremony practiced by Samurai was elaborate. Sen made it Zen.

In his fifties, Sen was tea master for two powerful shogun in Kyoto, center of style in Japan. Sen transformed the Way of Tea to an ultimate refinement in

---

14   Sen no Rikyu was born 1521 and died in 1591, by seppuku in Kyoto.

simplicity. Tea ceremony is practiced today just as Sen established the ritual four hundred years ago.

Sen designed tea bowls, in hand pressed clay, not uniform, wheel-made wares. In Zen, hand-pressed clay is imperfect, random and asymmetrical. There is no pretense in such bowls. Tea water warmers, ladles and serving trays were of similar design.

Sen cleared all clutter out of tea houses. Simple rattan mats supply the furnishings. He designed a brazier, recessed in the center of the floor, for the water kettle. The tea master brought a tray into the tearoom, with all necessary utensils, including a tea box.

Notably, Sen installed a small alcove as the focal point of a tearoom. In the alcove hangs a lovely calligraphy scroll, with a clever saying. On the floor in front of the scroll, Sen placed a flower arrangement, in ikebana, the asymmetrical floral bouquet. He even designed vases for flowers, much replicated today, in the random form of nature.

Tea Ceremony at Morikami Gardens

Sen was a trusted member of the inner circle, able to serve tea to shogun. Serving tea to politicians was deadly. Shogun Toyotomi Hideyoshi was known for his temper. When he became angry with Sen, the tea master was invited to perform seppuku, ritual suicide, which he did. Sen died at age seventy in Kyoto. His tea ceremony is everlasting.

In a Sen devised tea ceremony, the experience begins upon approach to the tea house. This is a time to decompress from stress of the outer world. Stone steps to the tea house are randomly set, through a garden. Leaves or petals are freshly strewn along the path. No noise, clutter, or litter is allowed to destroy the moment. Conversation is calming.

The door to the tea house is intentionally low, requiring guests to bow to enter. Upon entry, sandals and shoes are removed. Legs are tucked into a sitting position. Guests sit in a row, with the most distinguished guest at the head of the line.

A tea ceremony is a display of civility. As each guest enters, they remark on the skill of calligraphy on the scroll, the wit of the saying and the beauty of the flower arrangement. Guests are appropriately attired in kimono. In formal ceremony, black kimono are worn.

Demurely and silently, the host enters with the tea tray. Items are gracefully removed from tray to floor by the host, as if performing ballet movements. Guests see the tea container, tea bowls, ladle, tray of sweets and towel to wipe the bowls. Although everything is immaculately clean when brought into the tea house, guests watch the host clean their bowls again. The display exhibits respect for guests.

Each bowl of tea is prepared separately for each guest. Tea used in a ceremony is matcha, a powdered form of green tea. Available today in loose powder and bags, matcha tea is high in antioxidants. It has a naturally sweet taste. Cream and sugar are not part of the Japanese tea ceremony. Tea in bags is never used. A tea brush whisk is used to mix tea in hot water, until frothy smooth. The first bowl is offered to the lead distinguished guest.

The tea bowl is offered with the design facing the guest. The civilized guest will remark on the fine design of the bowl prior to turning the bowl to take a drink of tea. Guests always drink from the plain side of the bowl. Then the bowl is passed back to the host.

A sweet is offered to offset any bitterness in tea and to further enjoyment in the ceremony. Offered to the leading guest, that guest takes the sweet tray and first offers a sweet to the next in line guest, who declines prior selection. Only then does the first guest take a sweet and pass the tray along. The offer and declination ritual goes down the line.

Guests leave the tearoom by backing out of the low door. Sandals go on outside. Guests remark on how lovely it was to share the experience. Tea conversation is always polite.

Culture as Art[15]

Imperial Palace Garden Tokyo

---

[15] See generally, Daniel Sosnoski, Introduction to Japanese Culture, Tuttle Publications, Tokyo, 1996.

Each medium of Japanese art is undertaken in the spirit of Zen. The wave of a brush is quick, imperfect and not subject to correction. Ceramics are styled as if random. In a form of flower arranging, stems are thrown into the vase, where they naturally land. Products used in art: clay, ink, paper and flowers occur in nature, a Shinto ideal.

Calligraphy – Japanese calligraphy is an art form. In hands, and sometimes toes, of the artist, quick brush strokes convey an emotion beyond the phrase conveyed in written language. Like a word spoken with emphasis or emotion, calligraphy artists have an identifiable style, which creates demand for their work. Calligraphy is performance art.

Calligraphy artists employ natural fiber brushes, taking up freshly ground ink in the water well of the ink stone. Solid color is shaved into water. A brush dipped in liquid is drawn quickly across paper before ink dries on the brush. Flourish, intensity of ink, thickness of line and a trailing tail are artistic determinations.

Paper is held in place with stone weights. The written message is finished with the block stamp seal of the artist. When copying a sutra of the Buddha, there is no seal.

Before printing presses, and typewriters with Chinese characters, books were copied by calligraphy artists. The hanging scroll in a tea house is expected to reflect the epitome of the calligrapher's style. Scrolls are dated by calligraphy experts, by styles evolving over time. In Japan today, Shodo, the Way of the Brush, is taught in the first years of school.

Ikebana – Ikebana is flower arranging. An arrangement may be a single flower. Usually, there are three flowers and exotic greenery. Asymmetry is key to an arrangement. There is always an imperfection, that is, a sense of being incomplete and of movement.

Since imperfection is a natural part of life, imperfection in a flower arrangement allows flowers to live. Ikebana literally means living flowers. Symbology of three comes from the East Asian trinity of heaven, humanity and earth. It is a Shinto concept. There is also the Buddhist concept of seven branches of wisdom, in which ikebana has seven branches.

After Buddhism was introduced in Japan in the seventh century, flower arrangements were offered to the Buddha and placed in temples. In Southeast Asia, perfect mounds of yellow mums are a common sight in temples. In Japan, flowers are often loose and falling naturally in a vase, offered in ikebana arrangements. By the sixteenth century, schools of ikebana opened to teach the art of flower arranging.

Incense – Incense in Japan was found in Buddhist temples and games played among courtiers in shogun palaces. Japanese incense is finely made and delicately fragranced of pure ingredients. Little cakes of incense perfume chambers of nobles and geisha.

Japanese nobles played a game of five incense. Of twenty-five little pillars of incense, the host picked five. Guests guessed the scent and recorded their answers on paper. The game required a trained sense of smell.

Haiku - Haiku is a seventeen-syllable statement, usually three short phrases, separated by a dash to indicate movement of thought. A typical haiku arrangement is a phrase with five syllables, followed by a phrase of seven syllables and another five-syllable thought. Phrases capture a moment of being. Haiku is simple, balanced, reflective thought.

Matsuo Basho was a popular, published, Japanese poet of the Edo period, in the time of the last shogun dynasty of the mid-seventeenth century.[16] Today, he is recognized as the greatest haiku poet of all time. Born into a Samurai family, young Basho was a page or cook to a Samurai, with whom he composed renku. Renku is a collaboration with two or more poets, composing alternating verses. When the Samurai died at age twenty-two, Basho went wandering, writing verse as he went. In haiku meter, Basho captured reflections on life of people he encountered, such as:

an ancient pond/ a frog jumps in/ the splash of water (1686) or
another year is gone/ a traveler's shade on my head / straw sandals
on my feet

---

[16] Matsuo Basho was born in 1644 and died in Osaka in 1694.

Haiku evokes vivid images without adjectives. The poet lives in the moment and is gone.

> Another Hemingway / without need for adjectives / the thought is profound

Origami – In Japanese, *ori* is folding and gami is *paper*. Paper was a precious commodity in seventeenth century Japan. Time-consuming, folded paper creations were cherished.

Paper butterflies, cranes and other birds decorated Shinto weddings and festivals. There were classic styles, which allowed cuts and coloring to enhance designs. Europeans received Japanese origami before Japan was closed to the west. Popular designs came back to Japan, when it opened in the 1868 Meiji Restoration. Today, designs incorporate cartoon characters. Colorful origami designs are painted on kimono.

Find origami today in tinfoil and heavy paper in folded sculpture. Making folded art permanent is a western concept. Japanese origami is symmetrical yet impermanent.

Bonsai – The art of grooming miniature trees is a thousand-year skill in Japan. It is an art form imported from China and cultivated in Japan during centuries of isolation. Bonsai are grown in small containers to mimic the shape of full-size, although imperfect, trees.

Grooming trees to become bonsai requires years of patience. There are no quickly created bonsai, although small, sculpted, container trees are used in manicured landscaping today, within and beyond Japan. Strictly speaking, sculpted greenery is not bonsai.

To quickly create a small tree defies Zen/Shinto concepts of patience and contemplation. Natural growth develops the design. A bonsai begins from a seedling or cutting and develops through root and branch pruning. Like so much of the culture of art in Japan, simplicity in design of bonsai is deceiving. There are traditional shapes, to best reflect nature in a Wabi-Sabi relationship with the natural environment, held to a small scale in bonsai. A random branch, creating asymmetry, is not actually random.

Containers for Japanese bonsai are smaller than those used in Chinese bonsai. Attention is on the container, like ceramic bowls in a tea ceremony. Japanese bonsai have no decorations or miniature figures as in Chinese or Southeast Asian garden diorama.

Today, century-old bonsai are prized as are bonsai by award-winning design artists. Tools of bonsai are specialized. Simplicity and randomness in the art take skill and patience.

Rock Garden – Japanese stone gardens are unique. It is not that Japanese care little for flowers. They adore flowers in abundance and plant cherry and other blooming trees in masses. A rock garden performs a distinct purpose in Japanese life. They are gardens for contemplation of self, in relation to the cosmos. As such, there is permanence of rocks and impermanence in linear designs in sand or crushed stone pebbles. Rock gardens provide an essence of purity in a Zen/Shinto environment.[17]

In ancient times, before shrines and temples, stones on the landscape served as place-markers and housed spirits, the kami. Stone shapes in a garden represent islands, surrounded by combed waves of sand, like waves in the sea. Raking sand is an art form. Japanese stone gardens of reverence and solitude date to 2500 BCE. Today they are found outside temples and shrines and in home gardens across the globe.

Components of a rock garden include a natural feature, the rock, in an open space, the contemplative environment. Water features, such as a pond or waterfall may be incorporated into the garden. The garden is an embodiment of nature, scaled to home size. Use of sand creates a dry waterscape, inferring purity of water and endless waves.

---

[17] See generally, Stephen Mansfield, Japanese Stone Gardens, Tuttle Publishing, Tokyo, 2009.

A garden offers protection from bad karma. An upright stone embodies the spirit of Buddhist origins on mythical Mount Maru of India, known as Shumisen in Japan. The rock must never be placed in line with support beams of the house, or in the northeast. Devil's Gate is in the northeast. The Chinese had enemies in the northeast. They were Manchurians, who came to Beijing in 1644 and usurped the Ming dynasty.

In Zen Buddhism there is no superstition. Way of the Buddha removes preconceived notions of superstition and looks inward to enlightenment. Sitting in a rock garden is an ideal setting for contemplation, with few, if any, distractions. When there is turmoil in the world, there is peace and solace in the garden. It is no coincidence that Zen priests were among landscape designers to the shogun.

Enjoying Japanese Culture Today

National Museum Tokyo

Sake Ceremony

When Japan opened in the nineteenth century, western artists were in awe of Japanese art. Monet and Whistler painted scenes of geisha in kimono and experimented with wood blocks. Their paintings of Japan are distinguishable from Japanese art. Impressed as they were with Japan, French and American art did not embody Zen concepts.[18]

Ryoan-ji Rock Garden and Tenryu-ji, both in Kyoto, date to 1450, when each was installed next to a Zen Buddhist temple. Today they are open to the public to enjoy, although for contemplation, less visited sites are appropriate. Unless the visitor has attained enlightenment, at most, only fourteen of the fifteen rocks in Ryoan-ji will fill their view at any one time. Also in Kyoto is the sixteenth century Daitoku-ji, with its stunning, intricate arrangement of rocks. Wander the garden and contemplate impermanence of human existence amid permanence of stone.

---

[18] See Whistler's Japanese period paintings up close at the Smithsonian Freer Museum of Art, Washington, DC.

Japanese culture, expressed in art forms, has so permeated lands beyond Japan that rock gardens are found in Australia, New Zealand and Delray, Beach Florida, at Morikami Museum and Gardens. Morikami is dedicated to cultural history of Japan.[19]

When in Japan, rent a kimono to wear when visiting temple sites. Try writing with an ink brush and folding origami. If creating something that takes much effort to look effortless is frustrating, consider attending a tea ceremony. Kimono dress is not required. Be certain to compliment the host on inspirational calligraphy and beauty of ikebana.

---

[19] Sadly, Morikami Museum has retired its library. It has a full-scale tea house for lessons. Enjoy tea ceremony classes in Himeji Castle in Kyoto.

Sakamoto Ryoma - The Last Samurai

Shogun, Samurai and Ninja

Romantic thoughts of old Japan raise irresistible images of Shogun, the ruler in fact of Japan; Samurai, elite warriors of Shogun; and Ninja, a cadre of secret agents. For seven hundred years, Shogun ruled Japan, wielding more power than the Sun of the Heavens, the emperor. Shogun rose amid warlord Samurai, descendants of excess sons of emperors and military leaders. Ninja were special forces, undercover operatives, from within Samurai. A strict code of honor pledged all in fealty to the Shogun, not the emperor.

Shogun ruled on behalf of the emperor of Japan. The first Shogun was appointed during the fifteen-year reign of the eighty-second emperor, the child emperor Go-Toba. Once appointed, clans anointed with the power of Shogun had no desire to step back. For over six centuries, from 1198, Shogun ruled supreme, often competing with emperors for power, though feigning rule on behalf of the emperor's wishes.

Fifty-first emperor of Japan, Heizei, only ruled from 806 to 809, a tumultuous time in the empire. While a prince in waiting, he fathered forty-nine children. To reduce the budget, over-extended by war and burgeoning palace staff, Emperor Heizei reduced his spare sons to commoners. Then he went into retirement. The sons called themselves Minamoto, meaning of the House of Origin. Heizei realized his error in retiring and came back to active control of Japan. Forces of an independent militia were in motion.

Minamoto went north to domain of Emishi people. They rode as warriors, wearing light lacquer armor and carrying curved swords. These were the first Samurai; the army of no one but themselves. Unable to rule, Samurai were elite soldiers, avenging wrongs for hire.

Samurai Warrior

Within Samurai a special forces unit of highly trained warriors became Ninja. Ninja wore black, as they operated quietly at night. Their weapons were magic and forces of nature.

The era of the shogunate was synonymous with development of an insular Japanese culture. Art, music and literature flourished. Shogun built magnificent palaces. Samurai were the educated elite of Japan. Ninja developed as finely tuned intelligence operatives, whose senses, physical agility and mental stamina were their secret weapons.

Over the era of the shogunate, there were clan wars to usurp one Shogun for another. There were wars within and between clans for turf. There were also long periods of peace, fostered by a strong, heavily militarized Shogun.

Shogun were dependent upon national isolation for continuity of survival. Arrival of Commodore Perry, in his Black Ships at Yokohama Bay in 1853, brought down the shogunate, without needing a cannon. Perry's arrival raised to a frenzy the inescapable debate over isolation building in Japan over the prior century. For fifteen years, Edo was a place of bloody streets, until 1868, when the last Shogun went into retirement and the last Samurai was assassinated. Then the shogunate era abruptly ended.[20]

Samurai myths were dispersed like sleeping powder blown from the palm of a Ninja. Lore of warriors was created by those who sought to live up to their image. Shogun kept Japan in a feudal state, long after the rest of the world entered the industrial age. Industrialized nations envied Ninja talent. When the emperor was restored in 1868, he and his descendants absorbed palaces and lore of the warlord era as indelible history of Japan, for its culture and as cautionary tales.

Shogunate Era

Shrine Tokugawa Shogun

---

[20] See generally, Romulus Hillsborough, Samurai Tales, Tuttle Publishing, Tokyo, 2010.

Emperor of Japan was just a title until the Meiji Restoration in 1868. Prior to that time, the group of islands were an amalgamation of fiefdoms, grouped under warlords. As many as two hundred and sixty or seventy warlords divided island turf.

People of Nippon, land of the rising sun, were united in language, bounded by geography and found connection in Shinto beliefs, that is, the power of the environment. Japanese people, then and now, revere their environment and ancestors. Buddhism came from China in the first millennium of the Christian era, as a means to enlightenment. Japanese were impressed by Chinese Confucianism, offering order in daily life.

Emperors of Japan had imperial military, which faced Samurai, the private armies of warlords. Warlords fought for turf, regardless of imperial authority. When a child emperor came to the throne, as eighty-second emperor, in 1183, advisors to the court leaned for support on the most powerful warlord, Minamoto Yorimoto.

Minamoto Yorimoto was a Samurai of Minamoto, original people clan. When the young emperor became an adult, Minamoto refused to cede authority to imperial advisors. Instead, he operated as a military dictator, under color of authority of the emperor. He established his capital at Kamakura, in part, to distinguish it from the capital of the emperor in Kyoto. The new era of Shogun began.

The Kamakura era was marked by continual turf wars. Losers in war, or those who failed to support the Shogun in battles, lost land. Shogun preempted authority of the emperor to give gifts of estates to loyal warlords, who brought their Samurai to defense of the Shogun. In the struggle over the right to gift land, the Shogun lost faith among the people. The emperor did not have power, although he was still the Son of the Heavens, he who must be obeyed in Japanese custom.

End of the Kamakura dynasty of Shogun came in 1333. Ninety-sixth emperor of Japan, Go Daigo, mustered military support to retake power and remove the Shogun. His effort failed, leaving Kamakura Shogun weakened and prey to Ashikaga warlords. Kamakura Shogun kept a pretense of ruling on behalf of the emperor. Ashikaga had no pretense of sharing power. Ashikaga Shogun ruled from 1336 to 1573, in their capital at Kyoto.

At first Ashikaga Shogun were consumed by cementing power against competing clans. Success of Ashikaga was in courting Samurai. For centuries, Samurai built a warrior fraternity. Ashikaga aggrandized Samurai by promoting their aesthetic side. Ritual, honor, and ceremony were heightened in importance.

Shogun and leading Samurai developed the tea ceremony. The Way of Tea was stylized and choreographed. No one dared laugh at men wearing long swords when they dressed for tea and entered the tea house ceremony. Ink brush painting and flower arranging were arts raised to perfection at this time. Ashikaga Shogun are remembered for aesthetics more than prowess on the battlefield.

Golden Pavilion – Kinkaku-ji

The third Ashikaga Shogun built a Palace of Flowers in Kyoto, putting a beautiful environment ahead of efficient administration, leading to downfall of the dynasty. In 1397, Ashikaga Shogun purchased the villa of a wealthy landowner and transformed it into a Buddhist temple, preserved as the Golden Pavilion, the Kinkaku-ji in Kyoto, a World Heritage Site today. Kinkaku means golden. Reflective thoughts were purified by gold.

Unfortunately, a crazed monk had less than pure thoughts when he set fire to the temple in 1950. It was rebuilt five years later to perfectly replicate the original.[21] Kinkaku-ji sits reflected in its pond, surrounded by garden. Souvenir shops are tucked out of view.

If the first shogun dynasty is characterized as a warrior society, and the Ashikaga dynasty is viewed as coaxing power with ceremonies, then the third, the Tokugawa dynasty, is a reflection of its founder, Ieyasu, the patient ruler. Tokugawa Ieyasu waited to attack the last Ashikaga shogun, when he was preoccupied with an attack on Korea and China.

Ieyasu instituted isolation in an effort to keep the peace in Japan. He decreed no guns and no Christianity. Much maligned in history for persecution of Jesuit missionaries, Ieyasu was aware of sectarian Christian wars destroying Europe. He did not want that for Japan.

Samurai Warriors and Aesthetes

Samurai began as excess sons of nobles in the ninth century. In the warlord society of early feudal Japan, lords had personal armies. Since the lord fed the army, wealth of the lord determined the size of the force. Powerful warlords kept a contingent of Samurai.

Samurai were more than soldiers. Among Samurai, a code of conduct developed, a way of fighting, rules of punishment, preparation for death and style of dress. The Way of Samurai was courage. Their manta was to face death until it defeats you.

Killing is inconsistent with Buddhism. To justify killing, Samurai developed an ethical code. In the Way of Samurai, killing is justified against a tyrant, to quell a rebellion, against treachery, to take power from weakness, when the land is in chaos, when there is a leadership vacuum and for vengeance. Vengeance stories date to the twelfth century. In 1873, the emperor outlawed the Way of Vengeance. War of greed was dishonorable.

---

[21] Wooden temples with gold-leaf facie require periodic restoration, with or without a fire.

Samurai Ensemble

Just as cowboys are nothing without a horse, a Samurai was known by his sword.[22] Typical arms in Japan before the fifteenth century were bow and arrow, spears and poles. The Samurai *katana* reached mythical status. The long, narrow blade was honed very sharp and slightly curved. The two handed, single grip allowed experienced sword masters to cut through thin metal helmets, severing a head in one quick swipe.

Swords were worn over the left hip. In the robe sash, also on the left, was a short dagger. In close combat, short weapons were preferred. If the sword broke, the dagger was useful. Sword testers were important specialists. They tested swords on live prisoners.

---

[22] Masculine gender is used, although there were female Samurai. Lady Tomoe Gozen fought as a Samurai in clan wars in the thirteenth century. She is chronicled in *Tale of the Heike*, written in 1330, which regarded her as brave and beautiful. She was an excellent horsewoman and archer. Her long sword severed heads in battle.

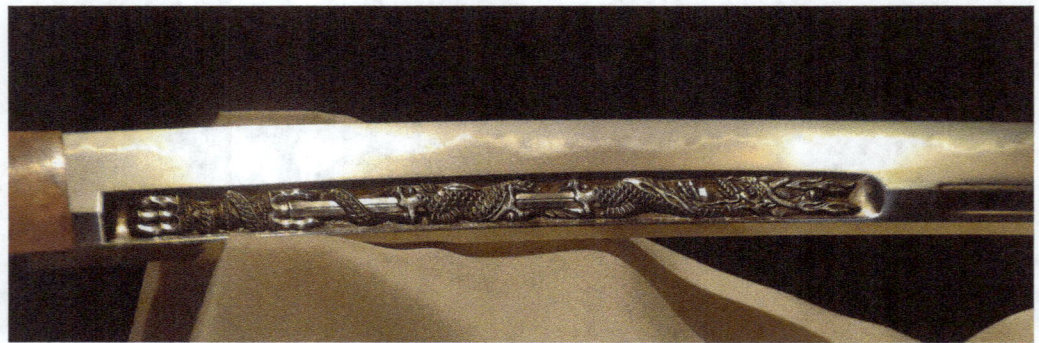

Samurai Sword Detail

In 1543, Portuguese traders beached in Japan. Among their offerings were guns. The last Samurai, Sakamoto Ryoma, is often pictured and depicted in statues with his right hand inside his kimono. Some say he has his hand on a law book, others say it is a gun.

Far from being destructive of society in Japan, guns are credited with enabling large clans to unify Japan. Clans turned on each other, until one clan reigned supreme. The most powerful clan produced the Shogun, who kept the peace. For centuries, technology used to produce swords was altered to produce guns. Japan was self-reliant.

Until late 1500s, anyone could wear a sword. Brawls after theatre performances were often deadly. Shogun decreed only Samurai could wear a sword. There were sword hunts to collect swords of common folk. Samurai had status. Status was displayed in a sword.

As an egalitarian Buddhist society, built on Shinto beliefs, where man strives for harmony with nature, there was no caste system until the Shogun era. As society became structured, Samurai were below nobles, that is below the Shogun. Peasants, craftsmen and merchants came next, in that order.[23] In the nineteenth century, as the Shogun lost power and merchants had funds, often loaned to Samurai, a Samurai redeemed debts by adopting a merchant into his Samurai family. Merchants then had swords and status.

---

[23] The thinking was that peasants grew food, craftsmen created products, while merchants made income from the efforts of others.

Samurai began as warriors for hire. *Ronin* is the name for independent Samurai. Samurai pledged to a lord, or *daimyo*, owed loyalty to that lord. Breach of loyalty was punishable by *seppuku*, a ceremony where dishonored Samurai commit *hara-kiri*. In seppuku, a Samurai fatally slits his abdomen and a second Samurai honorably beheads the dying Samurai, before he exhibits pain.

Samurai battle costume was ritualized. The tunic and skirted portions were twisted fibers over leather, plaited into a fabric tile, assembled by leather thongs. Head pieces were protective and decorative, clearly displaying rank and group. Later tunics were made of lacquered leather. Helmets were decorated metal. The appearance of a group of Samurai would intimidate the enemy, unless they too were Samurai.

The position of Samurai was inherited. Samurai boys began at age five to attend Samurai school, in addition to a local school, which taught classic arts of calligraphy and poetry. At Samurai school, boys learned when to fight and when not to fight. Skilled Samurai had confidence in an ability to vanquish a foe. Key to being a Samurai was practiced restraint.

Samurai learned to live in the rough during battle. They learned to swim in armor. They also learned martial arts. Karate means hand in Chinese. Chinese concepts were highly developed in Japan's centuries of isolation. Concept of a black belt did not exist.[24]

Samurai developed as a pack of warriors, organized under a leader of exceptional skill. Over centuries, Samurai were fraternal by school. Identity of a Samurai was based on family and school. Leaders of notable schools wrote books of Samurai philosophy.

In times of peace, Samurai extended ritual to all aspects of life. Tea ceremony began in a Samurai school. As denizens of culture, young Samurai were schooled in manners.

In the nineteenth century, Samurai saw their lifeway declining. Few had sponsoring lords. Carrying a sword in Edo was passé. Diplomacy replaced battles. When the Son of the Heavens, the emperor, was restored to rule, paid armies replaced Samurai. Swords were pawned by descendants. Battle armor went into museums. International scholarship replaced classical ways of learning in Japan.

---

[24] Black belt is a modern concept. Headbands, belted jackets and trousers are traditional garb.

Ninja - Special Forces

Among Samurai, Ninja were specialists. Wearing black was part of traditional garb. Ninja most often worked at night. Ninja practiced *shinobi*, that is, the art of deception.

Ninja were *shinobi-ninjitsu*, that is, spy commandos of Samurai warriors. Jitsu means hand combat. Ninjitsu means defeating the enemy using espionage. In short, Ninja.

Ninja required training above that of Samurai. Ninja worked at night to vanquish enemies with potions, or blow sleeping powders on sleeping warriors, so they would not wake while the Ninja collected intelligence on the opposing army. Other Ninja worked undercover. Appearing as peasants or craftsmen was a cover for gathering information.

Ninja Hiding Inside Himeji Castle

When duty called, the Ninja put on dark garb, packed a special kit and went to the castle of an enemy. They knew how to measure a moat and silently climb a stone wall. When light was needed, they lit a ball of dust in their palm, or sent a light dart across the room. They could enter a room of sleeping Samurai and know who is sleeping and who is not. A puff of sleeping powder blown to the wind of a wakeful guard retired the sentry.

Ninja knew house designs. They knew where to move at night not to be detected. They could sense and avoid loose floorboards. Creaking floorboards betrayed a Ninja.

To be a Ninja is to fortify oneself to resist exhaustion, illness and hunger. True Ninja can make animal noises that sound authentic. They command charms and magic powders.

Most important to Ninja was the *Giyoshu Manual*, first written in 1690, of Ninja recipes that every Ninja memorized.[25] There are blinding powders and rice powder for the ground to reveal footprints of enemy forces. Ninja wrote messages in invisible ink.

---

[25] See, Anthony Cummins, Samurai and Ninja, Tuttle Publishing, Tokyo, 2015, p. 140.

Masters of deception infiltrated castle guards to incite internal derision. They left the name of an enemy on paper in a cemetery projecting doom. They left potions to rot rope needed by pursuing guards to slide down a wall. Silent, unseen Ninja were more feared than an oncoming Samurai with a sword. Ninja were invisible warriors.

In 1640, grandmaster of *Natori School of Ninja* wrote Natori Sanjuro Masazumi, the True Path of the Ninja. In the Meiji Restoration of 1858, the Natori school was abolished. If Ninja continue training today, only their masters know.

Last Shogun and Last Samurai

Himeji Castle of Shogun Kyoto

In 1853, Commodore Matthew Perry arrived at what is today Yokohama Harbor. He was prepared to use force to open trade with recalcitrant Japanese. Tokugawa Shogun was in power in his capital Edo, now Tokyo. Under prior Shogun, overseas travel, Christianity and trade with foreigners was banned for centuries. This Shogun realized the policy was as antiquated as wearing a sword. In 1854, he signed a treaty with the United States opening docks to trade and creating a fifteen-year rift among the Japanese population.

The treaty was cause for deadly ideological civil war, between those seeking Imperial Reverence and expulsion of barbarians, and those wanting an open country and freedom of movement. A third faction favored Imperial Reverence and an open country. That option required a constitutional monarchy in the model of Britain.

Itagaki Taisuke in Kochi

Parliamentary-royalists squabbled, unable to agree on a plan to present the modern-minded Meiji emperor. Brilliant Samurai transitional leader, Itagaki Taisuke, tried reasoning with warlords, likely future parliamentarians. The effort proved futile. He is remembered by a bronze statue in front of Kochi castle, where there is a statue to the lord's wife, who advised in a secret message, that support for the emperor was wise.

In the midst of civil war, with Russians advancing in the north and French and Americans firing on the ports, the Shogun who signed the treaty died. The last shogun, Tokugawa Yoshinobu was in power long enough to have his general sit down with the general of the emperor's fifty-thousand strong army and agree to a peaceful transition of power.

In 1868, Emperor Meiji was restored to power. He took residence in the Imperial Palace, vacated by the Shogun. He changed the name of Edo to Tokyo, the capital of Japan.

Samurai Sakamoto Ryoma was thirty-one years old when he was assassinated in Kyoto in 1867. He is revered in Japan as the last Samurai. He supported the emperor and championed democratic rule. His assailants were Samurai of the Shogun.

During civil strife, there were several young Samurai who saw the way of the future in return of the Son of the Heavens, the emperor, and stepped away from support of the Shogun. However, of those supporting the emperor, not all supported international trade.

Sakamoto Ryoma was born to a family of sake brewers in Kochi. He was only entitled to the lowest rank of Samurai, as he did not inherit an elite position. In 1853, seventeen-year-old Ryoma went to Edo to earn a mastery in swordsmanship.[26] It was the same fateful year of Commodore Perry's arrival in Japan.

Initially, Ryoma planned to assassinate the head of the Shogun's military, Itagaki Taisuke. Ryoma was pro-emperor and anti-westernization. Instead of assassinating the man, he became his protégé. An avid reader of political documents, Ryoma became convinced that the best resolution for Japan was a democratically elected, bi-cameral parliament, on the model of Great Britain. He wrote a treatise on the *Eight Proposals*, outlining an ideal government, in a combination of the British form, with concepts from the United States.

---

[26] Ryoma was not a large man. He began sword training at age fourteen as he was bullied at school. He was never good at academics, despite his love for reading about governments and foreign constitutions.

Half the age of Itagaki Taisuke, and lacking formal schooling of the older man, Ryoma spread his message to youth and peasants. He was a charismatic leader from the old ways, showing a path to the new. He built a large following.[27] While traveling among the populace, Ryoma was attacked by Samurai of the Shogun, while at an inn, unarmed. He was killed, when he forgot the first rule of Samurai, to remain on guard and armed.

Visiting places of Shogun, Samurai and Ninja Today

Tourists or Undercover Ninja?

In Giacomo Puccini's 1904 opera, *Madame Butterfly*, the soprano's father is a Samurai. Gilbert and Sullivan wrote the *Mikado 1885*, as a musical commentary on British politics. Costumes and settings of both productions are Japanese. Samurai characters are fiction.

---

[27] Ryoma liked to wear western cowboy boots under his Samurai kimono. He carried a sword and a gun.

To step into the world of Samurai, visit Himeji Castle in Kyoto, a World Heritage Site, and Kochi Castle in Kochi. Both are examples of the power of the Shogun to give bequests of large estates to faithful supporters. In cherry blossom season, the smaller, yet dramatic Hirosaki Castle in Aomori is a delightful walk among the blossoms.

For the height of the Shogun era, ascend the tower at Goryokaku on Hokodate, capital of the republic of Ezo, before Japan was united. The French style star fort has a moat. View the fort from the top of the tower and then walk the park or boat on the moat.

Ryoma and Itagaki Taisuke would be pleased to see Japan today. The legislature they envisioned is the government of Japan. The emperor has survived in a ceremonial role. Present-day Samurai warriors wear blue suits and carry cell phones and briefcases. They command businesses across the world. As to Ninja, they would not be Ninja if they were obvious. They could be anywhere.

84 | Cruise Through History – Itinerary XV Ports of the Far East, with Indonesia

1945 8/9 11 02 AM

Hiroshima & Nagasaki: The Bomb and Modern Japan

Hiroshima and Nagasaki evoke thoughts of the atomic bomb. There were explosions the world had never seen and never wants to see again. Blasts ended a world war and began cold wars to avoid new world war. For Japan, after the bombs was a time of rebuilding.

From the time Japan reopened itself to international trade in 1868, it was a nation focused upon industrialism and maintenance of a strong military. Those priorities kept Japan out of colonialism overtaking Southeast Asia. Japan became an independent world power.

Japan fought China for control of Korea in 1894. In September 1931, Japan entered Northeast China, then known as Manchuria. The occupation lasted through 1945.

Invasion of China began in full force in the fall of 1937, with the bombing of Shanghai. By September 1940, Japan allied with Axis forces in World War II and promptly advanced in French Indochina, Malaysia and Dutch Indonesia. Dutch Indonesia held coveted oil.

Japan brought the United States into World War II on December 7, 1941, when it bombed the US naval station at Pearl Harbor, Hawaii. From June 3 to 6, 1942, Japan engaged the US in the critical sea battle of World War II, the Battle of Midway. Although the battle was a stunning loss for Japan, Japanese forces vigorously defended the Allied landing in Okinawa. Allies took Okinawa at the cost of 300,000 casualties, most of them Japanese.

Despite heavy losses at sea and on land, cessation of the War in Europe, in May 1945, and the Potsdam Declaration of Allied and occupied countries, calling for surrender of Japan in July 1945 and threatening utter devastation of Japan should it fail to do so, Japan persisted in pursuing war. Japan seemed ready to fight to death as Samurai. Japanese people revered their emperor as god and remained obedient to traditions of honor.

On August 6, 1945, the US dropped an atomic bomb on Hiroshima. Eighty thousand people died instantly and one hundred thousand more suffered fatal radiation and concussive effects. On August 8, Russia declared war on Japan and entered Manchuria. On August 9, a bomb was dropped on Nagasaki, taking forty-two thousand more lives.

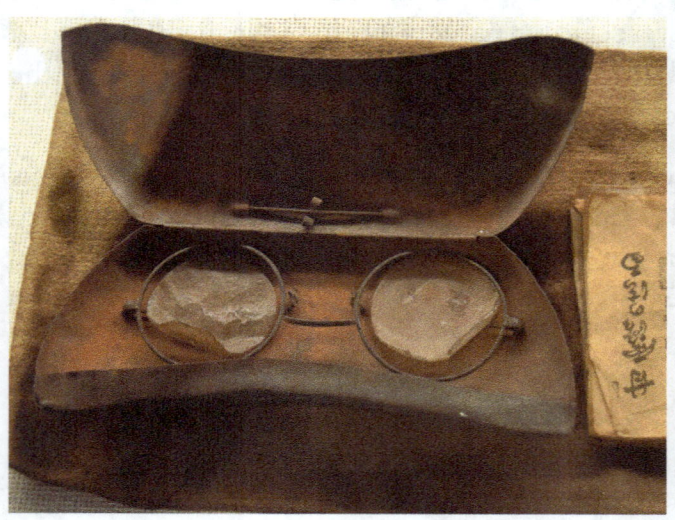

Poignant Memory

When Time Stopped

August 12, US President Franklin Roosevelt died, and Harry S. Truman became president. On August 15, Japan surrendered. Russia entered north Korea at that time. US troops, six hundred miles away in Okinawa, sped northward.

From August 15, 1945 to 1952, Japan was a country occupied by foreign governments, principally the United States and Great Britain. General Douglas MacArthur commanded demilitarization of Japan, overseeing a new constitution, in which the emperor was no longer a deity. The nation devastated by war, was rebuilt. The rebuilding era formed the view of Japanese in the humanity of their occupiers. This is the story of rebuilding Japan.

Rebuilding and Remembering in Hiroshima

Hiroshima Genbaku Dome 1945 (public domain)

The US defined its role in Japan, in the post war years, as a comprehensive political, economic and social reformer.[28] The usual first acts of a conquering general were punishment and restitution. A devastated economy yielded little compensation. A demoralized people, needing compassion, looked at occupiers for help to rebuild.

MacArthur excluded from the new government high-ranking military and wealthy landowners, who favored military campaigns of the past. He instituted land reform, splitting large land holdings and business conglomerates, whose profits were fed by war. Beneficiaries were small businesses in an atmosphere of free market capitalism and women, who gained rights and privileges previously only afforded to men.

In a bit of irony, Japan, twice rebuffed in attempts to control Korea, was a big beneficiary of the Korean War. Supplying war materials boosted the Japanese economy. United States' Cold War with Russia turned Japan into a US ally and military base venue. The 1949 Communist takeover of China prompted the US to negotiate a treaty with Japan, the 1951 Treaty of San Francisco, which hastened the conclusion of occupation.[29] Reparations were exonerated, a prohibition on shipbuilding was lifted in 1952, and Japan was on its way to rebuilding the nation. Rebuilding was accomplished by the Japanese people.

Devastation to central Hiroshima was complete. Although radiation as a consequence of bomb fallout caused sickness and death, immediate effects were concussion from the blast, four-thousand-degree heat in the blast area and radiating outward, carried by winds raging at five hundred yards per second. Buildings instantly turned to rubble, glass incinerated, and people disappeared. Beyond ground zero agony was perceptible. Within the zero area, devastation was beyond comprehension. A thirteen square mile circumference of ground zero was reduced to ash, if not by the initial blast, then by fire.

Prior to the bomb, Hiroshima was home to four hundred and twenty thousand residents. One year post blast, one hundred and forty thousand were dead. The

---

[28] See, Office of the Historian, US Department of State, Occupation and Reconstruction of Japan, 1945-1952, history.state.gov. last accessed May 7, 2019.

[29] United States ended the bar on Asian immigration, instead setting a low number of allowed entry visas.

city went dark. Businesses in the industrial city and transportation hub were gone. All but two of sixteen hospitals in the city were gone and only two dozen of several hundred doctors survived. Two thirds of the city schools were demolished.

Bulldozing the city was never an option discussed. Survivors immediately began rebuilding. Even before the second bomb dropped, Hiroshima residents saw power and water restored to homes.[30]

Hiroshima branch of the Bank of Japan opened two days post blast, although dozens of employees perished. Other banks opened in its concrete building, though there was only a partial covering from rain. Notably, southern Ujina Railway station, out of the main area of destruction, moved supplies to stricken Nagasaki within days of the second bomb.

On September 17, 1945 good and bad effects of a typhoon struck Hiroshima. Wind and rain disrupted tent hospitals. Radiation clouds dissipated in the storm.

American presence in rebuilding Hiroshima was largely in facilitating materials into the city. The US received criticism that it was biased against Hiroshima, a military town and place of war material production. Hundreds of Japanese volunteers poured into the city to aid the stricken and hasten rebuilding. Rebuilding was an effort of people, given supplies.

By 1946, civic leaders proposed visions for city reconstruction, including a memorial. In the 1949 Hiroshima Peace Memorial City Construction Law, center city land was designated a memorial park, dedicated to peace.[31] The law established a memorial zone regulating buildings in and around the zone. It facilitated funding peace memorial projects. Hiroshima rebuilt, without forgetting its part in history. A 1949 competition solicited designs for a Peace Memorial. By 1950, projects rose on Peace Boulevard.

---

[30] The Hiroshima Peace Institute of the Hiroshima City University launched in 1998 to produce information on the Hiroshima experience in the interest of working toward peace and elimination of nuclear weapons. Hiroshima-cu.ac.jp. last accessed May 7, 2019.

[31] The Hiroshima Peace Memorial City Construction Law, pcf.city.hiroshima.jp. Last accessed May 7, 2019.

The Peace Memorial included planting one hundred and twenty thousand trees, recalling fatalities from the blast. Trees came from throughout Japan. The entryway Peace Bridge is graced by designs from Japanese sculptor Isamu Noguchi. The bridge is a city landmark.

Children left without parents or other guardians, known as A-Bomb Orphans, were not forgotten. Schools promptly opened providing a sense of normalcy. American journalist and professor of ethics, Norman Cousins, an advocate of nuclear disarmament, began a Spiritual Adoption program, in which twenty dollars a year was solicited from Americans for the care of an orphan. For a decade, the program supported A-Bomb Orphans.[32]

Today a bullet train connects Hiroshima to major Japanese cities. Just beyond the train station is the Peace Memorial Museum, where visitors encounter stone steps retrieved from debris of Sumitomo Bank. Permanently embossed on stones is the outline of a human, incinerated by the blast and etched into history on stone.

Rebuilding and Remembering in Nagasaki

The bomb exploded over Nagasaki was three times as powerful as the first bomb. It fell north of the city, in a small village, with far reaching impact. Of two hundred thousand residents, three-fourths perished. In rebuilding, Nagasaki created Peace Park Memorial, at ground zero. A cable car connects recent and older history, including the Dutch era.

Nagasaki sits in a southernmost harbor in the string of Japanese islands. It was a first stop for Portuguese, then Dutch traders as they came up the coast from China to Korea.[33] Christian missionaries traveled the same route, when making initial stops in Japan.

---

[32] Norman Cousins, born in 1915 in Union City, New Jersey and died in 1990 in Los Angeles. He was a proponent of peace and advocated truth in the media. He taught a sense of humor aided good health.
[33] Tempura battered and deep-fried seafood and vegetables, popular in Japan, began as Portuguese dumplings.

Hypocenter Cenotaph

Nagasaki was a fishing village in the sixteenth century when Jesuit missionary Francis Xavier arrived in 1549, to bring Christianity to Japan. Christianity flourished in southern villages, to the extent it did not exclude ancestor worship and allowed private regard for kami, spirits of the natural world. That people retained their emperor as Son of the Heavens, bothered the missionary. He was pleased to build churches and schools.

Christianity was popular until the third Shogun of the Tokugawa dynasty, who knew about religious wars raging through Europe. To avoid violence spreading to Japan, the Shogun closed Japan to the world in 1638, then persecuted Christians. Only the Meiji Restoration in 1868, that is the return of the emperor and opening of Japan to the world, brought Christians in Japan out of hiding and back into churches.

In Nagasaki, Christian church building blossomed in the mid-nineteenth century. The Christian story of the city is recognized as a UNESCO World Heritage Site. Christian heritage sites are part of the old harbor area, left standing after the bomb. Oura Cathedral, named for Oura Sumitada, the first Samurai district governor, or daimyo, to become a Christian, is the oldest church in Nagasaki.

Nagasaki Today

During the era of isolation, Dutch traders, non-proselytizing Calvinists, were allowed into Nagasaki, even after expulsion of Portuguese. Dutch books were permitted as they were non-religious. To obtain knowledge of Western and classical texts, Japanese scholars flocked to Nagasaki. The tradition of Nagasaki as a learning center continues today.

From 1641 to 1854, Dutch traders were relegated to an island in Nagasaki harbor known as Dejima. The area was a small island, where comings and goings of the Dutch were easily contained and observed. Today Dejima is attached to the mainland of Nagasaki.

On Dejima, Dutch lived amid warehouses and alongside docks allotted for their ships. The Dutch trading company rented the land from Japanese nobles, about the size of an estate, less than four hundred feet long. The small bridge allowing access to the island was gated at night. From this bastion in the Far East, Dutch traders made fortunes trading in silk and sugar. Secretly, traders sold books.

In 1868, Nagasaki was the first Japanese port opened to Westerners. Already popular with Chinese merchants, hundreds of whom had homes in the city, British and Russian traders came to the port. Nagasaki grew as an international city, ahead of Tokyo.

Emperor Meiji designated Nagasaki a production city for the Imperial Navy. The harbor was filled with dry docks. Industrial production grew in Nagasaki through war years of the early twentieth century, when Japan occupied Manchuria.[34] When the bomb fell north of the harbor, shipbuilding facilities remained. They were closed during the Allied occupation, then reopened in 1952.

Blast in Nagasaki

Nagasaki was an Allied conventional bombing target in 1945, aimed to disable shipbuilding. Bombing did little to stop production, although it caused children and many civilians to evacuate the area prior to the atomic bomb. Prior evacuation reduced the number of bomb victims, although many children were orphaned. Today the harbor is hardly recognizable from pre-1945, due to proliferation of new and larger facilities.

---

[34] Mitsubishi arms factories employed ninety percent of the Nagasaki labor force until 1945.

Visiting Hiroshima and Nagasaki Today

Bomb Museum Going Down in Time

Today people in Hiroshima and Nagasaki define their proximity to Ground Zero. The second bomb fell to the north, in Urakami Valley. It exploded at an altitude of 1,800 feet, spreading radiation a greater distance than in Hiroshima.

Ground Zero is demarked in both cities. In these areas of eerie openness, visitors instinctively fall quiet. A column left standing in Nagasaki, was several blocks from Ground Zero. It was moved to the memorial to exemplify the magnitude of the blast. In Nagasaki, a torii, arched entry to a shrine, was left in situ, now enclosed by housing.

Both Peace Parks are green space within high density, vibrant cities. Locals and visitors mingle, meandering past statues dedicated to peace. Museum displays are sobering.

Glover Gardens was home to Thomas Blake Glover, a Scot, who was a merchant and consultant to the Japanese in 1863. The gardens, historic house and café are quiet spots in busy Nagasaki. They offer a view of historic western life in Japan.

Peace Park Fountain

Peace Monument

The iconic bright orange torii gate, standing in water of Hiroshima harbor, is the entrance to Itsukushima Shrine. Great Torii Gate is the ultimate Japanese photo opportunity, for visitors to Miyajima Island and its floating Shinto shrine. Stand in the shrine to reflect on the shogun era in Japan, the destruction of war and the heritage sites dedicated to peace.

Kabuki, Noh, Doll and Comedy Theater

Theatre in Tokyo

In Japan, the Way of Culture is imbued with Zen Buddhist principles of deep reflection into meaning, expressed with simplicity. Physical arts of pottery, painting, flower arranging, calligraphy and paper folding are reflections of Zen. In live art of the theater, Zen mastery is seen in various forms, most emanating from the tenth century. In 1400, a playwright compiled a style manual of Japanese theater in *Fushikaden*, the Ways of Being and Non-Being, that is, Zen expressed in Noh dramatic theater.

Japanese are also adherents to Shinto philosophy, a lifeway respectful of traditional views of social custom. Several forms of theatrical performance, combining Zen and Shinto, evolved in Japan. In Japanese theater, audiences seek moments of beauty, introspection, reverence for history, intellectual curiosity and raucous good fun.

Theatrical performance in Japan, received in early forms from Korea and China, began in rice fields, dry riverbeds, street corners and Buddhist temples, from the sixth to tenth century. Rakugo, a form of storytelling, and Noh drama theater, emanated from temples. Doll theater and Bunraku slapstick comedy began as entertainment in rice fields, from which it evolved to complex puppetry and Manzai, contemporary stand-up comedy.

Ironically, it was a woman, whose performance is credited with launch of Kabuki theater. Her popular success, and schools for actors, so intimidated a Shogun, that he banned women from performing on stage. Today, Shogun are history and women are actors.

Powerful Shogun were patrons of actors, elevating actor status from peasants in fields to celebrities in ornate theaters. When theaters became too popular, and actors too attractive to audiences, other Shogun banned theater from cities, or halted performances. When allowed to thrive, theater came forth from temples and mansions of aristocrats, to streets of major cities. Japanese theater in its Zen mastery is a cultural institution.

Japanese cities most associated with theater are Edo/Tokyo, Kyoto and Osaka. These were domains of Shogun and venue for their castles. Most early forms of theater began in Osaka. Kyoto, long a cultural capital, developed a theater district when respectable nobles cast actors from their mansions. During the Meiji Restoration, theater decreed by Shogun off limits to well-mannered Samurai, became public entertainment for all.

This story is a historical-theatrical review of Japanese theater from rice fields to major tourist attractions, in various forms. Often excursions to theater in Japan are experiences in sounds discordant to western ears. Attend Japanese theater, as Japanese people do, armed with knowledge of historical components and classical stories from Japanese literature, ready to enjoy technical skill, imbued with Zen soul. This is *kata*, the style, of Japanese za, the theater, found in Kabuki, Noh, Manzai and Rakugo theater experiences.

Fushikaden – The Flower of Noh

Early Style Outdoor Noh Theater

Buddhist priests, looking out from temples in the fourteenth century, saw people gathered in rice fields enjoying dances. Buddhism came to Japan in the sixth century in waves. Temples competing for adherents saw an opportunity to attract new members.

Once chanting within Buddhist temples developed into recognizable melody, priests engaged singers to perform at festivals. Later, rice field dances were incorporated into dignified festival performances. Zen expression grew synonymous with entertainment.

In 1349, a festival performance, staged in a dry riverbed near Kyoto, attracted a huge crowd. Spectators pushing for a better view of the stage overwhelmed the actors. Some spectators grabbed swords used as stage props. Actors pursued the thieves. The riverbed erupted into a riot. Fame of the Kyoto event spread across the land to Osaka.

The Kyoto incident left an impression on Kwanami, a sixteen-year-old Buddhist priest.[35] He combined knowledge of Zen and observation of performers to innovate a polished form of dramatic theater, now known as Noh theater. Kwanami became head of a famous *za* troop, which by 1374, garnered a powerful patron in Shogun Yoshimitso. The Shogun was inspired by Kwanami to develop Kyoto into a cultural-military-religious capital.

Kwanami's son, Zeami, studied movements of his father, seeking to distill in words the essence of *kata*, that is, form and style of the Noh actor. Zeami also wrote for the theater. Imbued with Zen philosophy, Zeami wrote, *every day is a good day.*

From 1400 to 1418, Zeami laboriously applied his brush to writing a comprehensive manual on the mind of an effective actor. He entitled his work, *Fushikaden*, literally, Transmission of Style and the Flower. The flower is a reference to the Enlightened One, who twisted the stem of a flower in front of a group of disciples. The message of Buddha was that the flower is visible **and** a vessel of fragrance. In Zen, the Way is conveyed in being and non-being. *Fushikaden* is read today by actors, practitioners of martial arts and masters of tea ceremony, to learn elements of grace in its physical presence.[36] In theater, the skilled actor masters technique, yet it is his *kata* that propels an inner essence, conveyed to the audience, which renders the performance special.

In Noh theater, there is a main actor, who always wears a mask, and a secondary actor, who enhances action. The secondary actor is the first on stage. He explains the drama. Since Noh plays are drawn from classic literature and historic events, audiences know the story. Attendees today arrive at the theater with copies of the script. Seated to the side of the three-sided auditorium, is the chorus of eight to twelve members. The chorus sings the actor's words, portrayed by the main actor in movement. The chorus also chants, adding drama, much like the chorus in Italian grand opera.

---

[35] Kwanami was born in 1333 and lived to 1384.
[36] Zeami, Fushikaden, written 1400-1418. A copy found in a used bookstore in 1908, was published. By 1940, Fushikaden was regarded as a classic of Japanese literature. William Scott Wilson, translation of Fushikaden in English, Shambhala Publisher, 2013. Zeami (Seami) was banished in 1434, at age seventy-one for refusal to release his copy of Fushikaden to the shogun. He lived to 1443.

Noh dance is expressed in five movements. The secondary actor has a repertoire of three movements. Props are few. The lead actor may carry a fan or sword. The fan becomes imagery for falling cherry blossoms, waves in the sea, a rising moon, or an arrow.

Noh Performance (public domain)

There is no scenery in Noh theater, so costumes are important. Costumes are exaggerated robes, in great color and of quality workmanship. Actors cross a bridge to enter the nineteen-foot square stage, made of highly polished cedar. Off stage, the orchestra consists of three-string instruments and drums. Drums and wood clappers keep the tempo of the performance. The audience is alerted by a flute, at the beginning of the performance and at crescendo moments. Drama is restrained. Anger is an emotion, while violence is an action. Noh theater is non-violent Zen expression of emotions.[37]

---

[37] See generally, Arthur Waley, The Noh Plays of Japan (1921), Tuttle, Tokyo, 1976.

Not every experience in Noh theater is serious and slow-paced. Buddhist monks recognized the value of comedic interludes. Acrobatic or slap-stick humorous performances during intermission, known as Kyogen, were brought from rice fields to the stage. Kyogen recurred between acts in Kabuki theatre. Kyogen are short, with no attempt at literary value. In Kyogen, a clever servant outwits his master, a bridegroom dodges a disastrous union, a thief is foiled, or a devil is unmasked. It is all good fun.[38]

Doll Theater of Osaka – Inspiration to Live Actors

Noh plays draw scripts from notable Japanese literature, presented in formal language. Auditoriums for Noh were originally located on stages, within mansions of wealthy nobles. In the streets and fields of Osaka, common people were excluded from Noh entertainment and felt abandoned by entertainers, cloistered in palaces of patrons.

In streets of Osaka a new form of entertainment emerged. So called Doll Theater began a rise in popularity in the late sixteenth century. Dolls began as bobbing heads on a stick, while the handler recited a story. Some doll faces were specialized to the story and had two faces, beautiful and demonic. When movable eyebrows were added to a doll, a new era opened in theater.

In the seventeenth century, wood replaced clay dolls. Wooden dolls received legs and feet, so they could dance. They had arms and hands, so they could gesture. Mask styles from Noh theater became puppets in Doll Theater. As dolls became more intricate, replicating human movement, they required more handlers. Doll handlers were kept in view of the audience, on three tier stages, necessary to manipulate realistic movement of dolls, which grew three to four feet in height.

In 1684, a ballad singer, Takemoto Gidayu established a Doll Theater. He employed writers to create scripts. Material was adopted from Noh theater, in addition to lighter, short pieces. Dolls wore wigs and Noh style costume.

---

[38] Arthur Lindsay Sadler, Japanese Plays, Tuttle, Tokyo, 2010, reprint of 1934 edition, Paul S. Atkins forward.

For the next eighty years, Doll Theater was widespread in Japan, eclipsing popularity of live entertainment.

In the mid-eighteenth century, new entertainment, in the form of Kabuki, captivated audiences and restored human actor preeminence. Kabuki incorporates stories, movement and music of Doll Theater. Original Doll Theater enthralls audiences today.

Kabuki – Beauty in Tableau

Kabuki Theatre (Edo Tokyo Museum)

Dance is the oldest form of dramatic expression in Japan.[39] Slow, sliding, rhythmic steps and an occasional stomp in Noh, together with posturing of puppets in Doll theater, inspired dance in melodramatic form, brought to flower in Kabuki theater.

---

[39] Adolphe Clarence Scott, Kabuki Theatre of Japan, General Publishing Company, Ltd., Toronto, 1955, p. 82.

In the early seventeenth century, a young, beautiful, ceremonial dancer named O Kuni captivated audiences in Kyoto with her festival dance.[40] She added flourishes to traditional dance steps. O Kuni joined a male partner and an orchestra of flute and drums, to keep the beat and add tone. Students flocked to her. Owners of *za* emulated O Kuni's Kabuki theater. After her death in 1610, students proliferated her formula.

In 1629, the Shogun, concerned with provocative female dancers, or jealous of the popularity of O Kuni and her financial success, issued a decree prohibiting women performing in Kabuki. Next he banned women choreographers. Kabuki theater was devastated. Young men began performing female roles.

When young male actors proved attractive to audiences, the Shogun issued a decree, which required young men to appear less attractive by shaving their frontal hair. Actors portraying male roles shaved the top of their heads, or wore a balding wig, with hair pulled into a knot. Actors portraying female roles wore wigs, set back on their forehead. Later in the seventeenth century, Shogun closed all Kabuki theaters. Doll theater increased audiences. Closure lasted two years, until Kabuki resumed by popular demand.

Samurai, elite soldiers and courtiers of Shogun, were prohibited from attendance at Kabuki. Light entertainment was considered a lack in discipline for military men. Mid-nineteenth century Kabuki included more acrobatics and slap-stick humor than classic literature. When the Meiji Restoration restored imperial rule, removing power of Shogun and rendering Samurai unemployed, Kabuki theater was open to everyone. The result was attendance at theaters of educated, intellectual audiences, who demanded traditional quality Kabuki.[41] Kabuki themes in its Renaissance included witty heroes, chivalrous and honorable, as well as strong characters, who rose in stature by helping the weak.

In O Kuni's Kabuki, the lead actor danced, accompanied by an orchestra, but did not sing. The original format is unchanged. Actors dance, gesture and pose.

---

[40] Scott, at 35.
[41] One Shogunate era prohibition on Kabuki remains intact. Stories in Kabuki may be historical fact, or mystical, never subjects of contemporary politics. Typical stories are drawn from classical literature.

The on-stage orchestra provides rhythm to keep pace, melody for drama and mood. The best actors are great dancers. Many Kabuki poses are adapted from Doll Theater. Kabuki performances end with actors together in a final pose, or tableaux. This is the curtain call of Kabuki theater.

Kanze Sakonn in Performance (public domain)

Costumes in Kabuki are colorful and carefully made. Originally actors wore clothing of common folk. They were street actors on a stage. As actors became celebrities, costumes became extensions of the stage character. Universal in Kabuki is the *tabi*, the white sock, which rises over the ankle and has four clasps. *Tabi* accentuate dance steps and poses.

In Noh, the lead actor always wears a mask. Kabuki actors wear makeup. Typically the face is white with black lines and red accents. Handsome young characters have rouge and red at the corner of their eyes. Demons have mouths outlined in black. Old people have blackened teeth. Black facial lines emphasize emotion.

There are three types of Kabuki theater: historical styled stories, which may be fiction; stories from lives of people, which display human character; and performances consisting solely of dance. In Chinese Kabuki theater the stage is bare, as in Japanese Noh theater. In Japanese Kabuki, the theater is colorful and decorated by cherry blossoms, painted backdrops and gates on stage to symbolize house walls, or city boundaries.

Japanese Kabuki has always been open to innovation in technology. Lighting today is extensive and part of creative set design. Kabuki theaters of wood were subject to fires. When Shogun banned Kabuki from cities, theaters were clustered in city outskirts, near modest homes of workers. When fire raged, as it did several times in Edo between 1804 and 1844, the entire theater district was at risk.

New theaters, built of stone, crumpled in the Tokyo earthquake of 1923. Fortunes in theatrical masks and costumes were lost at that time. During World War II, Tokyo was bombed. Many great Kabuki actors were lost to the theater between 1940 and 1949.

Kabuki theater today revives traditional theater, sometimes of twelve-hour performances. There are short performances for tourists. Both are performed in modern buildings, replicating traditional set design, costumes, music and dance. Stories in Kabuki are adaptations from Noh and Doll Theater. When masks are used, they have moveable jaws, a holdover from Doll Theater. In Kabuki, visitors will see the Way of Theater: the real and imagined, as well as the innovative and traditional. Such combination is consistent with Shinto and Zen, the Way of Life.

Classical Stories Across Forms of Japanese Theater

Noh-stage Today

Noh play, *Tomoe*, was adapted for Doll Theater and Kabuki. Details and story length may differ, although the basic story line is unchanged through time and form of performance. This story is of a young village girl and a traveling priest, often performed today.

The village girl believes her father arranged her marriage to the priest. When he visits, she flirts with him. He runs from the girl, to protect his honor. The priest hides under a temple bell. The girl turns into a serpent, which coils around the bell, crushing the priest.

Tomoe is popular as it involves a transformation. The innocent girl has a serpent within her. In Kabuki, transformation is displayed by throwing off a robe, exposing a different robe. In Doll Theater, the doll changes face. In Noh, the actor changes the mask. At the end, the ghost of the priest sings – *the water flows, indifferent to our fate.*

Tomoe in Kabuki features a dancing priest. Imagine a priest in an elegant pose, while surrounded by a chorus of priests, bobbing up and down in a moving circle. Give each priest an umbrella, to open and close as they go bobbing. Add music, colorful costumes, lights and stage set, and you have Kabuki.

Another staple of Noh and Doll Theater, adapted to Kabuki in the eighteenth century, is the *Story of Soga Brothers*. Soga Juro was age five and his brother Soga Gora was age three, when in 1177 their father was the victim of a political assassination. The Shogun assisted a murderous lord to locate and kill the boys, so they could not return for vengeance. The boys were well-hidden, while they grew to strong, young warriors.

In 1193, the Soga Brothers took their revenge. In a raid on the lord, Juro was killed as he slew the enemy of his father. Goro was captured and held in custody, awaiting execution. In the next scene, the Shogun has control of Goro's fate. The Shogun desires to pardon Goro. However, sons of the lord prevail in convincing the Shogun to execute Goro.

Story of the Soga Brothers is an example of historical drama, with factual origination, magnified over time into Japanese lore. Tenth century Japan was a cluster of lords, in contention to gain power and land. In the history of Japan, the Genji clan defeated other clan chiefs, one at a time, gaining preeminence. Within Genji, internal rivalry resulted in gallant warriors dying in palace revolts. Finally, the young and handsome Yoshitsune, who was also a skilled warrior, became clan leader. In an act of reconciliation, Yoshitsune lay his sword of victory upon a temple shrine. Many years, and several literary versions later, a temple priest retrieved Yoshitsune's sword, which he gave to the Soga brothers.

To lighten the scene, Kabuki includes *Takatoki*, a dance play. In the play, a rich man has a dog, which bites a poor, old woman, outside his mansion. The man refuses the woman compensation. He is haunted by dancing goblins, until he is humbled into payment.

From Doll Theater, Kabuki adapted the story of *Chushingura*, an eighteenth-century tale of forty-seven loyal retainers. The story emanates from an historical incident known as the *Ako Vendetta*. In the story, as in real life, a lord was taunted by his host for improper etiquette. The lord raised his sword in anger at his host. As punishment, the lord was ordered to commit ritual suicide, the seppuku. He did so. His estate was confiscated, as was the custom. When the estate was extinguished, the forty-seven retainers were adrift.

The forty-seven men avenged their lord by killing his enemy, then awaited their fate. When ordered to commit seppuku, they did so, in unison, on February 4, 1703. The play, reminiscent of the event, was first performed in 1748. Hundreds of scripts are variations of the original. The original play had eleven acts, requiring an eleven-hour performance.

Enjoying Theater in Japan Today

A review of Japanese theater reveals that beauty in simplicity does not arrive easily. All forms of Japanese theater are bound by rules, analogous to rules in a well-ordered society. Japanese theatergoers have expectations in form and content of a theatrical performance. They attend to escape daily life and see how actors express *kata* of *za*. As in Grand Opera, or Bolshoi Ballet, the libretto and score are well known by audiences. They expect a performer's skill to transport them through being and non-being, reality and illusion.

Traditional theater endures in Japan. Stories expressed in Kabuki, Noh and Doll theater today continue seasonal performance, much as westerners look to Charleton Heston, playing the role of Moses, parting the Red Sea each spring.[42] Themes in Japanese theater came west, when Seven Samurai were reimagined as Magnificent Seven.

Music in Japanese theater, discordant to western ears, conveys universal themes of human strife, emotion and transformation. In Noh, Doll and Kabuki theaters, dance, rhythm, poses and music convey drama, where language is no barrier. Watch and enjoy.

---

[42] In Japanese classic literature is a story of an infant found in a jar floating in a stream, after a flood, who was taken to the Emperor, who raised him. The infant grew to be a great actor. Zeami, *Fushikaden*, chapter four.

Nebuta Festival Float

Aomori – Ancient Jomon

Longhouse & Tower

Ancient Jomon people lived throughout Japan, when great pyramids were built in Egypt. They traveled long distances, trading between population centers. Jomon were not the first occupants of Japan, nor were they final Japanese forerunners. Jomon people blended with later arrivals, becoming Japanese people of today. In ancient Jomon society were beginnings of Japanese ceramic arts, reverence for water and cultivation of plants.

On the northern edge of the main Japanese island, near the port of Aomori, stands an ancient Joman village. It was discovered in the twentieth century, when the local government thought the site attractive for a baseball stadium. The massive site contains remains of one hundred and forty-five houses. At Sannai Maruyama in Aomori, secrets of the affluent, complex, egalitarian society of Jomon people were brought to light.

Aomori was a power center into the historic era. In the time of Shogun, the Tsugaro clan were preeminent. Tsugaro Shogun castle at Hirosaki, remains an enduring example of Imperial design. By backing the emperor in the civil war, which ended with the Meiji Restoration of Imperial rule, Hirosaki Castle, shrouded in cherry blossoms every spring, was spared destruction. Locals and visitors enjoy this quintessential Japanese historical park, as they cross the red lacquer bridge for moments of tranquility in the blossoms.

In this place, where the landscape holds thousands of years of Japanese history in open spaces, the museum at Aomori is dedicated to recent traditions. The Aomori Nebuta Matsuri is a summer festival, where colorful floats compete to impress crowds with color and imaginative interpretations of Japanese folk history. Nebuta Matsuri, summer festivals, are held throughout Japan. The Nebuta of Aomori is most spectacular.

This is a short story of ancient history in Japan, where Japanese culture was born. In one port stop at Aomori, it is possible to travel back sixteen hundred years, then move forward to nineteenth century formation of modern Japan and into a present-day festival.

Era of Ancient Jomon

It is not known when the first humans came to Japan from mainland Asia. It is likely people walked across ice to Japan before the end of the last Ice-Age.[43] The Ice-Age, known as Pleistocene Era, was from one hundred thousand to twelve thousand years ago. People, animals and plants of the era are known through fossilized remains.

Jomon were the next humans arriving in Japan. Time of arrival is uncertain, dated to at least sixteen thousand years ago by remnants of fired clay made into pottery. Four thousand years ago, Jomon developed high art forms of intricate pottery design, sophisticated architecture, enabling large communities to thrive, and long-distance trade, with other Jomon settlements, capitalizing on diversity of vegetation across the islands.

---

[43] C. Melvin Aikens and Takeru Akazawa, The Pleistocene – Holocene Transition in Japan and Adjacent Northeast Asia, Chapter 11, in Humans at the End of the Ice Age, Lawrence Guy Straus, et al, eds. Plenum Press, 1996.

Sannai Dwelling

Tracing development of culture is possible through fired pottery. Ceramics hold depictions of art and cosmology. Uses for pottery help define lifeways. Early pottery is seen with fingerprints of pinched clay and simple human figures, or religious objects. Eventually, artisans emerge, creating pottery as works of art, without religious or domestic purpose. Each phase of human development is seen in Jomon pottery.

Jomon used pots to store seeds, grains and nuts, mostly chestnuts. Chestnut trees were crucial to sustaining life in Jomon communities. Great pits were dug for chestnut storage.

Jomon culture thrived in Japan, in large communities, from 14,500 BCE, to 300 BCE, in part due to maximizing specialized food sources. Jomon people were hunter/gatherers. They cultivated mint, gourds, beans and grains, including millet, buckwheat and barley. Most diet staples, such as fish, chestnut and game, as well as other food plants, were traded across the long range of Jomon communities.[44] In the absence of war and transmittable disease, communities grew large, until they overpopulated a local environment. Communities shifted to new locations, returning to renew old sites with smaller populations, which grew again.

The calendar of Jomon life followed the seasons. Food sources were seasonal. Fish arrived near the shore in seasons. Herds of animals traveled the landscape, following food sources. There were seasons for harvest, fishing and hunting. Bounty shared across communities fed large populations with seasonal variety. In such bounty, artists thrived.

Over a millennium, lifeways of Jomon people adjusted to changes in the environment. When the sea retreated, and climate warmed, shellfish were no longer easy forage on the beach. People moved inland to find food. A thousand years ago, people made chipped stone axes. They made canoes for long-range travel, in search of food.

---

[44] Archaeologists discern cultivated plants from those left wild by comparing plant DNA. Cultivated plants have recurring DNA patterns, while plants left wild to mingle have a broader range of DNA.

Evolution of Jomon into modern Japanese, is of scholarly and social debate in Japan. Traits of Jomon people from South East Asia are seen in Ainu people and a blended offshoot of Ryukyus people. Another branch of Jomon, overcome by and blended with, later arriving Yayoi from Northeast Asia, are considered evolved people of modern Japan.

Note on Japanese and US archaeology: End of the Ice Age Aomori is geographically analogous to California. Both long, narrow landscapes, along the ocean, were inhabited by migrating people about the same time. US archaeologists came to Japan in the 1960s to 1980s, bringing their assumptions of cultural formation analogous to the landscape.

Junko Habu, a Japanese archaeologist, also educated in the United States, brought cross-cultural observations to her 1995 scholarly, scientific work, culminating in her thesis publication, *Ancient Jomon of Japan*.[45] Habu was impressed by US/Japan similarity in regard for other, early people, not regarded as ancestors. To the extent Jomon blended with Yayoi from mainland Asia, becoming modern Japanese, they are revered as ancestors. Cultural remnants of ancestors are respected in excavation, curation and interpretation. Archaeology of ancestors is done at government expense with pride.

In contrast, archaeology of Ainu, an offshoot of Jomon people considered others not ancestors, is of lesser regard. In Japan, relics of Ainu culture receive treatment as archaeological relics, not patrimony of ancestors, much like regard for Native American human remains and cultural objects received academic archaeological treatment as lesser regarded objects of others through the twenty-first century. Habu observed that European gravesites in the US are treated as human remains, while grave-goods and human remains of Native Americans are held by archaeologists as specimen.[46]

---

[45] Junko Habu, Ancient Jomon of Japan, Cambridge University Press, Cambridge, 2004.

[46] Observations of Habu are validated by the 1990 unanimous US Congress to rectify discrimination against Native Americans throughout academia by enacting the Native American Graves Protection and Repatriation Act, 25 USC 3001, et seq (NAGPRA). Japanese officials visited the NAGPRA Program in 2005, to learn how NAGPRA-like treatment could apply to Ainu burials.

Habu observed that after thirty years of archaeological investigation, there was little known of the role of women in Jomon culture, as though the role of men as leaders, warriors and hunters was the extent of critical knowledge of the culture. In committing the scientific sin of failing to control for bias in research, the almost exclusively male-led archaeological teams missed the opportunity to look broadly and comprehensively across available data retrievable from artifacts. Much information was lost in the process.

Sannai Maruyama in Aomori

Sannai Maruyama Museum

Existence of Jomon sites were known, in the 1950s, when the government began a baseball stadium in Aomori. Stadium construction was relocated, while Japanese archaeologists spent thirty years exposing the largest Jomon site in the country. Work is ongoing, increasing knowledge of Sannai Maruyama, a nominee to the World Heritage Site list.

Sannai Maruyama was occupied by Jomon people over fifteen hundred years. Over time, there was growth and ebb in residents, rendering the site a font of comprehensive knowledge of Jomon society. Archaeologists located seven hundred structures, including pit dwellings, long houses, graves and circular stone burials. Jars were found for use as burial jars, storage vessels, ceremonial use, simple cooking vessels and finely decorated pottery, made as coveted treasure. Pottery pieces in trash heaps, known as middens to archaeologists, help scientists track evolution of style, technological advancement and environmental change, seen in adaptation of lifeways of people.

Fragments of life, found in excavations, were charted to time and place, creating a matrix of early and middle periods of Jomon culture. The initial phase of Jomon existence was from sixteen thousand to nine thousand years ago. This is the time of rudimentary pottery. From nine thousand to six thousand-eight hundred years ago, Jomon experienced an early period of hunter/gatherer existence. During this time, arrowheads were elongated for large game, and smaller and sharper points for small game. Stone axes were common. The middle period of sixty-eight hundred to five thousand years ago is regarded the middle period. This was the high era of Jomon civilization. It was a time of creative arts and large, long houses holding group activities in winter.

Notable at Sannai Maruyama are changes in dwelling design and use over time. When the Jomon population became so successful that it grew too large to be supported by the local environment, people migrated to greener pastures. When Sannai Maruyama was reoccupied, maybe a century later, fewer people occupied the best of dwellings, which they modified, reflecting advances in design, or lessons incorporated from interaction with distant communities. While Sannai Maruyama, in the aggregate, had long habitation, not all houses had continuous occupation. By dating layers of habitation, through artifacts collected at different levels, archaeologists filled in their time matrix.

Yayoi people from Northeast Asia moved into Japan, beginning four thousand, eight hundred years ago, to the most recent, three thousand years ago. Yayoi were able sailors and hunters. Yayoi people had metal technology. They were adept at cultivating crops, notably rice. Cultivation of crops gave Yayoi an advantage over Jomon, still highly dependent upon seasonal gathering of seeds and nuts.

Yayoi were better able to remain in stable communities and withstand famine, when Jomon were forced to vacate communities in search of food. By 1,000 BCE, Yayoi overtook Jomon people, until Jomon blended into Yayoi, losing separate distinction by 300 BCE. Blending of people was not a function of war or conquest. It was a means to thrive.

In the late era of Jomon people, ceremony was growing in importance. Two large ceremonial mounds were built at Sannai Maruyama, from which fifteen hundred clay figurines were recovered. Hierarchy within the population was apparent in the late period. Archaeologists, always on the lookout for chiefs and followers, were stymied by the apparent egalitarian Jomon culture in the early and middle periods. The largest number of ceremonial objects appear in the late era.

In the late era, as Yayoi influence swept the island, groups of people migrated toward leaders, whether they were chiefs, or priests, to serve the top esculin of the social order. There is evidence of a growing number of chiefs, or priests, and fewer workers. In the creation of burdensome hierarchy, Jomon culture diminished. When there were fewer people to forage for food than there were people waiting to be fed, Jomon people were less able to survive than the Yayoi newcomers.

Sannai Maruyama was part of a trade network, where goods included jade, obsidian, asphalt and salt. Jade was carved into beads and earrings. Hard-rock obsidian was valuable to carve stone axes and as arrowheads. Salt water was heated in pots, until water evaporated, leaving salt crystals, a food preparation and preservation staple. Asphalt was used to waterproof reed buckets for hauling water and as an adhesive in building. Asphalt was used as glue to repair pottery.

From the early period, Jomon people created lacquerware vessels. Plant-based textiles were woven, with a twisted warp thread for added strength. Fabrics were lacquered to make them waterproof. Lacquered fabric worn as clothing was warm.

The process of making lacquer requires a sophisticated knowledge of transforming poisonous lacquer tree sap into refined liquid, to which color was added. Jomon people perfected use of red and black pigment, which was used to paint lacquerware vessels and personal adornment. Red lacquer painted posts, with black accents, seen in bridges and arches of the Shogun era, began in ancient Jomon communities.

Also found at Sannai Maruyama were amber, cinnabar, exotic shells, and mercury sulfide, used in red dye. Stone was often used for burials and lining storage pits, saving wood of nutmeg and cedar trees for canoe paddles. Giant nutmeg trees were felled to create tall structures, the use of which is still unknown.

Post Holes of an Ancient Tower

Today at Sannai Maruyama a metal shed protects six, large, empty pit holes, set in pairs, forming a rectangle. The post holes are almost six feet in diameter and six feet deep. Poles originally occupying the holes were chestnut. Purpose of the structure created from huge chestnut poles is unknown. Outside the metal shed, a tower was constructed, to approximate dimensions and architecture of a tower made from poles of the size indicated by holes. The tower was either another form of storage, or a lookout, or of ceremonial use, in the late period of Sannai Maruyama occupation.

Houses in proximity to the tower have raised floors. Archaeologists hypothesize that raised floor houses were used for storage, to keep grains and other foods from wet turf, or small animals. Other, smaller houses are set at ground level.

Research at Sannai Maruyama is ongoing. As a large site, representing the spectrum of Jomon culture, Japanese scientists located a museum and database to consolidate knowledge of Jomon people, found in fragments across Japan. Over time, as additional data is received, more questions will be answered. To date, the inviting museum of Jomon culture offers an opportunity to walk on a Jomon cultural landscape and into a cavernous longhouse. Sanai Maruyama is an introduction to ancient ancestors of Japanese people, evidencing early examples of high culture in arts and community development.

Japanese Era in Aomori at Tsugaro Shogun Hirosaki Castle

Hirosaki Castle

Not far from the cruise ship pier in Aomori, and Sannai Maruyama, is Hirosaki Castle, home of the Tsugaro clan of powerful Shogun. Tsugaro claim descendance from Genji, the clan regarded in Japanese history as uniting the country. In 1600, the head of the clan was rewarded by Shogun Tokugawa Ieyasu for loyal service, with a large estate and made lord of Hirosaki. In 1603, the first Tsugaro lord built Hirosaki Castle.

When Hirosaki Castle was completed in 1611, it was a three story, classic Imperial style Japanese square castle, made entirely of wood. The first castle burned, when struck by lightning in 1627. The ninth Tsugaro lord rebuilt the castle in 1810, just prior to civil discord, which divided lords and threatened Shogun existence.

In the civil war, which came to full fury in 1868, the lord Tsugaro of Hirosaki sided with the emperor. In the Meiji Restoration of 1869, lords of Hirosaki surrendered the castle to the government. In 1894, final lords of Hirosaki donated extensive, cherry tree grove grounds to the public as a park. Walls of the estate were removed, exposing the moat.

Red Lacquer Bridge at Hirosaki

In 1950, Hirosaki Castle was declared a National Important Cultural Property, which guaranteed preservation of the castle and surrounding park. Connecting access to the castle, across a gorge, is a red lacquer bridge, maintained in historic style.

Today, visitors to Hirosaki walk cherry tree lined paths to the red bridge and mount a viewing stand for views of Hirosaki Castle, restored to original beauty. Fortunate are those who arrive in April, when cherry blossoms are at their peak. In 1903, two thousand, six hundred cherry trees were planted on park and castle grounds. Each April, Hirosaki Castle on a hill, looks like it is rising from a snowstorm of cherry blossoms.

Today at Aomori Nebuta Matsuri

Nebuta Festival Float

Early each August, Nebuta Matsuri festivals occur around Japan. A spectacular Nebuta festival takes place in Aomori. After Nebuta processions end, elaborate floats represent too much effort and expense to land in a refuse heap. Since 2011, prized floats are preserved in Aomori Nebuta Matsuri Museum near the cruise pier.

Nebuta festivals are a riot of color and light. Creation of a float is a specialized art. Floats may be a singular subject from folk lore, whose Kabuki style face is familiar to Japanese theatergoers, or may be a crowded composition of heroes, beasts, and goblins from folk lore, gathered around a depiction of Mount Fuji. Scary faces predominate. Floats are lighted from within and are accompanied in procession by music.

Origins of Nebuta Festival are uncertain. There was an old Shinto festival of the dead, in which the dead arose, stomped the ground to remove dirt, and began to dance in celebration. Today, float attendants dance their way down the street to joyful crowds.

During a Nebuta procession, anyone may join and flow with floats along the route, as a *haneto* dancer, as long as they wear costumes. Bright red costumes are purchased or rented. Visitors in the spirit of the occasion are welcome to join the parade.

At the cruise ship pier in Aomori, there is a monument to harbor seals. Seals of these waters fed ancient Jomon people and contributed their skins to clothe Hirosaki lords of the castle. Today seals are not hunted. They are part of the historic landscape, which transports visitors through three critical episodes in the history of Japan, in one day.

Hakodate View Tower

Hakodate – Battle for the Empire

View from Goryokaku Tower

Visitors arriving at the port of Hakodate, on Hokkaido, the northernmost island of Japan, are treated to vistas of a sparsely inhabited place, always in view of Mount Hakodate. The volcanic mountain has been quiet for so long, that a cable car transports visitors to its peak, for a panoramic view of the harbor. The Battle of Hakodate in the harbor, from 1868 to 1869, was a final losing effort of the Shogun to maintain power over Japan.

Long ago, the northern island of Hokkaido was the scene of tension for Ainu people, descendent of Jomon people, considered *Others* not Japanese. As the population of lower islands of the Japan archipelago became land of Japanese lords, in nation formation, Ainu were pushed north, to Hokkaido, much like American Indians forced to Oklahoma. Several times, from the fifteenth to seventeenth centuries, tension between indigenous people and new arrivals broke into warfare. Ainu moved further inland on Hokkaido, avoiding Japanese cities on the coasts. Hokkaido's story must include Ainu history.

The spectacular visitor attraction in Hakodate is Goryokaku Fort. The sixty-two-acre park, a major cherry blossom viewing area, was built by Shogun in the nineteenth century, to garrison soldiers in the event of a Russian incursion. Built in the French Five-Point style, by French advisors to Shogun, battlements are backdrop to flowers and boats in the moat.

Goryokaku Fort was the Shogun last-stand stronghold in the effort to control Japan. This is where Shogunate supporters established an Ezo Republic. The republic was short-lived. Today, turf battles are picnickers claiming spaces under cherry trees for family dinners. Reflect on turbulent history in Hokkaido, before enjoying the beauty of lasting peace.

Ainu of Hokkaido

Japanese scholarship of Ainu regard them as ancient arrivals from the mainland, possibly Siberia. Lighter skinned than Japanese, Ainu held to traditional lifeways. They were hunters and gathers, who traded with emerging Japanese cultures. Pushed from land, Ainu and early lords were in constant conflict.

In the fifteenth century, Japanese lords built forts around Hokkaido, asserting presence, in the face of Russian expansion into islands and fishing areas. In 1512, Ainu people rebelled. They attacked and demolished twelve forts. For the next century, the north island of Japan was domain of Ainu. They hunted, fished and built communities. They practiced burial ritual and reverence for ancient spirits similar to Japanese.[47]

---

[47] Ainu use prayer sticks to honor their dead, known as *kamui*, similar to Japanese *kami* sticks.

As Ainu populations grew and resources became scarce, there were turf battles between Ainu groups. Capitalizing on dissention, in the mid-1660s, merchants of the Matsumae clan established a trade and fishing station in Hakodate. Clan ships carried armed soldiers to protect trade. There were minor skirmishes between Ainu and merchants, of no concern to merchants while Ainu lacked unity.

In 1669 an Ainu leader emerged, intent on unifying his people to defend the land. Shakushain was as charismatic as he was an able warrior. Ainu people of Hokkaido massed behind him. Matsumae clan soldiers were overwhelmed.

Word spread to Edo, that Ainu asserted land rights. Tokugawa Shogunate sent Samurai replacing Matsumae guards. At stake was more than trade at the harbor. Japan shifted in attitude toward Hokkaido, from rural backwater of Ainu, to integral land of Japan.

Shogunate Samurai had superior weapons to Ainu, in great supply. By the end of 1669, Shakushain was defeated. Random skirmishes continued until 1672, though Shakushain's career was brief. He and his warriors drank sake with opposing forces, in a truce offering. While Ainu warriors were under effects of alcohol, they were killed by Samurai.

Twelve decades later, another Ainu leader rose, in reprise of Shakushain. His campaign was also brief and inconclusive. Kanagawa Treaty of March 31, 1854, between the Shogun and US, opened Hakodate port to foreigners. Ainu had more than Samurai of the Shogun with which to contend. Sailors and merchants from the United States came to Hakodate.

Ainu retreated to interior villages of Hokkaido. The interior is as sparsely populated today as it was when Ainu first arrived. Opportunities for immersion in Ainu culture draw visitors from ports to experience ceremony and unique lifeways of Ainu. Today most Ainu live in Japanese style homes. Their children attend Japanese schools. Struggles today are on maintaining culture rather than competition for land.

Shogunate in Hakodate at Goryokaku Fort

Hakodate Moat

For three centuries, Russia and Japan explored the Kuril Islands connecting Russia's Kamchatka Peninsula to Hokkaido. Ainu claim traditional use of Kuril Islands, despite agreements, in which Japan gave up claims to Kamchatka and Russia abandoned claims to Hokkaido. The nations agreed to disagree on claims to the mid-range Kuril archipelago.

In the nineteenth century, uncertain of intentions of Russia, the Shogunate established forts on Hokkaido. The largest fort was Goryokaku, outside Hakodate. When ousted from Edo by the emperor in 1868, the Shogunate retrenched in Goryokaku Fort.

Begun in 1855, Goryokaku Fort is best appreciated from the viewing tower, opened in 2006. From the heights, the fort's five-point star stands out against the moat. The fort was the design of Marquis de Vauban, a French architect, the greatest military architect of his time, adapted to the site by Japanese architect, Takeda Ayasaburo. The star design enabled defenders to view approach of an enemy from any angle. Vauban designs were utilized up until the early twentieth century, around the world.[48]

Tokugawa Shogunate utilized forts on Hokkaido to monitor Russian activity and as military garrisons during Ainu uprisings. During the Boshin War, the civil war between the Shogun, striving to maintain power, and the Emperor of Japan seeking to regain power, Goryokaku was the last bastion of the Shogun, ousted from Edo (Tokyo) Castle.

In the Battle of Hakodate, the Imperial Navy used its secret weapon to eliminate the Shogun Navy. On land, eight thousand Imperial troops, overwhelmed three thousand Shogun troops, taking Goryokaku Fort, and driving the Shogun from power. Surrender of the Shogun occurred at nearby Benten Daiba Fort, another star fort by Takeda.

Since 1913, Goryokaku Fort has been a public park, with picnic grounds, boat rides on the moat, and tours of restored historic buildings. Goryokaku is a wonderful venue for *hanami*, cherry blossom viewing. Once a scene of war, it is now a place of beauty and relaxation among hundreds of cherry trees.

Secret Battleship with Many Names

In 1866, the Shogunate purchased an iron-clad battleship from France, with three guns on deck. The state-of-the-art ship had inner struts of teak, for buoyancy. Built in Bordeaux, the ship was not ready for delivery prior to outbreak of civil war between the Shogun and Emperor. Emperor Napoleon III of France did not wish to commit international crimes by selling war machinery to the Shogun in the midst of civil war, so the operation went covert. The ship was named *Sphinx*, as though intended for Egypt.

---

[48] French King Louis XIV relied on Sebastien Vauban, 1633 to 1707, to design forts, castles, and fun fireworks. See Vauban Five-Point forts, World Heritage Sites, notably, Saint-Martin-de-Ré and Mount Dauphin in the Alps; Willemstad, Curaçao; Kastellet, Copenhagen; and Fort McHenry, Baltimore, Maryland.

CSS Stonewall-Kotetsu *(Public Domain)*

American intelligence agents in France detected the scheme and cried foul. France reacted by selling the *Sphinx* to Denmark. The Danes named the ship something quintessentially Danish. Denmark enjoyed peace, so they sold the ship to the Confederacy. The Confederates named their new ship the CSS *Stonewall*.

CSS *Stonewall* was plagued by storms crossing the Atlantic. By the time it limped into Havana Harbor, in May 1866, the US Civil War ended. The Confederacy no longer existed. When the CSS *Stonewall* sailed into the Washington Navy Yard in November, it was greeted by agents of the Shogun, on a ship-shopping trip. In early 1867, the Shogunate purchased the ship from the US for $400,000 (1867 rates) and named it *Kotetsu*.

Neutral in the Japanese civil war, the US withheld delivery of the *Kotetsu*. By the time *Kotetsu* was released from Washington Harbor and delivered to Edo, in March 1869, the Shogunate conceded Edo to the Emperor, who renamed his capital city Tokyo. Meiji Restoration of power in the Emperor and building modern Japan was underway. *Kotetsu* was delivered to the Imperial Navy.

Admiral of the Shogun Navy, Enomoto Takeaki, accepted loss of Edo to Imperial control, yet refused to concede defeat of the Shogunate. Under command of Takeaki, the entire Shogunate Navy of eight ships sailed to Hakodate, without waiting for *Kotetsu*. In Hakodate, the Shogunate set up the Ezo republic. Operation central was Goryokaku Fort. Takeaki named himself president of the Ezo Republic and Admiral of Ezo Navy.

Meanwhile, Emperor Meiji reconstituted the Imperial Navy, around the *Kotetsu*. Vessels of loyal merchants repurposed to naval vessels. The Imperial fleet sailed to Hakodate.

In the Battle of Hakodate, from December 1868 to June 1869, Kotetsu, the French-built ship, intended for the Shogunate, played a pivotal role in defeating the Ezo Navy. In the battle, the Imperial Navy launched eight steam-warships, of which one ship was sunk. The Ezo Navy had five steam-warships, after a typhon in transit to Hakodate. Led by *Kotetsu*, the Imperial Navy won a decisive battle and ended the Boshin (Civil) War.

Once the war ended, *Kotetsu* was renamed *Azuma*. The ship next saw action in 1874, in Taiwan, which leads to another story.[49] *Azuma* sunk in a typhon and refloated, enabled by its teak interior. Decommissioned in 1888, *Azuma* ended in a scrap pile by 1889. Metal sheeting was repurposed for electric generators in 1895. It was a new era.

---

[49] Japan's Taiwan Expedition is known in China and Taiwan as the Mudan Incident a dispute begining in Ryukyu Islands. Qing China left Taiwan. Ryukyu is within Japan today.

Visiting Hakodate Today – Cherry Blossoms at Goryokaku Fort

Hakodate Hanami – Cherry Blossom Time

Today Aomori, on Honshu, the main Japanese island, and Hakodate, across the Tsugaru Strait on Hokkaido, are linked by a railway running through Seikan Tunnel, opened in 1988. Seikan was the longest under-sea tunnel and second deepest rail tunnel in the world when built. Construction of a tunnel was made necessary by a typhon in the 1950s, costing lives of ferry passengers. The rail line handles greater numbers of passengers safer and faster than the ferry. The rail line connects to Sapporo, making north island sights accessible to travelers.

Yokohama Meets Commodore Perry

Yokohama Perry Landing

When Commodore Matthew Calbraith Perry sailed into Yokohama harbor July 8, 1853, his world and Japan were forever altered. Commodore Perry is known for opening Japan to international trade by fiat. Gunboat diplomacy was his method. Perry was no diplomat.

Perry was an apt symbol of the age. The Perry family tree spread to landing of the *Mayflower* in the New World. Perry's first service in the US Navy was under his older brother. Commodore, an archaic title now, was the highest level in the US Navy.

Perry's timing was excellent. Russia, Britain, and France probed into Japan's seclusion. Two centuries earlier powerful Shogun protected Japan from havoc Christian sectarian wars created in Europe. The crisis was past. The last powerful Shogun was dead. The Shogun era was dissolving into rule by the Emperor of Japan. Perry stepped into and became part of a cataclysm of change.

Landing of four, black-hulled ships of the United States, referred to by Shogun as black ships of doom, was inside Edo harbor, Tokyo today. Not yet developed when Perry arrived, today Yokohama is a major commercial and cruise ship port. Within the ultra-modern port, the landing site of Perry is preserved.

Walk along Yokohama harbor park, look at your cruise ship, and imagine a black-hulled, steam, paddle roller in its place. In one direction are preserved nineteenth century buildings from Perry's time, in contrast to twenty-first century development. This story helps fill the time-gap. This is the story of Commodore Perry in Yokohama.

Perry Prior to Japan

Matthew Perry was born in 1794, in Rhode Island, to an Irish family with extended ties to William Wallace and arrivals on the Mayflower.[50] The Perry family farm near Newport is an historic property. Perry family served in the US Navy. Matthew first saw battle before he was twenty, in the War of 1812. He sat

Commodore Matthew Calbraith Perry (Public Domain)

---

[50] When serving as US representative during the Japan surrender ceremony of World War II, General Douglas MacArthur requested that he display the flag of his ancestor, Matthew Perry.

out much of the war, after sustaining an injury from an exploding cannon, while serving under his older brother.[51]

In Rhode Island, the Perry's were well represented in society. The first social hostess to give caché to tiny Newport was Caroline Perry, daughter of a US Naval captain, and niece to Matthew Perry. Caroline married August Belmont, banker to the Rothchild family. The couple spent summers in Newport. There are statues in Newport of August Belmont and Matthew Perry.[52] There are no statues to Caroline.

Recouping from injury, Perry's light duty included scouring the Barbary Coast of Africa for slave ships. Lawful importation of slaves to the US ended in 1807. Several times in his naval career, Perry hunted out slave ships and pirates to suppress the slave trade.

Perry established himself as a man of bold statement, when at age twenty-eight, in 1822, he resolved the nationality of Key West, Florida.[53] The history of land title in Key West is as quirky as Conch architecture. In 1815, the governor of Spanish Cuba gave a deed to Key West to Juan Pablo Salas, a Spanish Navy officer. When Britain gained Florida in 1821, Spain contended the Keys remained Spanish, as a part of Cuba.

Salas sold his land rights, twice. First, he sold Key West to John Geddes, a former governor of South Carolina, in exchange for a sloop valued at $575 US. Then, over dinner with a US businessman in Havana, Salas sold Key West to John W. Simonton for $2,000 in Spanish pesos. The two titleholders brought suit to clear title. Simonton, who had the greater weight in Washington, gained clear title. He recouped his investment by transfer of three-fourths of his land to three investors. Land nationality was left unresolved.

---

[51] Oliver Hazard Perry, of *Don't Give Up the Ship* fame, was commander of Erie-built *Lawrence* and *Niagara*, when he gave the American fleet its first victory over the British on Lake Erie in the War of 1812.

[52] Both statues by John Quincy Adams Ward are in front of the Preservation Society of Newport County. August Belmont initiated horse racing in Newport, as a high stakes event.

[53] See more on Key West in Cruise through History, Itinerary VI Ports of the Atlantic Coast of North America.

In 1822, Perry arrived in Key West, on behalf of the US, and planted an American flag. He renamed the adjoining island of *Cayo Hueso*, bone island to Native Americans, as Thompson Island, in honor of Smith Thompson, Secretary of the Navy. The US Navy presence remained, while Native American burial recognition was obscured.

Besides routing out slavery and protecting US assets, Perry's passions were educating cadets and promoting new technology in the Navy. He developed curriculum at the Naval Academy. In the 1830s, Perry was at the Brooklyn Naval Yard, where he oversaw construction of the second naval steam ship, the USS *Fulton*. So enthusiastic was Perry over capabilities of steam warships, that he is regarded as the father of the steam navy.

In 1840, at age forty-six, Perry earned the highest rank in the navy, that of commodore. When the US went to war in Mexico, in 1846, Perry led part of the US fleet. He personally led a ground assault in Tabasco, during the Siege of Veracruz.

When there were no wars to fight, Perry returned to hunting slave ships. He remained part of US naval talent reserve. Ready for his next challenge.

Japan Prior to Perry

Yokahama Ancient Tomb Site

Japan was formed by emperors, who rose above regional power elite, becoming god-like sons of the heavens. Removed from people, and from daily chores of running a government, emperors acquiesced to Shogun to perform mundane aspects of rule. In 1183, a Shogun refused to concede power to a child-emperor. The age of Shogun began.

The first capital of a Shogun was Kyoto. For four centuries, Kyoto was the military, governmental and cultural capital of Japan. In all aspects, Shogun determined rules of society. Lords oppressed farmers. In return, Shogun ensured a period of peace.

In 1600, the Tokugawa dynasty of Shogun wrested power from other lords, gaining leadership of Japan. They moved the capital to Edo, as Tokyo was then known. Tokugawa Shogun built a beautiful castle in Edo, surrounded by gardens, still existing, now in the center of Tokyo. As a Tokugawa Shogun looked toward Europe, he was horrified by the degree to which sectarian religious rivalry caused bloodshed. He closed Japan to the west and enacted a brutal policy toward Jesuits and all missionaries. The closure policy remained in effect, until the arrival of Perry.

Though the arrival of Perry was a capstone event, igniting a civil war of ideology within Japan, the Shogunate system was already in decline. An emperor of a new era was gaining popular support, as though waking from a sleep of six and a half centuries. Common folk resented Samurai, complacent in their assumed superiority in society. Within Samurai ranks, there were warriors who supported return of the monarch.[54]

Shogun had physical power to close ports; they did not have ethereal power to contain economic effects of feudalism. Democratizing impacts of capitalism pierced Japan's veil. Samurai, supported by feudal lords, lived by taxing peasant farmers, at a constant rate. As the value of currency diminished, and cost of goods increased, taxes remained constant. Samurai became impoverished, while entrepreneur peasants flourished.

---

[54] Consider Samurai transitional leader Itagaki Taisuke, who attempted evolving Samurai to new purpose.

Wealthy farmers ignored Samurai and flaunted exceptions to Shogun rules. Common people of Japan regarded the Emperor as the Son of Heaven. By the mid-nineteenth century, Shogun were bureaucratic surplus, to an emerging democratic monarchy.

Perry in Yokohama

Yokahama Harbor

By 1852, the United States enjoyed robust trade with China. Japan remained sought-after and unattainable. The US was aware of Russian, French and British advances in Asia, with establishment of coaling stations and fishing fleets nearing Japanese borders. In addition, while shipwrecked Japanese sailors, rescued by American ships, were repatriated, American sailors held by Japan were imprisoned, or executed. The Shogun saw Americans as a threat to sovereignty. President Millard Fillmore viewed Japan as a problem to be solved. He turned to his problem-solver – Perry.

Perry's assignment was not debated in Congress, so it is not known what guidance he received. Perry knew the capacity of the American fleet. He was a veteran of planting the US flag and making firm statements of authority.

As his flagship, Perry chose the USS *Mississippi*, a steamship built under his supervision. When he reached Canton, now known as Guangzhou, China, the major international Chinese port of the time, Perry altered his flagship to the USS *Susquehanna*, a newer, side-wheel steamship, with a black hull. The former captain of *Susquehanna* was Fillmore's first choice to lead the US fleet into Edo. In Perry's string of fortuitous timing, the captain of the *Susquehanna* was relieved of duty, due to an unrelated incident. Perry assumed command of the Far East Squadron of the US Navy and its flagship.

Perry's choice of first landing in the Japanese archipelago evidences a keen sense of Japanese political structure. To characterize Perry entering Japan, as blasting his seventy-three-gun salute as he entered Edo harbor, fails to credit to his successful strategy, tactfully executed, prior to reaching Edo. His first port in Japan was Okinawa.[55]

Upon reaching Okinawa, Perry made his first audacious affront to the Shogun. He visited the king of Ryukyuan in Naha, rather than meet with the local affiliate of the Shogun. In further acknowledging authority of the local king, Perry entered into a trade agreement and purchased a parcel of land. Only heads of a country transferred rights to land or made treaties with governments. Perry knew he exposed Shogun weakness.

Perry also knew the Dutch maintained a presence in Japan, despite closure, in Nagasaki, on Kyushu island. On July 8, 1853, he led the US fleet past Nagasaki, to the outer reaches of Edo harbor, where he displayed firepower from his state-of-the-art cannons. Then he requested an audience with the Shogun, wrapped in a white flag of conciliation.

Shogunate officials were uncertain what action to take. The reigning twelfth Shogun was a strong leader, who successfully contained the Dutch in Nagasaki. Regardless of growing rebellion throughout Japan, spurred by repression of free thought, immediate concern of rulers in June 1853, was failing health of the Shogun. He died in July.

---

[55] Today, cruise itineraries follow Perry's route from Cape Town, across Southeast Asia; stopping for coal and water at Mauritius in the Indian Ocean, Ceylon, now known as Sri Lanka; Singapore, which was part of Malaysia; and the newly established British port in China of Hong Kong.

Assuming the Japanese needed time to organize a response, and not desiring an armed encounter, Perry sailed to Hong Kong to wait. Six months later, when Perry returned, there was a new Shogun. The thirteenth Shogun ascended by default, not ambition. Being Shogun lost its caché. In February 1854, Perry docked at Kanagawa, now Yokohama.

After a month of negotiations, a treaty was signed on March 31, 1854, with Perry representing the United States and an official of the Shogunate representing Japan. Known as the Kanagawa Convention, or the Treaty of Peace and Amity, the agreement opened a few ports for American ships. Perry made a cursory sailing around harbors of approved ports, including Hakodate on Hokkaido Island, before returning to the US. He knew the US Congress must ratify his actions to make them official. He did not know the tenuous nature of Shogun leadership.

Perry Legacy

Perry in Japan (Public Domain)

The Kanagawa Treaty divided the Japanese population. At times, the ideological rift was deadly. One faction promoted Imperial reverence and expulsion of foreign barbarians, while an equally outspoken faction wanted openness, freedom of speech and movement. There was a third faction favoring Imperial reverence and an open country. The third vision for Japan triumphed, resulting in a constitutional monarchy in the British model.

Amid civil unrest, the Boshin War erupted. This civil war between the Shogunate and Emperor ended with demise of Shogun and ascendency of Imperial rule in Japan by 1868. The last shogun, Tokugawa Yoshinobu was in power long enough to view the Emperor's fifty-thousand strong army and agree to a peaceful transition of power. Minor skirmishes continued for a decade, until people resolved to accept the new order.

In 1868, Emperor Meiji restored emperors to power. He resided in the Imperial Palace, vacated by the Shogun. He changed Edo, the Shogun name, to Tokyo, the capital of Japan.

For Perry, transition to life at home was far less turbulent. Congress eagerly ratified the Convention of Kanagawa. Perry was awarded a bonus and promoted to rear-admiral. Years of life at sea took a toll. He died in 1858 and was initially interred in New York. His final resting place is in his home city of Newport, Rhode Island.

Visiting Yokohama Today

Yokohama opened to foreign ships in 1859. The city quickly grew with American, British, and Chinese residents. Foreign trade brought new ideas and fashions. Yokohama soon had an English newspaper. Japan began exporting silk and expanded factory production.

Heavily bombed during World War II, Yokohama underwent extensive post-war redevelopment. Yokohama is a quiet place today, with an attractive walking area along the harbor, as part of Minato Mirai 21, a mixed-use development. Signature ornament of Minato Mirai is the 1993 Yokohama Landmark Tower. A favorite port stop for visitors and locals is the Cup of Noodle Museum. The minimalist food staple is a cult delight.

Yokohama Harbor Today

Do not look for Commodore Perry at Yokohama harbor. The Japanese memorial is in Perry Park, across the bay, in nearby Yokosuka, where Perry made his initial landing in 1853. His actions, seeming audacious to Japanese in 1853, are now regarded as a blessing.

KOREA

Busan & Jeju - Ancient Ways and Modern Adaptations

Isolated, insulated, occupied and independent, describes Korean people, on the peninsula and islands, who have survived for centuries adapting to circumstances. Stages of history are evident today, in hidden historical gems and unavoidable views of high-rise towers. Busan, the second city of Korea, never a capital city, a first foothold for ancient people and a last bastion for soldiers in the Korean War, is a vision of the new, first-world Korea. On Jeju Island, villagers, once isolated from the peninsula, then adopted by Korea, were often forgotten when foreign occupation, war and modernity came to the mainland. Visited together, Jeju and Busan offer two views of Korea, its history and its people.

On the peninsula, Busan is smaller and less dense, therefore more approachable, than its big sister, Seoul, the capital of Korea. A vacation destination for beaches, Busan retains vestiges of historic culture. It is the rising cultural city of Korea, home to rock music and film festivals, attracting millions of trendy culture seekers.

Blissfully ignored by the peninsula for most of its history, Jeju island is a life apart. One hundred and fifty miles south of Busan, closer to Japan, and two hundred and fifty miles from the Chinese mainland, Jeju-Do group of sixty-two islands sits at the confluence of the Yellow and East China seas, a transit point of migrating people in ancient history. Jeju Island developed mythology and cultural traditions unique from the Korean mainland.

This story examines Korea, holding the past and charging into the future, told through architecture, life ways and folk art. Mythical mermaids and rock music aficionados are joined in a look at Korea, more nuanced than guidebook views of a structured society. Koreans display their sense of humor. Visitors are enjoying the view.

Ancient & Modern

Ancient Ways on Jeju

Volcanic Terrain Jeju Island

Jeju island was formed by a volcano, bestowing the island with mystical lakes, above green plains. Basalt is the island bedrock. It was the building stone and artistic medium of ancient people, rediscovered in modern architecture and contemporary art.

Ancient people stopped on these islands in early migration from the Chinese or Korean mainland, on the way to Japan. Archaeological remains are of fishermen and potters. Lava tubes provided cave dwellings. Today, lava caves are a natural resource World Heritage Site. Early people were not sufficiently adept at farming to enable a large population. Until the tenth century, people lived simply, not far from the shore.

In legend, the first three men on Jeju emerged from holes in the ground. Fortuitously, a box washed up on shore containing all they needed to sustain life: three women, horses, cows, and seeds of grain. The island was named Tamna, the name of one of the men.

In the line of Tamna kings, there were periods of isolation, interspersed with contact with the peninsula. In the Three Kingdoms Period of Korea, two kingdoms visited Tamna. The ultimately successful kingdom, uniting and dominating Korea, the Silla, sent an embassy to Tamna. The visit established Jeju vassal states and collected taxes. No Silla officials stayed to rule Tamna. Of provinces of Korea today, Jeju is allowed local self-government. Cultural and language differences render local rule a practical option for Seoul.

In isolation, Jeju people developed language unique from the mainland. For five hundred years, from the tenth to the fourteenth century, Mongols controlled Jeju. When they left the island, they imparted so little to locals that indigenous island language endured.

Tamna kings had contact with Han dynasty officials from China and travelers from Japan. Since there are no cultural impacts from these visits, most likely Jeju provided a voyage stopover between mainland China, Korea, and Japan, just as the island is today.

Sometime around the fifth century of the current era, people of Jeju added fruits of the sea to their diet. Included were abalone, octopus, oyster, sea slugs, sea urchins and various types of algae. To reach the harvest, men dove below the water with a basket, fixed to their body with a reed or leather tie. As the Jeju population increased, and shallow depth sea life decreased, divers went deeper to retrieve a harvest.

Mermaid Monument

Over centuries, women replaced men, becoming *Haenyeo*, mermaids of Jeju. Historians speculate on various reasons for corps of divers becoming predominantly, then solely, women. Women were adept at holding their breath for up to three minutes, something men were unable to master. Women have fatty tissue, which keeps their bodies warm and able to sustain life in cold, deep water. Another Haenyeo theory is the population of men depleted, as conscripts for war, left women to feed families.

A bit of truth lies in all theories of origination of mermaids on Jeju. Mermaids today dive, as have their grandmothers and all island women in their memory. In early centuries, women wore cotton clothing, which weighed them down and made swimming difficult. Today mermaids wear wetsuits, flippers and googles.

In the Confucius society of China and Japan, women were subservient to husbands. By extension, historians assumed men of Jeju were predominant village leaders and food gatherers. However, Jeju was removed from mainland life in China and Korea, until the tenth century. From the fifth century, women dived for food. Matriarchs figure prominently in historic lore of China. On Jeju, matriarchs were leaders in society.

Silla control of Jeju, however minimal, ended in 935, when the Silla dynasty of Korea ended. Records of conquering Goryeo dynasty reflect that in 1105, Tamna was conquered and made part of Goryeo lands. Records and reality are inconsistent.

Mongol invasions of China and Korea in the thirteenth century did not go smoothly on the mainland. Rebel groups fought Mongols, even after kings capitulated. In 1270, rebels fleeing Mongol captors of Chinese and Korean provinces fled to Jeju. In Jeju, rebels controlled the island and banished the king of Tamna. Mongols pursued the rebels, bringing war to quiet, little Jeju. Mongols remained, enjoying the climate, although they were homesick for their traditional meat diet, plentiful on the mainland.

Mongols built little on the island during their stay. They imparted some vocabulary to Jeju speakers, making the local language even more unintelligible to mainlanders. Mongols wore leather and fur, a fashion statement enjoying longevity on the island.

When kings of the great Joseon dynasty of Korea sent Mongols back north in 1392, they replaced Mongols as overlords of Jeju. Joseon kings ruled Korea until 1897. Their capital was Seoul, known then as Hanseong. Joseon rule was a strictly structured society of Confucianism. Jeju, far from Seoul over the sea, was insulated from their confining ways.

So rigorous was Confucianism in Joseon society, that Buddhism was discouraged. Allowed deities were ancestors and the king. Life was relaxed on Jeju. People observed cosmology of the natural environment. Shamans guided spiritual relationships through the world of demons and afterlife. People of Jeju expressed grandfather worship in stone statues.

Using abundant basalt, *dolharubang* statues appeared across the island, documented from 1763. Affectionately known as *haru*, statues are three to ten feet tall of simple stylized human form, all with two hands toward their front, one higher than the other, and all wearing a mushroom hat. *Haru* have bulging eyes, broad noses, and thin mouths.

Haru are often compared to totem poles on the Korean peninsula, statues in China and Moa of Easter Island. Locally, statues are known as grandfather statues or guardians. In a nod to Confucianism, statues are placed in family units, with the grandfather prominent. In gift shops across Jeju today, *haru* come in all sizes, ready to grace gardens anywhere.

As guardians, protecting people from demons, *haru* are usually placed in pairs at gates and near homes. The Korean Cultural Center in Washington, DC placed two *haru* at the driveway entrance. Today, *haru* are seen guarding a beach or major street. They make appearances in comics, taking a light look at foreign visitors. *Haru* are happy Jeju icons.

Historic Busan

Among the oldest archaeological remains in Korea are in Busan. Early people migrated across northern plains of Asia and down the seacoast, east of the mountain ranges of Manchuria, to arrive at the Korean peninsula. At Busan people stopped at the sea.

When kings of the great Joseon dynasty of Korea sent Mongols back north in 1392, they replaced Mongols as overlords of Jeju. Joseon kings ruled Korea until 1897. Their capital was Seoul, known then as Hanseong. Joseon rule was a strictly structured society of Confucianism. Jeju, far from Seoul over the sea, was insulated from their confining ways.

So rigorous was Confucianism in Joseon society, that Buddhism was discouraged. Allowed deities were ancestors and the king. Life was relaxed on Jeju. People observed cosmology of the natural environment. Shamans guided spiritual relationships through the world of demons and afterlife. People of Jeju expressed grandfather worship in stone statues.

Using abundant basalt, *dolharubang* statues appeared across the island, documented from 1763. Affectionately known as *haru*, statues are three to ten feet tall of simple stylized human form, all with two hands toward their front, one higher than the other, and all wearing a mushroom hat. *Haru* have bulging eyes, broad noses, and thin mouths.

Haru are often compared to totem poles on the Korean peninsula, statues in China and Moa of Easter Island. Locally, statues are known as grandfather statues or guardians. In a nod to Confucianism, statues are placed in family units, with the grandfather prominent. In gift shops across Jeju today, *haru* come in all sizes, ready to grace gardens anywhere.

As guardians, protecting people from demons, *haru* are usually placed in pairs at gates and near homes. The Korean Cultural Center in Washington, DC placed two *haru* at the driveway entrance. Today, *haru* are seen guarding a beach or major street. They make appearances in comics, taking a light look at foreign visitors. *Haru* are happy Jeju icons.

Historic Busan

Among the oldest archaeological remains in Korea are in Busan. Early people migrated across northern plains of Asia and down the seacoast, east of the mountain ranges of Manchuria, to arrive at the Korean peninsula. At Busan people stopped at the sea.

Busan Bay

Busan, set back from the sea by a smattering of islands, developed as a port in the fifteenth century. It primarily received Japanese traders. Koreans do not have a history of seafaring. Formalized trade developed between Korea and Japan by 1443. Japanese pirates sailed among the islands, ignoring treaties.

Busan is home to a concentration of ancient burial tombs, indicating a large and stable early population.[56] Near Busan are sites of ancient iron ore mining. Weapons produced in Busan kilns were popular in tenth century Japan. Historically, Koreans were more focused on life at home than attempting to conquer others.

Japanese sailors collected knowledge of Busan defenses, or the lack of them. A pressed-earth fort at Dongnae was impressive, not effective. In 1592, a Japanese armada, carrying highly trained troops, landed and looted the city. The fort was expanded in 1707.

A great Korean naval commander, able to out-maneuver Japanese superior vessel strength, was Yi Sun-Sin.[57] All two dozen of his maritime victories were against Japanese adversaries. He is often compared to British Admiral

---

[56] See Bokcheon-dong Mound Tombs, and the Tomb Museum, with artifacts from before the sixth century CE.

[57] Yi Sun-Sin lived from 1545 to 1598.

Horatio Nelson for his brilliant tactical ability, as well as the fact that his government did not appreciate his efforts until after his death. A statue of Yi greets visitors to Yongdu-san Park today.

When Korea ended its Hermit Kingdom phase, at the end of the nineteenth century, Busan hosted merchant ships. Today, most of the incoming, and over half of exported goods, pass through Busan docks. A railroad line connects Busan to Seoul. Seoul is the governmental capital of Korea. Busan is the economic and cultural center.

Twentieth Century Jeju

A bloody mainland rebellion spread to Jeju in the mid-twentieth century. Known as the Jeju Uprising, independent-spirited people of Jeju revolted when their mother country was arbitrarily divided by foreign powers. Jeju objected to dual presidential elections.

In May 1948, people of Jeju island went into streets of Jeju City armed with weapons left behind by retreating Japanese forces. Rebels barricaded themselves in tunnels dug by the Japanese during World War II. People felt delivered from one overlord, only to be governed by puppets to the Soviet Union, China, and the United States.

South Korean troops on the peninsula went to Jeju Island to

Jeju Haru

put down rebellion. Korean troops had no desire to fire on other Koreans. On transit to Jeju, the troops rebelled.

In the rebellion, ten percent of the Jeju population of three hundred thousand perished. In response, the Republic of Korea instituted a National Security Act, making it a crime to disturb the peace. The act enabled political prisons, holding fifty thousand people.

Busan in Twenty-first Century Korea

Cruise Port Busan

From 1950 to 1954, Busan was the operations center for the government of the Republic of Korea. North Korean forces crossed the 38th parallel in August 1950, quickly overcoming Seoul and heading to Busan. Only the defended perimeter outside Busan kept South Korea on the map of nations today. Hundreds of thousands of people fled south to Busan, ahead of soldiers. At the war's end, many transplants remained in the city.

In 1950, Busan was not prepared to receive a large influx of people requiring shelter. People with few resources congregated in Gamcheon Village of south

Busan, an industrial area of steep hills. It provided marginal shelter of hastily built, multi-story, haphazard construction. After the Korean War, those who could, moved to better neighborhoods. The wartime town was a blight on the city. Gamcheon Village was set for removal.

Gamcheon Culture Village

Residents of Gamcheon Village were fond of their town within a city. They painted houses in bold colors, in defiance of steel and glass towers of modern Busan. A resident group obtained funding to make uninhabitable houses livable, so they could remain occupied. Instead of urban renewal with a dumpster, Gamcheon Culture Village was preserved.

Gamcheon Culture Village is culture-vernacular. It is the perfect place to join locals strolling through the former shanty town with ice creams in hand. Locals rent classic Joseon era clothing, then pose for photos. The village invites unapologetic tourism.

Pre-1954 Korea was predominately an agrarian country. Impacts of World War II caused resettlement of people from farms to factories. The end of war began a cosmic shift in society. Not all factory workers wanted to return to farms. In the dynamic twentieth century, factory workers easily transitioned from war-time production to new technology of consumer goods, technology devices and automobiles. Korea went from a Third World occupied country to a First World tiger economy.

Sections of Busan today are still referred to as marketplaces. Instead of acres of street stalls, markets are shopping streets, that wind across major thoroughfares and small side streets. It is easy to become lost in Busan, intrigued by a maze of shops.

Nurimaru APEC House

In 2005, Busan was host to the Asia-Pacific Economic Cooperation meetings. Built for the event, Nurimaru APEC House, with a panoramic view of the city, is open to the public.[58] It is a stunning example of Korean twenty-first century architecture, in a garden.

---

58   Nurimaru is Korean for World Summit.

For a livelier side of culture, enjoy the Busan Film Festival. Begun in 1996, submissions are highly competitive. Busan is the premier film festival of Asia. Loud and colorful is the Busan Rock Music Festival, held on a Busan beach every August since 2000. Over a million people attend each year. Busan sends a message to the world that turbulent history and reliable automobiles are not the only reasons to think of Korea.

Visiting Jeju and Busan Today

Haeundae Beach

Today on Jeju, Haenyeo pose for cameras and demonstrate skills for visitors. Haenyeo are diminishing as there are many other options for women in industry and professions. Diving is a skill that requires practice. Many women of Jeju prefer to spend time at universities. Support for skilled mermaids comes from the United Nations cultural arm, which recognizes Haenyeo as Intangible Cultural Heritage of Jeju.

Ubiquitous at gift shops are *haru*. Since they are a light-hearted representation of the independent spirit of Jeju, there is no cultural slight in a haru refrigerator magnet. *Haru* of basalt are a double memento, as basalt is the indigenous building material of Jeju, now used for homes in daring architectural designs.

Decades from the Jeju Uprising, people are resigned to two Koreas. Politicians focus on democracy, stewardship, and economic success. Jeju people feel part of South Korea. Disputes are focused today on stewardship of the environment. Conversion of precious old forests to tangerine groves ended, with some economic success, but no desire to continue turning forests to farms on Jeju. Jeju is treasured for its natural landscape.

Wars destroyed the fort at Dongnae and some cultural sites. Japanese intended Shinto to replace Buddhism. Koreans do not forgive occupation behavior. People now welcome Russians and Americans, despite the nations waging hot and cold war on their turf.

For a lovely Busan experience, wander the tree-lined road of Youngdu-san Park. Admire pagoda style buildings, dragon statues, the site of the original port and the Nurimaru APEC House, then head down to Haeundae Beach. The beach is where locals go. Along the beach periphery are high rise apartments, where hard working locals aspire to live.

CHINA
BLENDED HISTORY
CHINA-KOREA-JAPAN

Chinese Tomb Style Garden Monument

Conquering emperors of China thought themselves kings of the world. They looked inward at the expanse of their domain. Japanese emperors believed the sun rose to shine on them. They looked west, on whom the sun descended, to conquer vassals under their majesty. Emperors of Korea believed they held paradise, poised between two aggressive military powers. They decided territory preservation, not expansive action, was the best course. The western world looked upon the three domains as the Far East - places of mystery, cultural novelty and trade opportunity.

Tokyo Pagoda

China, Korea and Japan derive from an ancient past, in which the cultures of each informed and interacted with the others, developing into distinct nations. Despite Chinese anthropological claims of an origination of homo sapiens in China, the Peking Man theory has receded to understandings of migration of peoples of the world from Eve in Africa, although earlier dates and more frequent migration patterns are now known. Japan and Korea each developed toward a homogeneous people, while China melded diverse people into one nation.

Even when the nations kept outsiders from their harbors, they traded goods and ideas amongst themselves. At times they were competitors or aggressors. Ideas or technology received, became unique in separate development over time. It is almost impossible to tell the history of any of the three without mention of repeated interaction. Their histories are strands of a braid interwoven over time, with commonalities and diversions.

China has a history of warring bands more or less conquering the larger landscape, becoming dynasties of power, whose greatest enemies were internal. As Confucius, the fifth century BCE sage said of China, *when it is apart, it must come together, and when it is together, it must come apart.* Wisdom of his words is repeated in history.[59]

Pre-Yangtze Dam Village Fortress

---

[59] Confucius was a minor Chinese court official to the emperor, who lived from 551 to 479 BCE.

Korea, much desired by China and Japan as a base from which to attack each other, was briefly occupied by each. In over two thousand years of written history, Korea has withstood aggressors, whether they were neighbors, or Europeans, until 1950. Before 1945, Korea was one of the oldest united states of the world, from the fourteenth century.

Japan's one dynasty ruled through one hundred and twenty-five emperors. Its thin string of islands ranges from balmy Ryúkyú in the south, to chilly Hokkaidó in the north.[60] The Meiji emperor in the nineteenth century became a model reformist, in part to convince Great Britain there was no moral imperative to colonizing the already modern Japan.

The 1950 Korean War was a climaxing event in the blend of history that altered Korea's future. Japan set events in play, when it occupied Korea in 1910, then forfeited its hold in 1945. The United States and the Soviet Union ended World War II and began the Cold War in Korea. China entered the fray, increasing stakes in a war, with no declared peace.

A complete history of each country is beyond the scope of a short story. This story is a brief introduction to the dynamics of China, Korea and Japan, to offer an understanding of nuances of culture, as a prelude to visiting special sites in all three.

Developing Cultures through Interaction

Early humans migrated from Africa to China in a southern route across India and Southeast Asia, before coming past the Yangzi River to the Yellow River near Beijing. There they were joined by humans coming across a northern route through Mongolia and southward toward Beijing. Ancient Tianyuan Cave, and Upper Cave the home of Peking Man, attest to early humans in China. Such a large population flourished in that part of China, at such an early date, that Mao hoped to prove his people originated near Beijing.

---

[60] Ryúkyú is the same latitude as the Bahamas, while Hokkaidó is the same latitude as Quebec.

Chinese Money Tree

Early Han Burial

Early humans migrated from China to Korea and from Korea to Japan, although there were other migrations to Japan that went through neither China nor Korea. People took the northern route across Mongolia and Manchuria into northern Japan, while others migrated from southern Asia to southern islands of Japan. Several migration waves occurred over thousands of years.

Today, the historic population of Korea is a homogenous people of Korean speakers. Migration of Vietnamese and other Asian people to Korea is a recent dynamic, as Korean rural dwellers seek spouses from far afield. Japan is a largely homogenous population. Indigenous people, on the northern island of Hokkaido, are a small minority.

An interesting note to early human migration routes, is that they are similar to the route of Buddhism to China, Korea and Japan from northcentral India in the first century CE. Two-thousand-year-old trade routes followed the same path from the Arabian Peninsula into central China and the Yellow River valley. Early trade routes did not flow directly to Korea and Japan. Evidence of early trade indicates Korean and Japanese traders came to China. Japan sent monks to China to learn about Confucian ethical society.

Landing Site in Korean Text

China was master of the Silk Road economy. Korea and Japan learned silk-making techniques from China, although Chinese silks remained superior. Korea learned to weave cotton from China. Korean cottons did well in the Silk Road marketplace. Japan came to market with high quality metal goods, including swords. Japan learned initial metallurgy skills from China. Interaction furthered technology for all three.

All three countries began settlements that developed into fiefdoms of war lords. In China, the first big royal dynasty was the Han dynasty of the second century BCE to the second century CE, about the time of the Roman Empire. Han rulers made the brilliant discovery that war was costly to population and resources. Their formula for a cohesive and compliant domain was bureaucratic administration to collect taxes, and a regal emperor, whose ceremonies allowed people to leave the fields to celebrate. Identifying with majesty of a ruler, spread a feeling of stability and peace among the people.

Han emperors were masters of foreign relations. Rather than conquer Korea or Japan, their kings were invited to receive titles from the great Chinese emperor. Foreigners were impressed. Titles bequeathed by the Chinese had status. Japanese merchants were given gold seals to stamp trade correspondence with an aura of authority and prestige.

Chinese Warlord

Writing began in China in the fifteenth century BCE. Initially, Korea and Japan adopted Chinese characters. Classical Chinese is known as Wenyan. Only experts in calligraphy had mastery of language. Although second century CE Han emperors transitioned to Baihu, or vernacular, Wenyan, also known as Mandarin, continued as the language of civil service exams in China until the twentieth century. The exam was a test of culture more than suitability for office.[61]

Hangul alphabet replaced Wenyan in Korea in the fifteenth century CE. Classical scholars resisted change, while women quickly adapted, producing popular literature. Today, Korean language is a cultural icon. In Japan, Chinese characters, known as kanji, combined with vernacular, becoming kana. Added vocabulary, necessary for worldly experiences, resulted in kanji and kana mixed with katakana, creating complex language.

Korea and Japan adopted Chinese paper making techniques by the fifth century CE. In the sixth century, China printed the world's first paper currency. The idea of paper having value in trade was rejected as a silly idea in Korea and Japan. In China the practice ceased.

Political Independence and Nation Building

The name China comes from Qin, pronounced Chin. In the third century BCE, Emperor Qin built more than five hundred miles of stone-paved road to transport soldiers and rice. He built walls across hill tops, which sixteen hundred years later Ming dynasty emperors covered in stone to create the Great Wall of China. In 219 BCE, Qin cut a canal from a tributary of the Yangzi River, connecting the West River to a tributary of the Pearl River, giving his people a waterway from Hong Kong into central China. He enabled reliable food sources, avoiding periodic famine.

Qin was obsessed with immortality. He heard legends of people toward the rising sun, who held the secret to long life. Twice he tried to sail to Japan.

---

[61] Chen Duxiu, faculty of Beijing University and a founder of Chinese Communism with Mao Zedong, advocated use of Baihu, also known as Guoyu, as the national language. John Keay, China: A History, Basic Books, New York, 2009, p. 481.

Great Wall of China

Frustrated by large sea monsters, Qin built a scale replica of his palace for his tomb and let everyone know it had an artificial lake of poisonous mercury, to deter looters. The tomb has not been located.

Terracotta Soldiers in Qin's Tomb in Xian

In 1974, a man digging a well near Xian, the area Qin's tomb, dredged up terracotta life-size limbs. Eventual excavation of Qin's Terracotta Soldiers revealed three pits of terracotta statues, modeled from people in Qin's army. The largest of three pits has 3,210 statues, standing in rows of infantry. Tomb robbers looted armor adorning statues, just after Qin died. Loss of armor has not deterred thousands of visitors each year from marveling at Qin's world. His memory is immortal.

Qin was the last ruler in a succession of Warring States, which depleted empires in the desire for total conquest of China. In the prior Shang empire, lasting to 1027 BCE, oracles heated bones and wrote fortunes told in bone cracklings. The Zhou dynasty followed from 1027 to 221 BCE, when copper was mined and building a Great Wall began. More might be known of Qin, but historians worked for Han emperors. Knowing that reputations are made by those writing history, Han marginalized accomplishments of Qin, to make Han greater by comparison. Beware politicized historians.

There were five imperial dynasties in China from Han in the second century BCE to the Qing dynasty in 1912. The first Han emperor united most of China by 90 BCE, including Manchuria, northern Korea and west toward the Caspian Sea south of Tibet. Confucius advised emperors to lead rituals not armies. The advice was well taken by Han. Emperors built tombs to their ancestors. Royals were buried in full body jade suits. A usurper unseated complacent Han. From 618 to 907, the Tang dynasty ruled China.

Feeding Population Along Grand Canal

Tang emperors cut the Grand Canal, a World Heritage Site, early in the seventh century. The transport corridor facilitated rice grown in the south to reach the hungry north. Japanese pirates enjoyed use of the canal.

While Europe was in dark ages of the crusades, the Song Dynasty ruled China from 960 to 1279. Song emperors looked inward to reforming government administration and expanded an academy of scholars. Gun powder and the magnetic compass were in use. When Niccolo and Matteo Polo arrived, Dadu, now Beijing, was a sophisticated city.

The Song were gone by 1279. Mongols from the north usurped the Song and ruled a united China to 1368. Since Genghis Khan fell off his horse and died in 1227, Khans were more adept at conquest than proficient administration. Chinese culture and population went into descent, although unnoticed by the Polos, as they marveled at China.[62]

The Ming dynasty presided over a united China from 1368 to 1644. It was an era of high culture. Chinese tea, porcelain and silk were prized in Europe. The Forbidden City was built in Beijing. The Great Wall was connected and covered in stone. Often portrayed as a defensive wall, Ming used the wall as a transport corridor across the hills. Emperors went along the wall in sedan chairs, stopping at the same towers visited by travelers today.

While Ming emperors sponsored artworks, Ottoman Turks conquered central Asia. Mongols took control of India. In 1644, Ming emperors invited Manchurians to cross the wall to help quell rebellion in their capital. Manchurians came into the city and took charge. They changed their name to a more elegant sounding Qing. Qing emperors had Manchu mustaches. Styles and priorities of Chinese royals changed.

From the fourth century BCE three kingdoms, Koguryo, Paekche and Silla, developed from a bevy of feudal warlords in Korea. By 676, the Silla kingdom ruled a united Choson, pre-empire Korea, and had the strength to expel the Chinese. Until the nineteenth century invasion by Japan and colonization in 1910, Korea was a united people, of a single language and culture, with stable borders. It was the Hermit Kingdom.

---

[62] Mongols were able horsemen, who often slept in the saddle. Genghis Khan may have fallen in his sleep.

Korean Style

Between warring giants, Korea's growing population, well supplied with rice, built an independent civilian government, structured by Confucius. A small military defended the borders. Most resources were focused on agriculture and artistic culture.

Surrounded by sea, Choson people were not seafarers. The inhospitable coast foiled several Japanese invasion attempts. Seoul was founded in 1404, on a rare spot for a harbor. Silla pirates attacked Japanese cargo ships, until the nations established a treaty in 1600.

History of modern Japan begins in 710, when the *Chronicles of Japan*, *Kojiki*, were begun, to the exclusion of prior books.[63] In a combination of myth and fact, gods created Nippon, land of the rising sun. The land was so wealthy, that

---

[63] *Kojiki* was originally written in Chinese. Only women wrote in hiragana. They were prolific. Sei Shónagon wrote the *Pillow Book* in 1002, of her time attending the empress. Written as a diary, it is a peek into court life, without political bias. Another lady-in-waiting, Murasaki Shikibu, wrote *Tale of Genji*, a novel written as fiction, based on fact, and a depiction of life in court society.

in 1274, Kublai Khan, the great Mongol warlord, came to conquer. He first needed to reach land. A storm ravaged his ships and sent survivors to shores of Korea. He came back with fifteen thousand ships, on which many troops died of disease before entering the Korea Strait. Before reaching land, a 200 mile an hour hurricane destroyed the fleet. Those sailors who reached Japan were killed on the beach. The Divine Wind of the Sun God protected Nippon. Kublai died in 1294. There was no third armada.[64]

Japan is a Buddhist country. Ritual of governance was organized in Shinto, Way of the Gods, until 1945. Shinto is viewed as a religion. If good governance is a religion, so it was.

Japan was ruled by one continuous dynasty, in which heads of a few noble families wielded enormous power. They were warrior shogun of legend.[65] Shogun were effective to corral warlords. Shogun were Buddhists, and killing is not condoned in Buddhism, so shogun made killing in the emperor's name an act of honor. Shogun acted, not on orders of the emperor, rather on what he knew the emperor to have wanted. Interpretation of emperor desire differed between Shogun, leading to power struggles. After threat of invasion by Mongols subsided in 1294, Shogun fought among themselves.

While Shogun engaged in war, a merchant class engaged in trade. Ink painting and Noh drama flourished in ornate palaces, behind high walls, surrounded by moats. Contact with China was constricted during the late Tang dynasty, in the tenth century. Japanese artisans, informed by Tang arts, unknowing of the growing Ming style in China, took Tang style in clothes and artistic expression, formed into styles uniquely Japanese. Tea ceremony, garden design, clothing and architecture were highly ritualized in Japan.

For two hundred years, through the sixteenth and seventeenth centuries, Japan was secluded from the outer world by edict of Shogun. Lore of persecution of Jesuit missionaries emanates from this era. Shogun excluded western

---

[64] Numbers of ships have grown in legend over time. Records kept were often written as symbolic and poetic.
[65] In the ninth century a Shogun took 200 children and trained them to fight. These were Samurai, warriors of no one but self. Elite Samurai were Ninja. See the story of Shogun, Samurai and Ninja.

missionaries, to protect Japan from religious wars then raging in Europe. Japan had sufficient armed camps of Shogun and Samurai, without bringing religious war into a Buddhist land.

World Trade, War and Economic Dominance

China Imperial Architecture

The nineteenth century was a pivotal time for China, Korea and Japan. Each was an independent nation state, with unique national identity. Then they opened to the world.

China opened to European trade in the sixteenth century, when it gave Portugal a trading station at Macau. The Dutch were refused a mainland port in the seventeenth century, so they opted for Taiwan. The British sailed to an uninhabited area across the harbor from Macau in 1830, and demanded rights to establish a trading station, known as Hong Kong.

Englishmen exported tea from China from 1691, through a crown monopoly granted to the English East India Company. Since England had no trade goods of interest to China, English traders paid for tea in silver. To end the drain on English silver, when tea drinking was the rage, the East India Company traded opium, grown in India, to China, where it was exchanged for tea. Opium use in China quickly became a health problem for the Chinese. The reformulated government of England as Britain, imported the lucrative commodity of tea in England, obtained without cost to Britain, using Indian opium.

By 1830, the British crown replaced the Company. Crown agent Lord Napier would only deal on a government-to-government basis and not with Chinese merchants as in the past. Chinese emperors did not deal directly with port agents. Napier was ordered to leave the port. He refused and called for British warships from India. China halted all trade. Napier returned to Macau where he died.[66]

China demanded that Britain stop importing opium to China. Britain claimed they were insulted when referred to in official correspondence as Yi. Yi means foreigner. British agents interpreted the word as barbarian.[67] In the end, China asked only that Britain trade something less vile for tea. Britain received control of Hong Kong in 1840. British Hong Kong was expanded in 1880.[68] The Opium War began a new era for China of making treaties with governments instead of war.

In 1853, Commodore Matthew C. Perry sailed into Edo Harbor, the capital, now Tokyo, and demanded the Japanese open trade or he would open fire. Perry demonstrated his cannon power. Japanese, in a power transfer from Shogun to emperor, negotiated a resolution granting open trade and ushering Perry's ship into the harbor at Yokohama.

Perry's timing was fortunate. The Meiji emperor of Japan ended the two-hundred-year control of the Tokugawa family as Shogun. Government vested

---

[66] William Napier, 9th Lord Napier, born Kinsale, Ireland in 1786 and died in Macau in 1834, of dysentery.
[67] In Korea, the classic age of Korean culture is the Yi dynasty, from 1392 to 1910. Yi is a matter of semantics.
[68] Hong Kong has its own story in this Itinerary.

in an elected assembly, in which all people were enfranchised. The rule of law, and law of nature, replaced Shogun edicts. Japan opened to western knowledge. Known as the Meiji Restoration, the wise emperor presented Japan to Britain and the US as an equal, not as a potential colony.

In 1866, a United States merchant vessel, the *General Sherman*, arrived in the Korean harbor at Pyongyang, demanding Korea open itself to trade. The ship was ordered to leave. Instead, it fired on people on shore and burned fishing vessels. The *General Sherman* had difficulty sailing away in low tide. Locals burned and sunk the vessel.[69]

An 1884 Seoul food crisis gave Japan and China an opportunity to upstage each other asserting dominance in Korea. Crisis was averted by treaty in which Japan, with its display of superior military forces, received Taiwan from China. Russia challenged Japan in Korea.

In 1905, tension between Russia and Japan exploded in the Battle of Tsushima in the Korean Strait. Japan devastated the Russian navy. United States President Theodore Roosevelt brokered a peace arrangement, in which Japan received half of Sakhalin Island, north of Hokkaido. Roosevelt received a Nobel Peace Prize for his efforts.[70]

Emboldened by its show of strength over Russia and China, in 1910, Japan invaded Korea and its portion of Manchuria. Korea ended its era of unbroken independence, when it became a Japanese colony. During World War II, Japan extended occupation to all of Manchuria. Chinese maps today name the region Northeast China, not Manchuria.

Victory in the Battle of Tsushima emboldened Japan's image as a dominant sea power. Japan exited the League of Nations in 1933 and invaded China in 1937. The United States embargoed all goods to Japan in 1940. In 1941, *the*

---

[69] Facts surrounding the *misunderstanding* remain in dispute. The incident is celebrated in North Korea for deflecting foreign imperialism.
[70] The Nobel Prize awarded Roosevelt was the first Nobel awarded to an American politician. Japan lost control of Sakhalin Island to Russia in 1945, in the aftermath of World War II. Russia and Japan continue to dispute ownership of Kuril Islands.

day that will live in infamy, Japan bombed Pearl Harbor, United States navy base in Hawaii.[71]

World War II Allied HQ in China

The end of World War II, in the context of East Asia, was the immediate beginning of the Korean War. Events happened in quick succession to result in a war, governed by a truce, where peace has not yet been declared. As so many facts remain in dispute, the following is an overview, to complete the story of twentieth century China, Japan and Korea.

Korea was a Japanese colony from 1910 to 1945. During thirty-five years of Japanese occupation, Korean government and economic systems were replaced by Japanese government officials, businesspeople and bankers. By 1940, assimilation to Japanese culture was in full form. Korean media and printing were halted. Korean people were required to adopt Japanese names. People

---

[71] Franklin D. Roosevelt's radio address on December 7, 1941, called *the day one that would live in infamy.*

were relocated to work in the war effort. Life was similar in Manchuria. After World War II, there was chaos in Korea. Manchuria was absorbed into China as Northeast China.[72]

World War II ended in Japan so abruptly that there was no plan for transition of Korea to independence. After declaring victory in Europe, Roosevelt and Stalin discussed a gradual transition for Korea, lasting decades. On August 6, 1945, the United States dropped an atomic bomb on Hiroshima. On August 8, Russia declared war on Japan and began to enter Manchuria. On August 9, the second bomb was dropped on Nagasaki. On August 15, Japan surrendered. Russia was at the time entering north Korea. United States troops were six hundred miles away in Okinawa.

On August 12, President Franklin Roosevelt died, and Harry S. Truman became president. Colonel Dean Rusk was given hours to draw a plan for Korea; to appease the Soviet Union and leave all Korea communist. The plan seized upon an arbitrary division of the country at the 38th parallel on the map, which put the Korean capital of Seoul in the south. August 13, U.S. President Truman approved the plan. Stalin also approved.

North Korea immediately became a communist state and held elections for president. The dynasty of Kim Il Sung began. South Korea held elections in which dictatorial Syngman Rhee was chosen. The south declared its president the national leader of a single Korea. The United Nations recognized the Republic of Korea in the south.

In response, the north, the People's Republic of Korea, shut down power transmission from the north to the south. Seoul was without power. There was no effective government organization in the south, where violent rebellions erupted.

United States withdrew troops once an election was held. Kim, with Soviet support, came across the 38th Parallel on June 25, 1950. Seoul fell quickly. Truman appealed to the United Nations for a War Resolution, not waiting for authority from the US Congress.

---

[72] Manchu people lived in the area, a traditional homeland of Korea.

By August 1950, war was at a stalemate at a perimeter around Pusan, the southeastern port city, now Busan. Truman deployed General George MacArthur, his best and worst decision of the war. Brilliant tactician, MacArthur landed his eighty thousand marines at Inchon, south of Seoul, liberated Seoul and cut off supply lines to the North's troops. By April 1951, Truman and Stalin agreed to end the war, by setting the line back at the 38th Parallel. The war might have been a ten-month police action of the United Nations. Instead, the war dragged on for two more years.

There were several matters that preempted cease-fire and forever avoided real peace. General MacArthur, in the euphoria of the field, issued a public statement that there is no honor without victory. Truman immediately fired MacArthur, although the damage was done. Stalin was suspicious of each move by the United States. The Cold War began.

China entered the war, offering a ceaseless supply of humans in waves of assaults on United Nations forces. Casualties mounted on all sides. Meanwhile, the US and Soviets dickered over placement of a demilitarized zone and terms of a prisoner exchange. The UN preferred a voluntary return, allowing North Korean forces to remain as civilians in South Korea, if they chose. North Korea and China demanded return of all prisoners.

The Korean War ended with an armistice on July 27, 1953. Full peace was coopted by the Cold War and US desire to maintain atomic weapons in Korea. Kim Il Sung consolidated power, directing the North Korean economy to heavy industry and military production. He was succeeded in death by his son Kim Jong Il in 1994. In 2008, Kim Jong Il died of a stroke, leaving the country to his son, the current leader, Kim Jong Un.[73]

South Korea's post war years were turbulent. There were few government and business leaders after thirty-five years on the sidelines. The first civil elections were held in 1992, four years after the 1988 Seoul Olympics. North Korea demanded to co-host the Olympics in a country still outwardly planning for unification. When the demand was refused, North Korea called for a boycott. Cuba and Albania observed the boycott. China did not.

---

[73] Kim Jong Un was born in 1983 or 1984. He holds a degree in physics.

Cultural Preservation – Unique and Enduring

Enduring Market Economy

In 1991, the Soviet Union dissolved. North Korea was left to its own economic future. Just before his death in 1994, Kim Il Sung acknowledged problems of a country without Soviet support. Kim Jong Un inherited a country with firm control of a government and a failing economy. Power output of North Korea in 2014 was one percent that of South Korea.

South Korea now leads Asian Tiger economies. Along the beach in Busan today, visitors see a dense skyline of high-rise apartments. Streets are thick with new cars. Hyundai Motors, started by Korean native Chung Ju Yung, with government support, returned the national investment with one of the most successful automobile manufacturers in the world. Hyundai employees have incentives to purchase new cars every few years. The middle class is large and growing in South Korea, where unification is rarely mentioned.

Cruise visitors to Seoul or Busan find the ports lively and prosperous. The biggest issues facing Koreans today is the high cost of education and declining birthrate due to women in universities and work force, enjoying emancipation of a western-style country.

Further reading on China, Korea and Japan: Gina L. Barnes, China, Korea and Japan, Thames and Hudson, London, 1993; Mario Bussagli, Oriental Architecture, Electra, Milan, 1981; Jonathan Clements, A Brief History of Japan, Tuttle, Tokyo, 2017; Cho-Yun Hsu, China: A New Cultural History, Columbia University, New York, 2006; John Keay, China, A History, Basic Books, New York, 2009; Don Oberdorfer & Robert Carlin, The Two Koreas 3rd ed., Basic Books, New York, 2014; Michael J. Seth, A Concise History of Korea, Rowman & Littlefield, Lanham, 2016; Daniel Tudor, Korea: The Impossible Country, Tuttle, Tokyo, 2012.

Beijing – Forbidden and Inviting City

Forbidden City Entrance

Two icons of Chinese history face off across Tiananmen Square. The fifteenth century wood and lacquer Forbidden City faces south, the priority position, and the twentieth century cement cube of the People's Republic of China Tomb of the First Premier faces north. The Square spans six hundred years in China, from ancient empire to world power.

Ming emperors knew they were supreme Celestial Rulers, at the center of the universe. As proof of his power, Emperor Yongle came to Beijing, at the center of his empire, where in 1402 he built a palace in the center of the city. It was an imperial city within a capital city. The emperor lived in the inner sanctum, where he ruled from the harmonious center of the world. Only those serving the emperor entered the palace. To all others, it was the Forbidden City.

Emperors of the Ming dynasty ruled the expanse of China from the mid-fourteenth century to 1644. In the final and fateful year, they sought help of Manchurian warlords in putting down a rebellion, which threatened the Forbidden City. Manchurians crossed the Great Wall, by invitation. They so liked what they saw that they ejected Ming and pronounced themselves Qing, Celestial Rulers of China. Qing found legitimacy in association with Ming by preserving the Forbidden City and continuing its artistic legacy.

Twenty-four Celestial Rulers of China lived in the Forbidden City from 1420 to 1925. Each built on traditions to create a life of structure and harmony. Emperors were expected to keep peace with nature and guarantee abundant crops.

This story focuses on three Celestial Rulers, all Qing, putting a face on Forbidden City occupants. Qianlong, known as Hongli, extended China to its farthest extent during his reign of 1735 to 1796. Then he came home, to rule the world, write poetry and collect art.

The Dowager Empress, Cixi, ruled from 1861 to 1908, on her own, or as guardian of young emperors. Her controversial reign launched stories and films. Strong female defenders of tradition, who instigated reform, were difficult for palace biographers to accept.

The final Qing emperor and final Celestial Ruler of China, last occupant of the Forbidden City was Emperor Xuantong, known as Puyi. Born in 1905, Puyi was emperor at age three, deposed as ruler in 1911 and homeless in 1925, when the Forbidden City became the Palace Museum. Puyi transcended the Imperial Era to the People's Republic of China.

This is a story of the Forbidden City, as a city within a city, and of three of its occupants. It is an introduction to the maze of corridors and palace temples visited by fourteen million people each year. More than an assemblage of wood and lacquer, the Forbidden City is integral to Chinese history and culture. After almost a century in denial of its importance, yet thankfully preserved, China now invites visitors to explore the Forbidden City and Tiananmen Square, to know China.

Ming Dynasty Celestial Capital

Entrance to Inner Court

More than a country, China is a sub-continent. Han Chinese rulers presided over empires built, divided and built again for more than two thousand years. There were capitals of the empire in the north and south, none of which were Beijing, except for a short period when Mongols displaced Han Chinese and settled in Dadu, also known as Beiping.[74]

The great Kublai Khan came into China, when other Mongol descendants of Genghis Khan conquered north India. In India, Mongols became Mughals, great emperors, one of whom built the Taj Mahal. In China, Mongols were better warriors than administrators.

---

[74] Han is the ancestral group of the majority of indigenous Chinese. The vast empire of China engulfs several ethnic groups, speaking several languages. Han Chinese speak Mandarin. Genghis Khan captured Peking in 1115, known as Beijing in Mandarin, so named in 1402.

In 1368, Han Chinese returned as the Ming dynasty of rulers. The third Ming emperor wanted his capital in the north, from whence came invaders, Mongol or Manchu. He changed the city name to Beijing.

Emperor Yongle usurped his nephew, taking command of the empire begun by his father, and earning the name Black Dragon. Yongle dredged the Grand Canal, built in the seventh century CE. He joined walls built over the prior millennium, creating the Great Wall of China. Then Yongle built a capital city.

Yongle had a vision for his capital, developed while he lived in Kublai Khan's thirteenth century city. To repopulate the Mongol city with Han Chinese, and build his palace, Yongle relocated ten thousand landless Chinese families from north of the city. One hundred thousand laborers were required to build the palace.

The Mongol city of Dadu was inspired in design by Arab architects. Unlike haphazard, meandering streets of old Han cities, such as Guangzhou, known as Canton, Dadu had a liner design. The original square city was surrounded by a larger square, which later adjoined a rectangle section. In innermost walls kings held court. In the outer city, armies quartered. The royal city encompassed a water supply, as security from siege.

Yongle embraced the entire Mongol city for his capital, in which the inner city had a further inner square, housing the Imperial City. Inside the Imperial City, Yongle drew a further rectangle for his palace compound. Imperial City had ten-foot-high walls. The palace compound within had fifteen-feet-high walls. Only the emperor, his family and courtiers could enter the palace compound, which became known as the Forbidden City.

Ten thousand people lived in the Forbidden City at its height under Qing dynasty rulers. Four hundred cooks prepared meals for the multigenerational royal family, a growing body of women of the emperor and former emperors, and more than a thousand eunuchs, the castrated men who served the royal court in the inner-most sanctum of the inner city. Everyone had a rank. Accoutrements of life depended upon rank.

In the outer court of the Forbidden City were monks, palace guards and sedan chair bearers, for royal transport within the Forbidden City. For the emperor to traverse the Forbidden city, carried in a sedan chair, from southern to northern gate, took ninety minutes. Although the city plan is lineal, in harmonious division into quadrants and further quadrants, corridors created a maze within the palace.

Empire administrators, military officials, and other high-ranking employees of the empire, lived in the Imperial City of Beijing. Business with the emperor was transacted at one of two gates of the Imperial City leading into the Forbidden City. Low level Forbidden City courtiers worked at the gates, from which messages went through channels in the palace, until high-ranking assistants consulted with the emperor.

Beijing lake was within the Imperial City. An offshoot stream supplied water to the Forbidden City. On islands within the lake, royals, including emperors, built summer palaces, known as Lake Palaces. When Mao Zedong took command of the People's Republic of China in 1949, he lived seventeen years in a Lake Palace of Qing royals.[75]

Outside Imperial City walls, in the Inner City, lived people who built the city. Yongle's conscripted workers built homes and temples in the Inner City. Centuries later, Qing dynasty emperors brought their elite Manchu Banner Guards to live in the Inner City. Working folk, craftspeople and merchants were relegated to the Outer City. The Outer City was often referred to as the Chinese City, while the Inner City was the Tartar City.

North of Imperial City, still within the Inner City, on the concentric axis of all four cities, is a traffic intersection, with the Kublai Khan era Bell Tower and the Ming era Drum Tower in the center. Processions starting at the towers came south to the base of Coal Hill, in the Inner City, at the north gate to the Forbidden City. Coal hill gave symmetry to the Imperial City, in the feng-shui of water below and mountain behind. Coal Hill is man-made from dredging the palace moat. Ming called it Prospect Hill, protector from Manchu enemies from the north. When Manchu usurped Ming and became Qing, the new rulers renamed the hill for its use in storing coal.

---

[75] Mao Zedong died in 1976.

By 1860, when China opened to foreign trade, embassy houses of foreign governments were built in the Inner City. The first luxury hotels of the city were built in the area. Mao limited the height of hotels in the Inner City, making certain his home, and its telephone lines, were not in gun range. The foreign section, known as Legation Quarter, is between the Imperial City and the southern wall of the Inner City, where it adjoins the Outer City.

A statement is attributed to Chairman Mao, when looking out from Communist Party offices, at the three cities: Inner, Imperial and Forbidden; exclaiming he was impatient to see them filled with factories. Fortunately, Mao also saw himself as keeper of Chinese culture and history. Despite his failed Great Leap Forward and Cultural Revolution, when millions of Chinese died, little was built. Forbidden City was locked and preserved.[76]

Life in the Celestial Center of the World

Walls of the Forbidden City enclose one hundred and eighty acres of densely packed, though orderly, palaces and gardens. Most inhabitants spent entire lives within the walls. Three hundred years of Ming dynasty porcelain, paintings and lacquer furniture, joined acquisitions during Qing dynasty emperors, creating an inventory of millions of objects. Scrolls of literature and philosophy joined records of palace business and emperor diaries.

The south half of the Forbidden City, the Outer Court, is open to visitors today. This was domain of servants, eunuchs and officers of the Imperial household. High officials of the empire had offices near the East Flowery Gate, through which vital information came to the emperor. Halls of Literary Glory, containing schoolrooms and library, were here.

---

[76] Looting of the palace occurred in 1860, by British, French and American forces during the 2nd Opium War, a trade war; from 1911 to 1924, by palace eunuchs, until expelled by Emperor Puyi; in 1925 by Nationalist Chinese troops; in 1937 by Japanese occupation forces; and in 1945 by liberating Nationalist troops. During the Cultural Revolution, Red Guards, indignant young people, entered the palace to smash objects.

Forbidden City Hall

Visitors to the Imperial City today enter under Chairman Mao's picture above Meridian Gate and proceed on bridges over golden waters to the Supreme Imperial Gate. A dramatic succession of three oblong red buildings, with marble balustrade-lined stairs and oversize Ming roofs, are Halls of Harmony. These are ceremonial halls for coronations, weddings and special days of the celestial calendar.

East of Halls of Harmony is the Hall of Honoring Ancestors. It is steps to this temple from the Hall of Peaceful Old Age, retirement home of emperors. Co-founder of the People's Republic of China, and first premier, well-loved for humanism, was Zhou Enlai. His memorial service was held in the Hall of Honoring Ancestors, despite objections of Mao. Mao relented after students demonstrated in Tiananmen Square in 1976.

Only royal family were admitted through the Gate of Heavenly Purity, to the Forbidden City. In inner sanctum rooms were bedrooms of emperors, where they had private moments with the empress, a mistress, or other women of the court. Private rooms for women were in six palaces on the west side of the Forbidden City, now Palace Museum offices. Private rooms for men were in palaces on the east side. The Great Theatre was on the east side, among palaces for men.

Forbidden City Inner Gate

Five-toe dragons were iconic symbols of Han dynasty emperors. Each wardrobe item of the emperor displayed five-toe dragons, relegating other royals to dragons with four-toes or fewer, under penalty of death. Forbidden City has twelve thousand dragon images.

Every design feature of the Forbidden City is imbued with meaning. Emperors resided in palaces under yellow roofs. Only the emperor wore yellow. Heirs-in-waiting slept under green roofs, a sign of growth. Spines of pointed roof lines held figurines. The more figures dancing on the roof, the higher the rank of the person below. The mythical number of rooms in the Forbidden City is 9,999, the harmonious number of the universe. There are 8,886 rooms. No emperor had time to count the rooms and know the deficiency.

Yellow Roofs & 4-Toe Dragon

Roof Detail

The Forbidden City is Ming design, with Ming decoration, under Confucian guidance. Qing rulers adopted Ming heritage, without assimilating to Han Ming. They expressed Manchu heritage in clothing. Ming rulers wore silk robes and slippers. Their beards were short. Qing drew from frontier horsemen heritage wearing boots, furs, and leather vests. Qing beards were long and pointed, with Manchu mustache. Exemplary of Ming/Qing adaptation without assimilation is Qianlong, a great emperor of the Qing dynasty.

Qianlong (Hongli) was the warrior-poet emperor, whose sixty-year reign, from 1735 to 1796, stopped a year short of his grandfather, to respect his ancestor. Hongli never vacated palace rooms in the Hall of Cultivation of Character, living three years after abdicating to his son.[77] In his long reign, Hongli expanded borders of China west and south, fought back Mongols, then came home to sit for portraits and write poetry.

To Hongli, collecting art was a means to display power. His collection extended prowess on the battlefield. Jesuit artists painted him as a military victor, in the European style. He was also painted by Chinese artists. He added contemporary pieces to his Ming collection of carved jade, porcelain and bronze sculpture. By associating with Ming art, Hongli added credibility to his rule as a Manchu Qing over the majority Han population.

For Hongli, it was not sufficient to hold objects unless their meaning was understood. He collected Books of the Four Treasures: classics, history, philosophy and letters. His maps, art inventory and diaries formed a valuable palace library.

Also remembered for his buildings, Hongli restored, repaired and expanded buildings within the Forbidden City. He orchestrated a home building project in the Outer City. Always appreciative of the restorative power of gardens, Hongli commissioned gardens in the Outer City, endearing him to common folk.

---

[77] Hongli died at eighty-seven in 1799. His son Jailing was a disappointment. Twice there were assassination attempts. Once a group of women of the palace tried to beat him to death to end his abuses.

Dragons on the Eaves

All of the activities of Hongli, military and domestic, were expensive. Part of the brilliance of the man was his means to raise revenue, to meet palace expenses. He taxed Inner City residents, the Banner Guards, who lived on palace stipends, even after military service. He gave loans to merchants, at high interest rates, and taxed salt.

At the end of a long day, reading field reports in Manchu and Chinese, Hongli retired to the Studio of Exhausted Diligence, on the east wall of the palace. There he relaxed with his inner circle. For him the palace was more refuge than cloister.

Qianlong (Hongli) was the last great emperor of the Imperial era of China. Among his descendants there were none who inherited his talent or skill in military affairs. The next skilled ruler of China was an empress, not an emperor.

Dowager Empress Cixi ruled from behind a screen, as China lacked protocol for a woman to govern. Title of dowager meant Cixi outlived the emperor. Her power in the palace emanated from her ability to wield authority over heirs. To appreciate Cixi's skills in the art of palace intrigue, consider steps she ascended to arrive at her position.

Cixi Summer Palace

Women came to the palace in Imperial China the same way Hongli collected art. Some were chosen by the emperor and some were sent as gifts. There was only one empress, wedded to the emperor in an arranged marriage. The emperor could choose one Imperial noble consort, or chief mistress, two mere noble consorts, four regular consorts, six Imperial concubines and any number of honored ladies, ever present ladies and those who must comply. Everyone in palace life was ranked by status. A woman advanced in rank through bearing a son and by intrigue.

Cixi came to the palace in 1852, at sixteen, toward the lower end in rank. The emperor's reign began in 1851. Adept at palace politics, she worked her way up to a third position by the time she gave birth to the only son of the emperor in 1856.

In 1861, the emperor died and Cixi outwitted women above her in rank, becoming regent for her five-year-old son. Cixi was Dowager Empress at age twenty-five, despite the empress, widow of the emperor. The palace accommodated co-dowager empresses. They sat behind a screen, where Cixi's son, the young emperor, sat on a throne. Court administrators presented work to the emperor and orders came from behind the screen.

For fourteen years, Cixi ruled as regent and sole Dowager Empress, surviving her co-ruler. In 1875, when he might ascend to ruling emperor, the prince died at age nineteen from diseases, likely the result of his lifestyle beyond palace walls. The prince left behind a pregnant wife, who detested her mother-in-law. Before that child was born, Cixi adopted the son of a favorite sister. In so doing, she avoided another co-ruler and extended her time as regent for a much younger prince.

Pleased with her choice of Prince Gong, Cixi went into semi-retirement in 1889, after she arranged his marriage. In the mode of tradition, Cixi ruled based on advice of those with information beyond walls she could not cross, as a ruler and as a woman. Before retiring, she decreed an end to foot binding, a practice of Han women, that she considered barbaric. The practice continued into the nineteenth century in south China.

Cixi is credited with other decrees elevating the status of women, although effect of her pronouncements is unknown. Her husband was a weak ruler, who left the Forbidden City in a cloud of insurrection. Every emperor, from early dynasties to Qing, faced insurrection somewhere in the empire. Prior to 1840, and the press of western governments to open trade with China, threats to the empire were internal. Cixi was schooled in insular rule.

China was changing. Provincial governors became autonomous during the reign of Cixi and her predecessors. Southern governors had lucrative opportunities in trade with foreigners. Guangzhou, known then as Canton, was a major port. Pronouncements from Beijing meant little far from the capital.

Prince Gong was a reformer, which meant he was open to trade with foreigners, sending students to foreign universities and generally opening China to western ideas. Change threatened interests of palace traditionalists, largely keepers of ceremony and eunuchs fearful of retirement. Cixi often commented that eunuchs should not be trusted. The prince, desirous of nipping any bud of palace insurrection, placed Cixi under arrest in her Palace of Every Extravagance and planned execution of her closest advisors.

Stone Imperial Barge

The prince underestimated Cixi. She learned of his plans, preempted them and put him in the palace prison, which the prince intended for her. Cixi ruled until her death in 1908.

Much maligned by historians as causing the fall of the empire, Cixi shares that credit with a century of emperors before her, who failed to anticipate a changing world. True, her first act in semi-retirement was decorating her rooms, using funds budgeted for the navy. Defeat of the Chinese navy by the Japanese in 1894, is credited to her extravagance.[78]

Cloistered in the palace, without news of international events, Cixi was unaware of competition of Britain and France to colonize southeast Asia, or the race for Africa, in which Germany, France, Belgium, Britain, Italy Portugal and the United States divided up a continent between them. In two so-called

---

[78] Japan later defeated the Russian army and occupied Korea and Manchuria by 1910. Neither Russia nor Korea had a female sovereign. Cixi is often portrayed as the woman with long fingernails.

Opium Wars, actually pressure by Britain, France, Japan and the United States to gain favorable trade status in China, China gave up Macau, Hong Kong and Taiwan. In China, loss of status to foreigners grew into rebellion.

Throughout southern China, provincial governors either made lucrative trade deals with foreign governments or saw their centuries-old palaces sacked and burned. A British soldier wrote home to his mother, bemoaning the inability to thoroughly loot a palace before it was burned.[79] By 1900, anti-foreign sentiment grew from local demonstrations by men of a small boxing club, to a wide-spread Boxer Rebellion, which worked its way through south-central China to Beijing.

Imperial Tomb

---

[79] Letter home of Captain Charles Gordon in Lillian M. Li, Alison J. Dray-Novey and Haili Kong, Beijing: From Imperial Capital to Olympic City, Palgrave, New York, 2007, p. 109. In 1860, Lord Elgin, son of Parthenon Lord Elgin, led troops plundering the Forbidden City. China defended itself, causing the British to demand reparations, in the Treaty of Tianjin. The treaty gave Russia, Britain, France and the United States the Legation Quarter in the Inner City and the ability to bring opium directly to Chinese people.

Cixi gave support to the Boxers. Encouraged, they placed a siege around the Legation Quarter, homes of foreign government agents in Beijing. British, French, American and Japanese armies marched on Beijing to liberate fellow nationals. Cixi played into a choreographed take-over of Beijing as she slipped out the back gate of the Forbidden City.

Amid squabbling by foreign powers on partitioning China, Cixi slipped back into the city by 1902. Although the palace was looted, Cixi retrieved buried treasures. She gave receptions for wives of foreign officers. Japanese advisors organized a city police academy.

In 1908, Prince Gong died. The next day, in her last act of governance, Cixi anointed Puyi as the next emperor, at three years old. She knew she must act quickly. She died that day.

Puyi, last emperor of China, never had an opportunity to govern. In 1911, Sun Yat Sen returned to China from the United States establishing a democratic national government. Many Chinese wanted a constitutional monarchy like Britain. Nationalists would not compromise, though they never developed an internal organization, nor widespread support. China was condemned to forty years of war.

Caught amid cataclysmic forces, in a pivotal time in the history of China, Puyi was a helpless pawn. He was raised in the innermost Forbidden City as a prisoner of the Nationalist government. As a young man traditional studies were augmented by an English tutor, Sir Reginald Johnston. Johnston was an ally from 1911 to 1924.

Puyi was an intelligent youth, imprisoned by history, yet informed of the world through Johnston. Puyi cut his pigtail and required fifteen hundred men of the royal household to do so. In defiance of royal ladies, Puyi wore glasses, rather than be blind. Then he challenged eunuchs by announcing an inventory of palace treasures. Although a cloistered man, Puyi was aware of palace treasures for sale in antique shops.

During the night of January 27, 1923, a fire was set in the royal treasure storehouse. Six hundred items were recovered. The remainder were lost. Puyi was not fooled. He requested assistance from Republic troops to evict three thousand eunuchs from the Forbidden City. Then he built a tennis court over the lost buildings.

In 1925, Puyi was evicted without notice.[80] Only Japan offered him a home. In a play to his Manchu roots, while the Japanese occupied Manchuria, Puyi was installed as Emperor of Manchuria. Puyi was not fooled. He knew he was a puppet emperor. China lost any hope of a parliamentary monarchy. Sun Yat Sun died that year and was succeeded by his brother-in-law Chiang Kai-shek. Chiang moved the national capital south to Nanjing.

In 1937, Japan occupied China. In the wartime economy, Chinese people suffered depredations. Farm workers became factory workers in a forced march to modernization.

From the end of World War II, until 1949, Chiang was in a civil war with Communists. In 1949, Communist sieged Beijing. Chiang required ten thousand residents to stand in front of the Forbidden City to defy a Communist take-over. His actions were too little, too late.

On October 1, 1949, Mao Zedong stood on the balcony of the Gate of Heavenly Peace, where his portrait hangs today, and proclaimed birth of the People's Republic of China. Chiang fled to Taiwan. He took with him treasures of the Forbidden City.

Forbidden City within Beijing City

Tiananmen Square, in front of the Forbidden City, has always been the largest square in the city. It is the preferred venue of demonstrators. In 1919, protestors lamented Japanese occupation of Shandong Province, the beginning of the end of Nationalist China.

In 1976, the square, enlarged to accommodate Communist Party rallies of up to five hundred thousand, was the scene of protests mourning Zhou Enlai. Hundreds of protestors were arrested. Chairman Mao died that year. His tomb is in the imposing building facing the Forbidden City, where his picture eternally faces back at his tomb.

---

[80] For a portrayal of Cixi, Puyi and China to the Cultural Revolution, see the 1988 movie, *The Last Emperor*.

Inside Forbidden City

In later years, Tiananmen Square was enlarged to hold six hundred thousand people. In 1978, protests in Tiananmen Square included a democracy wall. Photos of those imprisoned for speaking out against the government were posted in silent protest.

In May 1989, a lengthy protest was timed for the seventieth anniversary of Communist Party governance of China. Martial law was imposed. Soldiers fired on unarmed civilians. It was a national crisis, viewed by the world.

Leader of the Communist Party of China, Deng Xiaoping realized economic reform was insufficient for people of China. Beijing, capital of China since 1402, home of Communism when Nationalists chose Nanjing, became the leading city of China in an evolution to Capitalist-Communism, a consumerist socialist economy.

As the architectural showplace of an advanced economy, bringing wealth through private enterprise, Beijing lost its historic look. World famous architect Rem Koolhaas gave China an icon building, stunning, yet placeless. McDonald's opened in Beijing in 1992. Foreigners resided in Beijing in conspicuous numbers.

The Forbidden City reopened as the Palace Museum. Thirteen hundred employees curated objects and managed visitors. An opening showcasing extravagant opulence of Imperial rulers, resulted in celebrations of culture. People of China did not wish to emulate Imperials as their Communist rulers long feared. Rather, Chinese wanted to know their path on the evolution to worldly, high-functioning, Chinese people.

Visiting Beijing Today

City Today

Today the Forbidden City is a World Heritage site, in part for its distinction as the oldest, largest, wooden structure. It is also a museum displaying objects in original settings.[81] The Chinese government restored the Forbidden City by 2020, the six-hundredth anniversary of its opening. China considers history a national asset.

In the aftermath of the Tiananmen Square massacre, China rebuilt its international image by hosting the 2008 Olympics. The Bird Nest stadium became an instant Chinese icon of the new China and modern Beijing. At a cost of $300 to $400 million, just to build the stadium, Cixi is vindicated. Legacies of culture are seen in the built environment.

Throughout Beijing, temples are restored, including Ming era, three-tiered-roof Temple of Heaven, Tian Tan, as part of twenty-five designated city historic districts. Tiananmen Square was enlarged in 2006, completing harmonious symmetry of Beijing.

---

[81] The collection is displayed in Taipei, Taiwan National Palace Museum and Nanjing Museum, China.

Today the Forbidden City is flanked on Tiananmen Square by the Great Hall of the People and the National Museum of China. Facing the Forbidden City across the square is the Museum of the History of Beijing. In the middle of the square is the Mausoleum of Mao and a pillar monument erected in 1958, with sayings of Mao and Zhou Enlai.

Walking around Tiananmen Square is a tour of six hundred years of history in China. There is much more to Beijing, of history and modern marvels of architecture and commercialism, completing the story of China today. Beijing is the center of a vast country and the Square is still the center of the Chinese universe as imagined by Yongle when he set his celestial compass on the Forbidden City in 1420.

Shanghai – Home of Old and New China

Window to the Past

The story of Shanghai takes place on the Bund, that magical bend in the Huangpu River of the Yangtze delta, where civilization began and grew in China. Looking at Shanghai today, it is hard to believe life existed in the city prior to high rise masterpieces of modern icon architecture. Imposing skyline of the Bund is, as it has always been, the face of success in China. Rice was grown here to feed people from the old times, and the Bank of China began to grow a nation here in the new times. While other cities were political and cultural capitals of China, Shanghai was the source and measure of economic wealth of an empire that built a nation of the world.

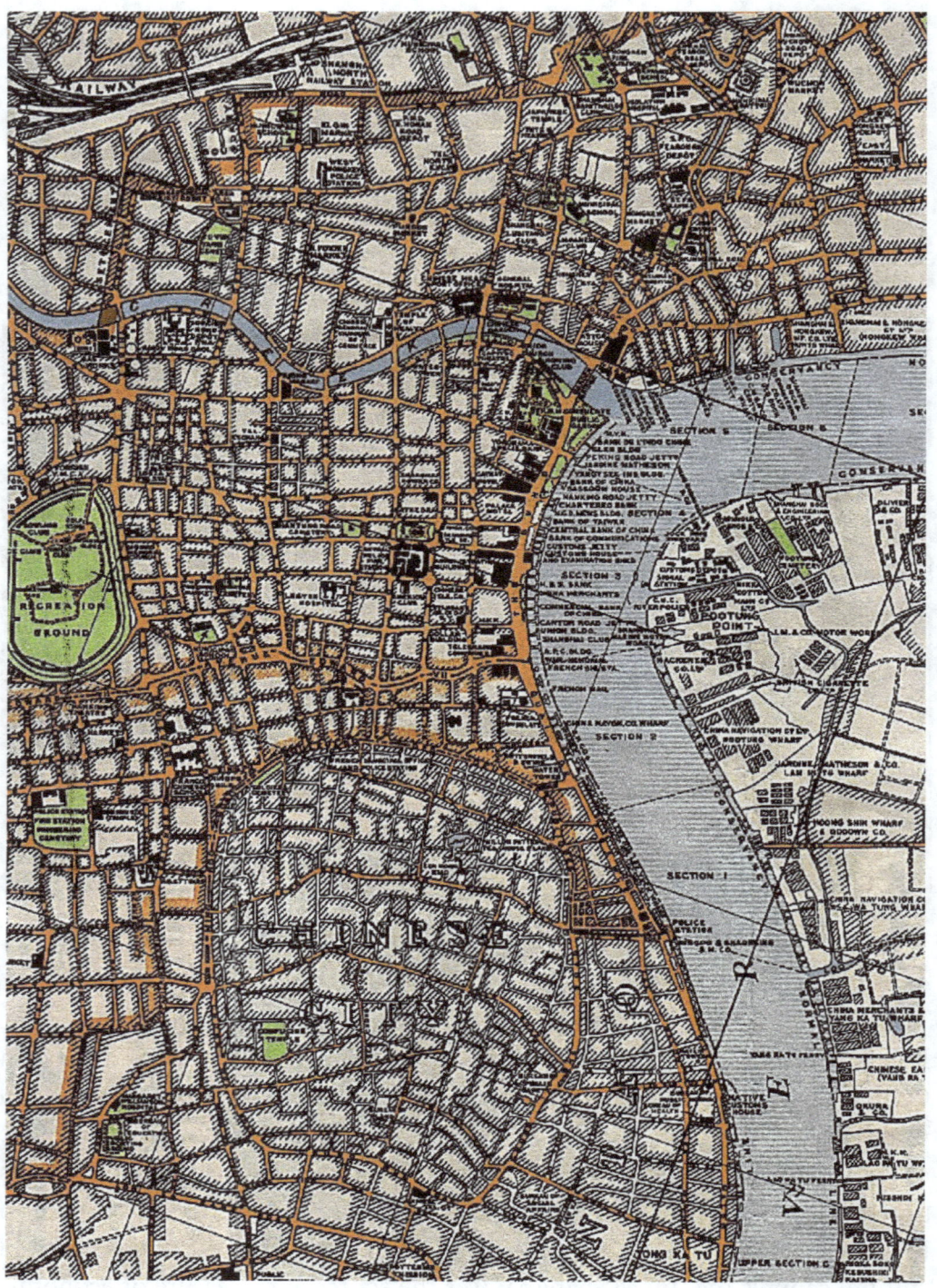

Shanghai 1933 (public domain)

Shanghai was and is a Chinese city, although for a century, from 1842 to 1949, it was home to more foreigners than Chinese. The little enclave of Chapei was surrounded by French and International land allotments, given to invading nations to settle a war, based on a pretext to advantage trade. Trade objectives were achieved. By 1900, Shanghai was one of the five largest trade ports of the world. Shanghai entered the modern world as three cities, attached by the Bund, a mile-long street. The world came to Shanghai.

Today, China is an economic master of the world. Mastery originated in Shanghai. It was achieved by Chinese entrepreneurs, who modeled foreign neighbors along the Bund and then surpassed them. The story of Shanghai is a story of Chinese achievement.

Shanghai is not immune to Chinese politics. From World War II to 1949, intrigue in Shanghai could fill several spy novels. The Bund was the last stand of the Nationalist Chinese government, before it left for Taiwan. That too, is part of the story of Shanghai.

In the context of a country where civilization of humans began, Shanghai has a short yet exciting past. Until it was bombed by Chinese forces, in error, occupied by Japan, and initially marginalized in the new China, Shanghai rivaled New York in trade and Paris in glamour. It has endured as a Chinese city, that is the economic capital of the nation.

Chinese Shanghai

So much of the growth of modern China, its international connections, and pivotal events of civil and international war, had connections to streets of Shanghai, that early history is often overshadowed. Shanghai began, not in 1841, upon arrival of British, French and American traders, but in centuries before the Christian era, along the Yangtze River delta. During the Song dynasty, the tenth to thirteenth centuries, the area *just above the water*, Shanghai, was a port for rice, shipped upriver to the Song capital and vassal towns.[82]

---

[82] The five main dynasties of China are Han, 3rd century BCE to 3rd century CE; Tang, 618 to 907 CE; Song, 907 to 1279; Ming, 1368 to 1644; and Qing, 1644 to 1911.

Old Town Shanghai Dragon Walls

Early Morning On the River

Shanghai was set back from the Huangpu River, on dry ground. High water tables made it difficult to build a walled city of stone closer to the river. Tall city walls, bits of which are seen today, protected town merchants and their wealth from pirates.

Feudal China was similar to feudal Europe. Warlords and their guards lived within walled fortresses. Farmers worked in open fields. In the Confucius oriented society of China, farmers were valued. Success of early China was in its ability to feed a large population. Armies capable of conquering territory and resisting conquest from the outside, such as from Japan, required a large population of warriors.

When Shanghai was first recorded as a city, in 1291, its population was three hundred thousand. Few people lived within walls in the area reserved for the elite. Farmers paid tax in rice. Warlords controlled the harbor. Peasants expected their lord to maintain an army to protect them from foreign incursion and slavery. City walls afforded protection from pirates. Walls did little to stop armies.

Early China was a Buddhist culture. The Buddha, who came from east-central India, had more followers in China than India. The essence of Buddhism is to live an honorable life. With few possessions, Chinese farmers lived little better than Buddhist monks. Monks lived in well-maintained, wooden temples and received rice as a token of faith. The Buddha preached an egalitarian social structure, much in conflict with the caste system in India. In China, farmers had status. They were poor yet valued.

Repeatedly over time in Chinese history, great dynasties fell to warriors who rose from agrarian roots. In the twentieth century, Marxist Communists understood egalitarian principles of Chinese people. They were better able to form a government than well-financed Nationalist Republicans. Chinese people revere ancestors, not lords.

In the land of fish and rice, people of Shanghai felt comfortable, far from aggressors, the Mongols and Tartars of Manchuria, invaders from the north. Emperors of Imperial China located capitals in the north, keeping armies within a short distance of northern borders. Food came from the south. Warlords of provinces, distant from the capital, had little reason to look beyond China for wealth. Necessities and luxuries of life, such as gold and jade, were available within their domain. Outsiders were devils or barbarians, or both.

Shanghai Old Style

Prior to the mid-nineteenth century, and arrival of Europeans, people of Shanghai lived as they had for centuries. Provincial governors, an army of bureaucrats in well-ordered Confucius China, leaders of the army, as well as traders, teachers and artisans, enjoyed a lifestyle that included art in their homes and gardens. Yu Gardens, in old Shanghai today, is a recreation of a bazaar for the benefit of tourism. It is modeled upon centuries old bazaars, amid waterways, meandering walls and gardens.

Home and garden design, including dragons on walls and roofs, mimic palaces of Ming emperors. Traditional style assured meaning and continuity in life. Quiet gardens were a place to contemplate one's bounty. Today, visitors slip through keyhole openings in walls to experience such moments.

For a vision of life, prior to arrival of Europeans, visitors take an excursion beyond Shanghai, down the Grand Canal, to little tenth century fishing villages of Tongli and Zhouzhuang, as well as to Suzhou, an administrative center of Imperial leaders since the third century CE. In these places, transportation is still tied to waterways. As early as the fifth century BCE, emperors who began the Great Wall in the north, fed their people and their armies with rice brought northward on the Grand Canal, as it meanders from Shanghai to Beijing. Connecting the canal to Beijing was accomplished in the thirteenth century. Although replaced for transport by railway in the nineteenth century, the canal was never abandoned.

Tongli Preserved Lifeways Along the Canal

In Tongli and Zhouzhuang, high, graceful, sloping and curved roofs of the Ming dynasty, so prevalent in the Forbidden City, are absent. Village houses are simple rectangles of white plaster walls, turned grey, and black, flat, unadorned tile roofs of homes of fishermen and rice farmers. Houses are small, stacked and tightly packed. Ground transport is by footpath, barely wide enough for two-wheeled carts. Slim boats still float through the canal, under small, arched bridges. Today local boats carry visitors.

In the Ming dynasty era of the thirteenth to seventeenth century, Suzhou was a regional center of silk manufacture. Canals began in Suzhou in the sixth century BCE, when roving bands of warlords preyed on villagers. The landmark of Suzhou is Beisi Ta, a Ming era temple complex, centered by the six-layer octagonal tower, open today for climbing.

Tranquility in Humble Administrator's Garden

Of many gardens around Shanghai, the Humble Administrator's Garden in Suzhou lures the most visitors. Begun in the twelfth century, and expanded by a city magistrate, who retired to the property in 1513, over two centuries, grateful successive owners, including a prince, added to the garden, until it became an expansive, enchanting retreat.[83] The garden includes several classic Zen Buddhist water-features in one lovely setting. Administrator Wang Xiancheng enjoyed the perfume of lotus flowers from a bench in the shaded pavilion.

International City

In 1840, British, French and American merchants desirous of expanding trade into China, incited incidents known collectively as Opium Wars. Battles were not fought to dominate trade in opium. War was aggression, by foreign nationals, into a country that did not want opium debilitating its people.

---

[83] The garden was divided in ownership until re-combined by the Chinese government in the 1950s. Known as Zhuozheng Yuan, the Administrator's Garden became a World Heritage Site in 1997.

Britain utilized opium from India as currency for tea. As a result of the war, Britain received rights to Hong Kong, and foreign nationals, including British merchants, were given duty-free ports in China, one of which was Shanghai. In foreign zones, foreign nationals were not subject to Chinese law.

Old Shanghai

Shanghai of the mid to late nineteenth century developed a curious arrangement, unique in the world. The walled Chinese city was surrounded by land concessions to the French, expanding west from the Huangpu River. Along the northern boundary of the French concession, an International concession to British and American merchants extended eastward along the northern riverbank, until the Chinese city was dwarfed by foreign land concessions. Within the International concession area, No. 1 Road, along the river, was a mile of foreign-owned buildings, known as the Bund.[84]

Chinese merchants were excluded from the Bund and from representation on the Shanghai Municipal Council. The foreign national area, on Chinese land, completely disassociated with Chinese people and their government. The only foreign-to-Chinese interaction occurred when Chinese silk merchants, and other Chinese sources of goods, brought products to foreign trade houses.

---

[84] Land area of the International concession was one hundred and forty acres.

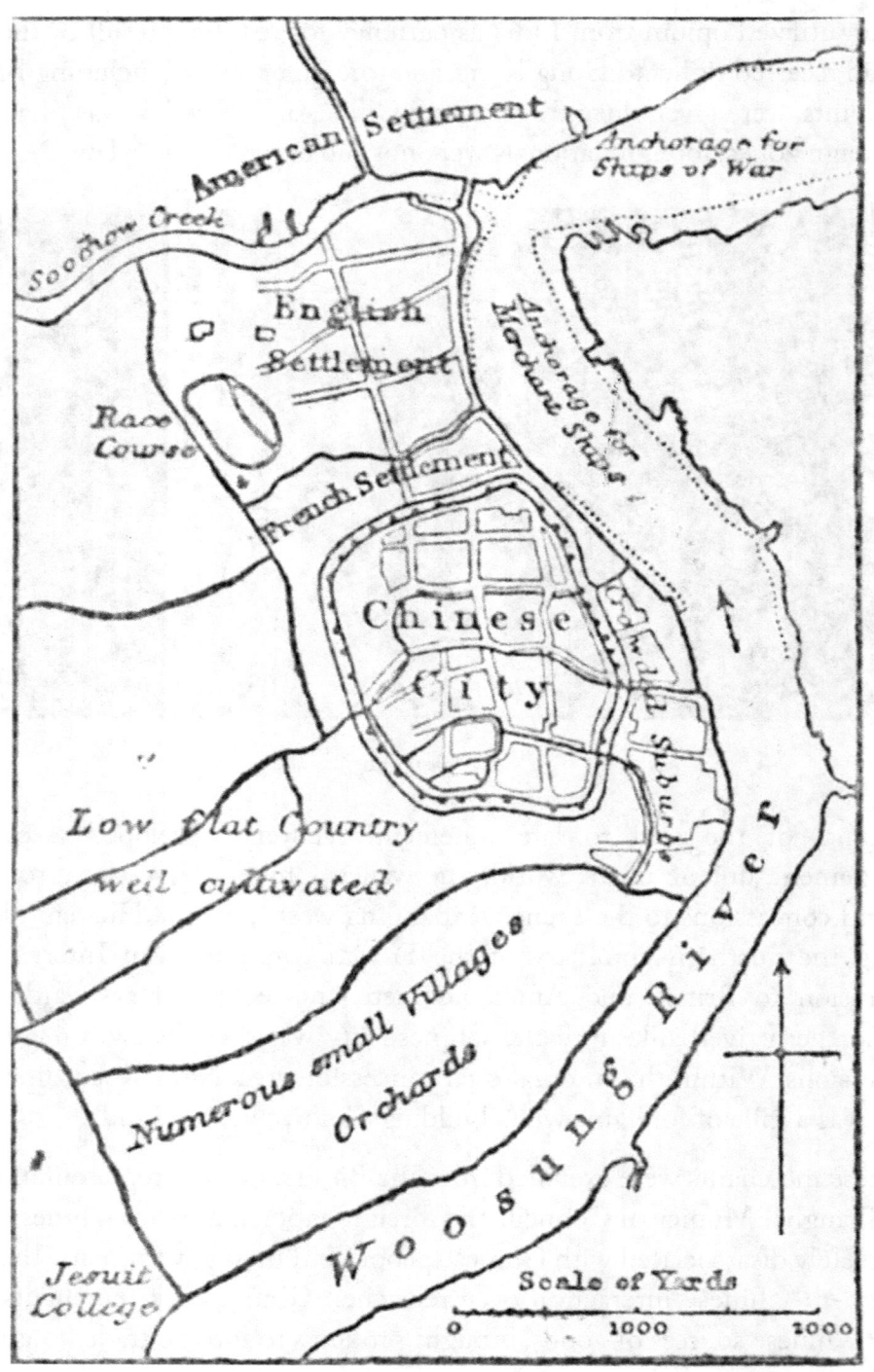

Shanghai City Sections (Public Domain)

An example of separated lives of city dwellers is the main shopping street Nanjing Road. Old Nanjing Road originated in the Chinese city, then extended in the nineteenth century into the French concession. Nanjing road, within the Chinese city, remained a produce and chicken market, where shops hung cages of songbirds, popular with the Chinese. When the street crossed into the French area, it was the site of multi-level department stores and mansions of elite foreigners.

Most important to merchants on foreign land concessions was the right of extra-territoriality, that is, exemption from Chinese law, including payment of Chinese taxes. Port fees were collected by British subjects and used to support port infrastructure necessary to accommodate British ships. So efficient were British administrators, that emperors delegated to them collection of customs duties due to the Imperial court. Emperors benefited from an increased volume of Shanghai trade.

Shanghai rapidly attracted all sorts of unsavory characters to the world's free-trade zone. No passports were needed to enter Shanghai. No questions were asked. Opium traders and adventurers were joined by gamblers and fugitives of the world. By 1885, it is estimated that only ten percent of the greater Shanghai population was native born.[85]

The Bund, Shanghai in 1926 (Public Domain)

---

[85] See, Stella Dong, Shanghai, Harper Perennial, New York, 2001, p. 75.

When the 1917 Bolshevik Revolution in Russia forced out supporters of the monarchy, known as White Russians, displaced royalists came to Shanghai. During World War II, when Jews escaping death at the hands of Nazis were denied entry into the United States and Great Britain, a fortunate few came to Shanghai. In Shanghai, they were given housing and financial assistance by early Jewish residents, becoming part of the Shanghai economy. In part, support for Jewish emigrees came from Iraqi transplant Victor Elias Sassoon, whose Sassoon House was the tallest building on the Bund.[86]

The nucleus of Shanghai commercial life was, and is, the one-mile section of No.1 Road, known as the Bund, or Magnificent Mile. Successive layers of history on the Bund reflect growth of Shanghai, as it became the fifth largest port in the world by 1900.[87] Original buildings on the Bund were trade houses, branches of business from Hong Kong, such as Jardine-Matheson and Dent and Company.[88] Prominent also were the Customs House and Shanghai Club, with its black stone floor and mahogany bar. Early wood buildings on the Bund were replaced by four-story brick structures.

In the 1920s boom era in Shanghai, notable buildings on the Bund were rebuilt from four to twenty-story skyscrapers. The neo-classical columned Hong Kong and China Bank, built in 1923, stands today at No. 12 Bund, renamed the HSBC Building. Next door, at No. 13 Bund, is the Customs House, originally built in Chinese Ming style, it was rebuilt in 1927, epitomizing Victorian British architecture, including a Big Ben style clock tower. The 1864, three-story Shanghai Club at No. 2 Bund, became a six-story Baroque ornate building in 1910. Today it houses the Waldorf-Astoria Shanghai Hotel. At No. 6 Bund was the first Chinese-owned bank, the China

---

[86] Sir Ellice Victor Elias Sassoon was born in Italy in 1881, educated in England, of a family from Baghdad. He died in the Bahamas in 1961. His father founded a Jewish settlement in Shanghai in the 1840s. Sassoon House, No. 20 Bund, housed the Cathay Hotel in 1926, now the Fairmont Peace Hotel.

[87] Five top ports by volume of cargo are: Shanghai, Singapore, Hong Kong, Busan, Guangzhou (Canton). Largest non-Asia port, ranked tenth in volume in 2017, is Dubai. As of 2019, the largest port in the United States was the Chinese container port of Long Beach. COSCO sold its interests to a consortium in 2019.

[88] The Jardine-Matheson Building, built in 1922, still stands at No. 27 Bund. It is now a retail center.

Merchants Bank, built in 1907, as it stands today, now a trendy Taiwanese-owned department store.

By 1902, talent and persistence enabled Chinese merchants, informed by experiences working with foreigners of Shanghai, to build businesses, which for some exceeded the success of their models. Regardless of growing wealth and prestige of Chinese-owned businesses, Chinese were denied entry to the Shanghai Club and from electing representatives to the Municipal Council. During the First World War years, when European goods were absent from the international market, Chinese of Shanghai and Hong Kong stepped into the void to export a greater volume of Chinese-made goods. Made in China became a world-wide hallmark.

Among early Chinese Chamber of Commerce members was Li Hung-Chang, who began the first Chinese steamship company in 1872. Li expanded his enterprise by purchasing bankrupt European firms. Pei Tsuyee, a Shanghai banker, is credited as a founder of modern banking in China. He was a governor of the Bank of China and advisor to the Nationalist government in 1935.[89] Great Wall cigarettes, another notable Chinese business, was founded by the Nanyang brothers in 1918.

In nightclubs and dance halls, the elite of Shanghai, European and Chinese, enjoyed lavish life in the city. Shanghai of the 1920s was the go-to place for glitterati of the world. Before she divorced, to marry the king of England, Wallis Warfield Simpson found Shanghai a real-world version of mythical Shangri-La. Cruise ships included port stops in Shanghai in 1920. Shanghai style was the rage in fashion magazines of Europe and America. The sedate qipao, a long silk dress of proper, elegant, Chinese women, was remade with a long side slit, becoming a popular, world-wide, fashion item.

In a lawless city of obscene wealth, an underworld flourished. Mob bosses and street gangs ruled with routine machine-gun executions for unpaid gambling debts. A leader of Shanghai's Green Gang controlled the opium trade, in

---

[89] Pei, born in China in 1893 and died in New York in 1982, is the father of I.M. Pei the noted architect. In traditional Asian style, family names are first and later reversed when westernized.

alliance with Chiang Kai-shek's Nationalists, affording mutual protection, as they split profits. Mob boss Du Yue-Sheng purchased an opulent mansion for use as a gang club house. Today guests experience splendor of the 1930s in the Mansion Hotel Shanghai.

One Shanghai tycoon was Charles Jones Soong. His life and his three daughters, Ai-ling, Ming-ling and Ching-ling, are part of the story of Shanghai, and its transition from pleasure palace to venue for the two most powerful political movements of twentieth century China. Ming-ling is better known as Madame Chiang Kai Shek and Ching-ling was Madame Sun Yat Sen. Their family saga has a Shanghai History Museum exhibit.

Mixing Family Business and Politics

Soong Sisters (Public Domain)

Charles Soong was a child of modest traders. He was educated in Christian schools taught by missionaries. Shunned as a missionary, he looked for opportunities in Shanghai. In a few years, he was prosperous beyond his parent's dreams. Never forgetting his debt to the church, one of the Soong businesses was printing Bibles.

Soong made a fortune manufacturing heavy machinery. During the First World War there were no European competitors. In 1919, when the Versailles Treaty ending the War gave German concessions to the Japanese government, which invaded Manchuria, Chinese patriots boycotted Japanese goods. Soong sent his three daughters to college in the US.[90]

Soong was a compatriot of Sun Yat Sen, whose independence revolution he generously supported. Ching-ling married Sun in 1915, three years after he was instrumental to overthrow the Qing dynasty and establish the Republic of China. Sun was the first president. Ching was loyal to Sun and his memory. He died in 1925. Ching-ling moved into the Sun house in Shanghai, where she hosted political philosophers.

Ai-ling married financial marvel H.H. Kung. They built a portfolio rendering them the wealthiest people in China. The couple continued the Soong role of financial involvement with the Nationalist government after Charlie died in 1919. Upon the death of Sun, Chiang Kai Shek led the government. Ai-ling introduced Mei-ling to Chiang. She became Madame Chiang. Kung and a Soong son were finance ministers of the Nationalist party.

1927 Wedding Soong Mei-ling, Madame and General Chiang Kai-shek (Public Domain)

---

[90] The girls attended Wesleyan College, Macon, Georgia. Mei-ling graduated from Wellesley College. Ai-ling was born 1888 and died in 1973; Ching-ling was born in 1893 and died 1981; Mei-ling was born in 1898 and died 2003.

Ching-ling was livid when she learned Mei-ling and Chiang wed. She regarded Chiang as an opportunist, not a revolutionary seeking independence for China. From her home in Shanghai, Ching-ling hosted communist academics and liberal thinkers of the era. She gave support to Zhou Enlai, who resided in Shanghai, and published critiques of Chiang.

Capital of Communist Capitalism

Zhou Enlai (l) and Mao Zedong (center-left) in 1935 (Public Domain)

In a girls' school in Shanghai's French Concession, in 1921, Zhou Enlai, Mao Zedong and others, formed the National Congress of the Chinese Communist Party. At the same time, Qing-ling was in the former home of Sun Yat Sen.[91] Then Chiang came to Shanghai.

---

[91] Both sites are open to visitors, as is the 1940s residence of Zhou Enlai, who directed Peoples' Army movements, even as Chiang's Nationalist Revolution Army was headquartered nearby.

The spring of 1927 was one of the bloodiest chapters in the history of Shanghai. Gang wars, Japanese occupation in 1937, and revolutionary war in 1949, paled in comparison. The event is known as the Shanghai Massacre. It was an act of random violence against communists, or anyone who might be, or seem to take an interest in, the Communist Party, perpetrated by the Nationalist Revolutionary Army. Between five and ten thousand people died in a few months. Only Ching-ling was immune to violence, out of respect for the memory of Sun. As word spread of violence, villagers joined the Communist Party.

Such was the personal rivalry between Chiang and Zhou, that when Japan invaded Manchuria, Chiang as the president of China, sent forces to look for communists in villages.[92] When Japan invaded Shanghai, Chiang offered a demilitarized zone. A slice of territory did not appease Japan. When full scale invasion of China by Japan was underway, Chiang mobilized his air force to bomb the Japanese fleet in the Shanghai harbor. In error, Chinese Nationalist bombs fell on Shanghai, not Japanese ships.

The period of Japanese occupation of Shanghai, from 1937 to 1945, was difficult for Europeans in Shanghai's International city and deadly for Chinese in the old city. The German invasion of France brought the French concession under control of Germany. In the overcrowded International section, the Municipal Council and Japanese of Shanghai refused to turn Jews over to Hitler's agent Josef Meisinger, when he visited in 1942. On December 7, 1942, Japanese bombed Pearl Harbor, the American naval base in Hawaii. The International city quickly evacuated eight thousand Americans and Europeans. Those who could not find space on ships, went to Japanese internment camps.

In 1945, peace abruptly came to the Asian theater. Mao returned to China from Russia and Chiang returned from the United States. Civil War resumed. Chiang required merchants to buy bonds. Chiang was well financed. Zhou had legions of people.

---

[92] Nationalist leaders wanted Chiang to join Zhou against Japanese incursion. When Chiang refused, he was kidnapped for two months in 1933. His life was threatened. Zhou stepped in, to save Chiang.

In 1949, Shanghai was the last stand of Chiang's government. He evacuated to Taiwan. On the plane with him was gold bullion of the Hong Kong and China Bank. The story of Chiang continues in Taiwan. Fate of contents of the bank is an ongoing dispute.

Shanghai residents, living in a commercial island within the Chinese mainland, and Red Guards, who took control of the city, eyed each other with curiosity. Over time, Shanghai was rebuilt. Mao built factories. People had jobs.

A middle class emerged after the Cultural Revolution of the 1960s. They returned to school. New leaders of China looked within China and at the world for opportunity.

Visiting Shanghai Today

Pudong (Creative Commons by Leonard G.)

A port stop in Shanghai is a visit to old and new China. In Tongli and Suzhou, old cities are preserved, allowing visitors to stroll paths and relax in gardens for introspection. Climb stairs of a centuries old Buddhist temple tower, shop for silk and enjoy a Chinese opera. In Shanghai's old city, wander from Nanjing

Road bird markets to elegant French/Chinese homes of Ching-ling, Zhou and the first home of the Chinese Communist Party. Museums are everywhere, from history to art, ancient and modern.

The story of Shanghai continues on the Bund. Today any international architect of merit strives for a commission on the Bund. Across Huangpu River in the Pudong district, where Pearl Tower, globes of the world, and some of the tallest buildings on the planet form a skyline, is a growing rival to the Bund. Shanghai harbor is an impressive skyline.

In a nation of three and a half billion people, Shanghai is the second largest city and the largest port in the world. Strolling along the river-side promenade, Shanghai does not overwhelm. In one Magnificent Mile is one hundred and fifty years of history to enjoy.

Po Lin Buddha Welcome to Hong Kong

Hong Kong – High Rises and Street Markets

The most densely occupied neighborhood in the world today is in Hong Kong. Two centuries ago, Hong Kong was a name given to barren rocks on a map of the Pearl River of China, that leads to Guangzhou, named Canton by the British. The rocks transformed in decades to a community built on trade, becoming a twentieth century wonder story.

Transition from bare rocks to marvel of commercial endeavor, on an appendage of a country that began the twentieth century in a declining monarchy, is credited to a small group, who fired no guns and led no armies.[93] Private, self-interested merchants and well-meaning bureaucrats, not governments, created an international port.

Birth of Hong Kong was launched by the Opium War. The Opium War was not about opium and may not have been a war. True, events bringing Britain and China to a face-off in 1839, began with a Chinese edict against opium sales and ended with British guns sinking Chinese boats. Of importance to history is resolution of tensions that left the British with rights in perpetuity to Hong Kong, uninhabited rocks across the bay from Portuguese Macau. Telling the story, by including personal motives and inter-country dynamics describes how bare rocks transitioned to a successful world port in decades.

Though China viewed Britain's control of Hong Kong as flawed, territory was twice added to the colony. Much maligned as imperialist and retaining Hong Kong beyond release of other British colonies, Britain always questioned the moral imperatives leading to the colony. It was a relief to China and Britain, as well as a benchmark of mutual respect, when in 1997, Hong Kong transitioned to China. History has a new milestone.

---

[93] Humans had settlements in the area from the stone age.

This is a story of Britain's entry to China and stunning growth of the most successful port of the early twentieth century. It provides insight to characters who seeded that growth. Before Hong Kong returned to China, it was a refuge from turbulence in China and elsewhere in Asia. That Hong Kong is home to seven million people and has not reverted to uninhabited rocks, despite repatriation to China, is part of the story, still unfolding. This is a story of one hundred and fifty years of action-packed history.

From Landscape of Barren Rocks to Densely Populated Trade Center

Hong Kong Old & New

Europe was enamored of Chinese silk from the thirteenth century, when Niccolo and Maffeo Polo returned to Venice from Beijing. Whether Marco Polo completed a return trip in 1295 is unknown. His colorful account, dictated to a scribe, while he sat in a Genoese prison, was almost as widely read as the Bible. When Ming dynasty emperors promoted the arts, between 1368 and 1644, silks, Chinese silk paintings, porcelain and lacquer chests thrilled European consumers and defined interior decoration. Christopher Columbus sailed west and Bartholomeu Dias sailed south, seeking sea routes to China.

Portuguese captains were aggressive on behalf of their king in establishing ports in the Far East. In China, a trading station allowed the Portuguese on the Chinese island of Macau, behind a privacy wall that exists today, established in 1547. Shortly after the Dutch East India Company was charted in 1602, it sought a trading station in China. Chinese and Portuguese authorities barred the Dutch entry, so they established a port in Taiwan.

The English East India Company, in competition with the Dutch and French East India companies, secured a base in India, at Calcutta in 1767. Denied a share of Portuguese Macau, the Chinese government allowed the British entry to the Pearl River in 1691, to trade from Canton.[94] Eventually, the British East India Company was allowed use of shops and warehouses. They were not allowed to bring families and establish residences, nor were they allowed a British-controlled compound, as they had established in India.

Eighteenth century Chinese society was structured on dictates of Confucius. In his ethical code for interaction in a just society, Confucius called for ordering society by function. At the top of the social ladder were rulers, then peasants. Peasant farmers were important producers of rice, the staple of life and a source of tax to the king. Next rung were craftsmen. At the bottom were merchants, taking profit and producing nothing.

Confucius was a fifth century BCE courtier. In his time, merchants siphoned goods meant for the king. Until kings learned to tax goods in commerce, merchants were of no use to royals. Merchants traveled across domains, exhibiting no loyalty to any single ruler. In China they were regarded as dangerous.

The East India Company (EIC) enjoyed a trade monopoly granted by the English Crown. Royal authority allowed it to make treaties and maintain soldiers to defend company property. The company was a joint commercial venture, spreading risks and costs across voyages. Self-dealing was prohibited. Flagrant self-dealing was so pervasive that company directors allowed space on company ships to transport side-trade of company officials.

---

[94] John Keay, China: A History, Basic Books, New York, 2009, p. 455.

Temple in Old Hong Kong

Operating in Canton, in concert with the East India Company were independent commercial agents. Houses of Agency provided on-site service to manage estates, collect rents on properties owned in foreign lands, collect debts and make freight arrangements for cargo. Successful agents built large import/export businesses. By 1822, there was a group of agencies in Canton, of which the leading two were Dent and Company and Jardine-Matheson. Dent's was a well-established London house. Jardine-Matheson grew from trade in Canton. Both houses quickly adapted to Hong Kong.

Peering into development of Jardine-Matheson affords insight to the cadre of merchants, support agencies and governmental bureaucracy, as it developed in Canton, and relocated to Hong Kong. The trader cadre called itself *Hongs*. Hongs created dissention in Canton, giving impetus to a war, intended to precipitate an independent trade station. Hongs desired a rocky patch known as Hong Kong, across the Pearl River Estuary from Macau. On that site, Hongs desired to relocate and build a superstar world trade center.

Dr. William Jardine was not formally educated, nor did he learn to spell. His introduction to business was as an assistant surgeon's mate on an EIC ship in 1802. He made sufficient funds on personal trade that in 1822, he set up a House of Agency in Canton. He charged the usual fee of five percent commission on sales of goods he brokered. The fee was less for gems and opium, as these items easily sold. As the need arose, Jardine added transit insurance and banking. His partner in these operations was James Matheson.

Matheson was from an old Scottish family. Educated at the university in Edinburgh, he went to Calcutta, India in 1819, as an accountant. He left the docile job to join a man importing opium in Canton. The man soon died, so he joined in partnership with another opium merchant. That man also died, leaving a partnership debt claimed by Matheson of £250,000.[95] Confucius warned about such men.

In 1833, the EIC charter was set for renewal in Parliament. Traders in Canton lobbied for open access to trade. Parliament liquidated EIC and gave £630,000 compensation to each partner.[96] The Crown became directly responsible for trade in Canton.

William Napier, Ninth Lord Napier, a Scott, was born in Ireland and educated at Edinburgh, as was Matheson, although Napier was a member of the Royal Society and socialized with a different crowd.[97] Napier represented Scotland in Parliament. Much appreciated by Englishmen, Napier failed to win hearts at home. In 1834, he was not re-elected. In Parliament since 1824, his friends found a new position for him as the first Crown representative to Canton. Napier knew nothing of Asia. It was expected that a man of good character would be successful at any job. His character was never in doubt.

The East India Company was a merchant organization. Napier was a representative of the Crown. His orders were to personally contact the viceroy of Canton, representative of the emperor, establishing continued trade between sovereigns.

---

[95] Frank Welsh, A Borrowed Place: The History of Hong Kong, Kodansha, Tokyo, 1993, p. 55.
[96] Amount of compensation is notable. Parliament awarded glorious service. After the Battle of Waterloo, grateful Parliament gave Lord Wellington £750,000. The same Parliament claimed poverty when asked to compensate traders in Canton £2million to avoid war. Note also, slight compensation to Horatio Nelson.
[97] Lord William Napier was born in Kinsale in 1786, and died in Macau in 1834, of fever from dysentery.

Protocol was a religion in China. Napier knew nothing of Chinese protocol, or rules of Confucius. Instead of petitioning the viceroy for a meeting, Napier went directly to Canton and demanded a royal audience. The Chinese were in shock at the offense. Foreigners were not to just arrive and travel in China. It was 1834. There were rules.

Napier made a display of force in Canton harbor. Guns were fired. Napier was granted a meeting with Chinese officials. Pending the meeting, the Chinese halted trade with Britain. When the Chinese arrived late for the meeting, Napier admonished them for the affront, accomplished nothing, and was left to make his own travel arrangements back to Macau. It was an arduous journey. Napier died in Macau of fever.

When the viceroy learned of Napier's death, he lifted the ban on trade. There was no war. Jardine and Matheson were disappointed. They hoped Napier would incite a war, the British would arrive with superior fire-power and the Chinese would capitulate and offer Hong Kong as a token of peace. Matheson, still hoping to incite war, wrote to Parliament demanding retribution from the Chinese for poor reception of Napier.

British trade in Canton grew in the five years after Napier's death. The British traded cotton and wool for silk and opium from India for tea. By paying for tea in opium, the British used a no-cost commodity to obtain the popular and profitable trade item. From 1830 to 1838, the number of cases of opium sold in Canton doubled. Chinese paid for opium in tea and bullion. The Chinese official in charge of Canton, Lin, was concerned that Chinese were ill on opium, while the British depleted China's silver bullion.

Lin ordered trade in opium cease, existing inventory burned, and traders punished. The British official, Charles Elliot, had traders produce their opium for burning. One thousand tons of opium burned on the shore at Canton, pleasing Lin. When Elliot presented Parliament the £2million debt owed to traders for lost opium, lords balked at payment.

Elliot's primary concern was punishment of traders found in the future possessing opium on their ships. His thought was, if a British subject faced punishment, it should be under laws of Britain and not China. Extra-territoriality, a concept basic to diplomatic agreements today, did not exist in Canton at the time.

While Elliot was discussing movement of bullion and extraterritoriality with Lin, Jardine-Matheson envoys stirred emotions of British officials in Calcutta. Jardine portrayed honorable Chinese traders as deceptive. Circumstances in Canton were depicted as dire. Life in Canton was restrictive. British and American sailors in a drunken brawl with Chinese left a Chinaman dead and the Chinese were demanding the guilty party turned over to Chinese authorities. Matheson was insistent that Britain needed an *insular possession*, that is, land of China, controlled by Britain. He repeated advice given to Napier, that Hong Kong was a fine option.

By 1839, circumstances between Britain and China were tense. Elliot wanted British captains not to sign an agreement submitting them to punishment by Chinese authorities, should opium be found on their ships, a condition to enter Canton. British ships waited in Macau, while American traders stood in for British ships in Canton.

One rogue British captain signed the agreement and entered Canton. Lin saw the move as weakness in Elliot's leadership. Emboldened, Lin ordered all British to leave Macau. Marooned on ships, the British community of Macau needed supplies. Elliot embarked on a small armed boat to obtain supplies on shore. Surrounded by Chinese boats, he fired. They fired back.

In the critical moment, when war was imminent, a British warship arrived from Calcutta, captained by Admiral George Elliot.[98] Elliot gave an impressive display of firepower. The incident ended, with a few Chinese boats sunk. Lin and Charles Elliot resumed talking.

China gave Britain rights to Hong Kong in perpetuity. Charles Elliot became the first British Administrator of the trading colony. Jardine and Matheson opened business in Victoria City, Hong Kong, across the street from Dent and Company. The cadre of Hongs moved in total to Hong Kong, where they were joined by banks. It was an instant port.

---

[98] Sir George Elliot and Charles Elliot were cousins. Sir George captained ships under Admiral Horatio Nelson during the Napoleonic War at the Battle of Copenhagen and Battle of St. Vincent.

Growth of the First Asian Marvel

Macau

Hong Kong grew in 1860, with a grant to Britain in perpetuity of Kowloon, across the inlet from Hong Kong. Population in Hong Kong and Kowloon expanded so rapidly, the Chinese were pressed by 1898, to add the New Territories, an adjoining group of islands, as a 99-year lease, not a perpetual authority of occupation. The Portuguese station in Macau was elevated in 1887, to a perpetual grant of authority. Thus, the insular country had two colonies within their lands. For the Chinese, the situation was preferable to India, where the British waged war until all of India was reduced to a colony of Britain.

Hong Kong developed as a little bit of Britain on the other side of the world. Gas lines and electricity were added to water and transportation infrastructure. The port expanded to receive growing traffic. Western dress, education and English language were the norm in Hong Kong, in sharp contrast to mainland China. Dramatic change was felt in big cities of Shanghai, Canton and Beijing. Starving farmers left villages for Hong Kong.

Recipe for economic success in Hong Kong was low taxation, an open port to all nations, low port charges, and multiple banks. Interest rates were not regulated, in the free-market competitive economy. The Hong Kong dollar was pegged to the US dollar.

As a British colony, colonial administrators managed Hong Kong to please traders. It was a difficult task, as some operated like pirates, less scrupulous than Confucian counterparts in Canton. As Hong Kong grew in trade volume, Canton receded from preeminence. During the 1950s Cultural Revolution, world trade was not China's priority.

Hong Kong was never a colony in the usual sense of extracting resources to benefit the colonizer. Rather, Hong Kong was allowed unbridled free-market commercialism, where port profits went to Britain, and all entrepreneurs had access to create benefits. Costs of administration and infrastructure were met by rents charged for buildings and port fees. Foreign direct investment poured into Hong Kong. The major crisis was building space.[99]

Refuge at the Tip of a Volcano

Hong Kong was from inception an international port of no government. Administrative budgets did not allow deficit spending. There were no social programs. Impoverished workers benefited from jobs in the open marketplace. The population was transient, that is, on site as temporary workers, returning home wealthy to retire. There was no provision for permanent population, requiring hospitals, or families requiring schools.

Hong Kong grew in resident population on long term assignment. Numerous agency houses, insurers, banks and shipping operations were joined at the turn of the twentieth century by manufacturing. To continue successful operation, Hong Kong required a large labor pool of lesser skilled workers, in a landscape with no existent resident population.

---

[99] There were bouts of plague in the early years.

Victoria Peak View

Labor flooded into Hong Kong. Initially, people came from mainland China, and over the decades from elsewhere in the Far East. Wherever rebellion, oppressive government or famine appeared, Hong Kong was a safe haven, offering peace and jobs.

In 1899, a boxing club of zealots grew in ferocity in China, until boxing as a hobby was forgotten. Mobs went from town to town attacking any show of western culture. People in western dress were attacked. Christian churches were destroyed. Known as the Boxer Rebellion, it was a populist purification of culture. There was no central leader. Rebellion was a flame that burst from province to province, until the government recognized a crisis and responded with soldiers.[100] Fleeing violence, villagers came to Hong Kong.

---

[100] Eleven nations sent troops to assist Chinese royals end the rebellion. Leaders were executed. China proclaimed an end to foot binding of young girls, established a national assembly of advisors from provinces and awarded college scholarships. Many scholarship recipients went to school in Japan.

The Crown colony was not a democracy. It did not enfranchise citizens. It offered a stable, free enterprise economy. By 1941, the population of Hong Kong was 1.6 million.

Regardless of intent of administrators, residents looked upon Hong Kong as home. They built temples and gardens. Although the cultural time depth of Hong Kong is less than two centuries, there exists abundant cultural vestiges of a melded people.

Temple Incense

Man Mo Temple in Hong Kong is an excursion into Taoist thought. Man is the god of literature and Mo is the god of war. The temple begs the question of which is mightier, the pen or sword. Pak Tai Temple, built in 1860, is dedicated to the warrior bringing peace. A temple frequented by locals is Wong Tai Sin, home of the god of gamblers. Visible from the air, when flying into Hong Kong airport, is the one-hundred-twelve feet high Po Lin Buddha. Climb 268 steps of the 250-ton Buddha and view Hong Kong.

Inside Incense-Filled Temple of Hong Kong

When Japanese forces invaded China in 1937, people fled to Hong Kong. By 1941, Hong Kong was occupied by Japanese troops. British and all bankers were imprisoned in Stanley Prison. Trade halted. Factory workers were force-marched to China. Population was reduced by two-thirds.

In 1945, Hong Kong came back to life. It was not life as it had been. Upon withdrawal of Japanese, China bid to take Hong Kong. British administrators, barely out of prison, quickly recognized resident Asians as part of Hong Kong society. Disparate living requirements for Asians, kept apart from British life, excluded Chinese from beaches and sites, such as Victoria Peak. In the new world order, barriers were removed, or at least reduced. Social services were included in the Hong Kong budget. New Hong Kong acknowledged a community of permanent residents, though citizens of no country.

Hong Kong population continued growth with refugees. In the 1950s, people fled war in Korea. In the 1960s and 1970s, Vietnamese fled war in their country. In 1962, seventy thousand refugees entered Hong Kong. By 1990, population approached seven million, on less than four hundred square miles of ground, three-quarters of which is green space. One neighborhood in Kowloon was the most densely populated place on earth.

Reversion

Mao Zedong disapproved of capitalism, sitting on fringes of China, providing a haven to refugees. In anticipation of the 1997 expiration of the lease on New Territories, British Prime Minister Margaret Thatcher and Chinese Premier Zhao Ziyang agreed on total reversion of Hong Kong to Chinese control. Britain ended its colonial era.

For Britain, Hong Kong was emblematic of successful administration of a colony built on free-market capitalism. Chinese wanted success of moving imperialists from their shores. By the 1980s, China moved from Marxist-Communism to capitalistic-communism. China did not want to lose face in an exodus of Hong Kong residents.

Hong Kong Street

China's solution to smooth reversion of control was a policy of *One Country, Two Systems*. At midnight on July 1, 1997, Britain handed Hong Kong to China as a Special Administrative District. Special rules for Hong Kong were set for fifty years.

By the terms of the Basic Law, Hong Kong is an inalienable part of China. It has authority for fifty years to be governed in separate executive, legislative and judicial systems. China is responsible for defense and international affairs, not interfering with operations of Hong Kong entities. A similar arrangement devised for Macau in 1999.

Visiting Hong Kong Today

The future of Hong Kong and special status are unknown. The Chinese mainland economy is an international powerhouse. Singapore, Vietnam and

Korea vie for preeminence in world trade with China. Tension grows when leaders discuss politics.[101]

Feng Shui Hong Kong

Visitors to Hong Kong are struck by the density of development. Hong Kong holds the world's record for the number of high-rise buildings at the harbor. Icon towers abound in Hong Kong, where architects competed for representation in the skyline. Kowloon is so densely populated that people move as a fluid mass at street intersections. Space for tai chi is found on above-street walkways. Still, there are open spaces for street markets.

Hong Kong is known for shopping. It is a world center for pearls and pearl jewelry. Almost anything that can be bought anywhere in the world can be found in Hong Kong.

---

[101] See The Economist, Has one country, two systems been a success for Hong Kong? June 29, 2017, electronic edition, last accessed April 21, 2019.

Yuan Po Street Bird Market

Port excursions include a visit to Po Lin Buddha and city view from Victoria Peak. Few colonial era buildings remain, although there are vestiges of Japanese occupation, seen in pagoda style roofs tacked onto Victorian architecture. Hong Kong is a unique experience. Enjoy Asian fusion cuisine, where it was invented, and leave plenty of time for shopping.

TAIWAN

Cross Currents of Culture

Taiwan was previously known as Formosa, the Republic of China in exile, a Japanese Colony, and a Dutch commercial outpost, always at crosscurrents of control by external powers. Never docile, nor compliant, its indigenous groups, made subservient, were never extinguished. History of Taiwan was a bouncing line from uprising to uprising.

Taiwan's story is written several ways, depending on the author, and intended audience. This story is ecumenical, not judgmental. Inclusion of political history is unavoidable. Taiwan is floating, searching for identity in the modern world.

Taiwan sits at the confluence of the East China Sea and South China Sea, across the narrow Formosa Strait from the great body of mainland China. Ironically, first arrivals were Austronesians, that is, people of the Philippines, to the south, and from Malaysia. Chinese people arrived slowly from the third to sixth century of the current era, then as part of Chinese diaspora from the mainland in recent centuries.

History of Taiwan is related to its closest neighbor. When famine or war drove Chinese people to relocate, Taiwan was an easy option. Almost two million Chinese came to Taiwan in the late 1940s, with fleeing politician Chiang Kai-shek. Relationship of Taiwanese to Chiang, was akin to disdain for the Dutch and Japanese. All three held a veneer of an imposed national organization in Taiwan, their reluctant host.

Emphasis of this story is on cultural identity of Taiwan. Cruise visitors encounter diverse cultures in a port stop in Taipei. It is a people-to-people experience, which enthuses travelers. Video games featuring bold, iron-clad warriors and ghostly heroes, come close to reality of Taiwanese history.

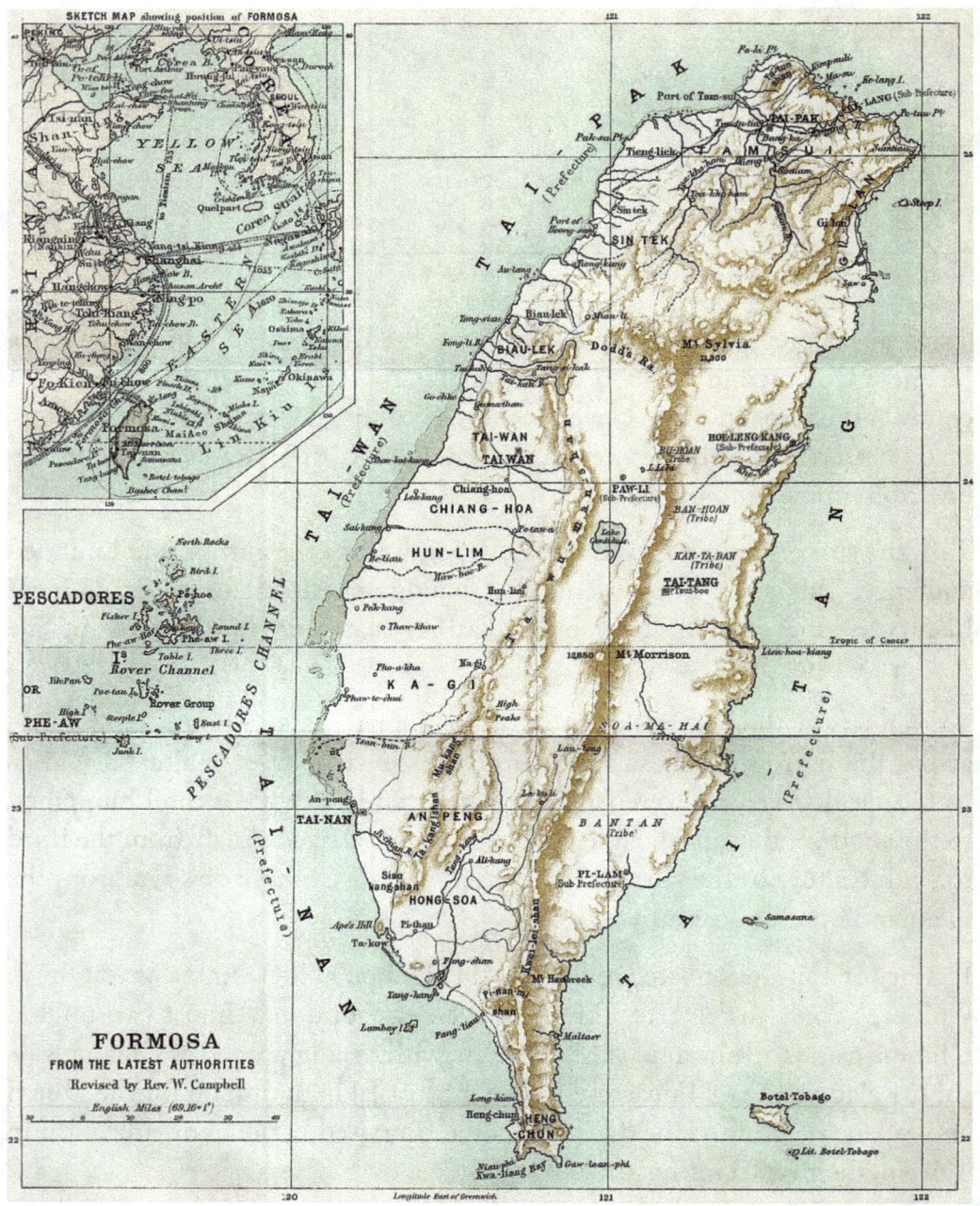

1896 Map of Taiwan & Pescadores with China to West (Public Domain)

A Brief Cultural Tour of Taiwan

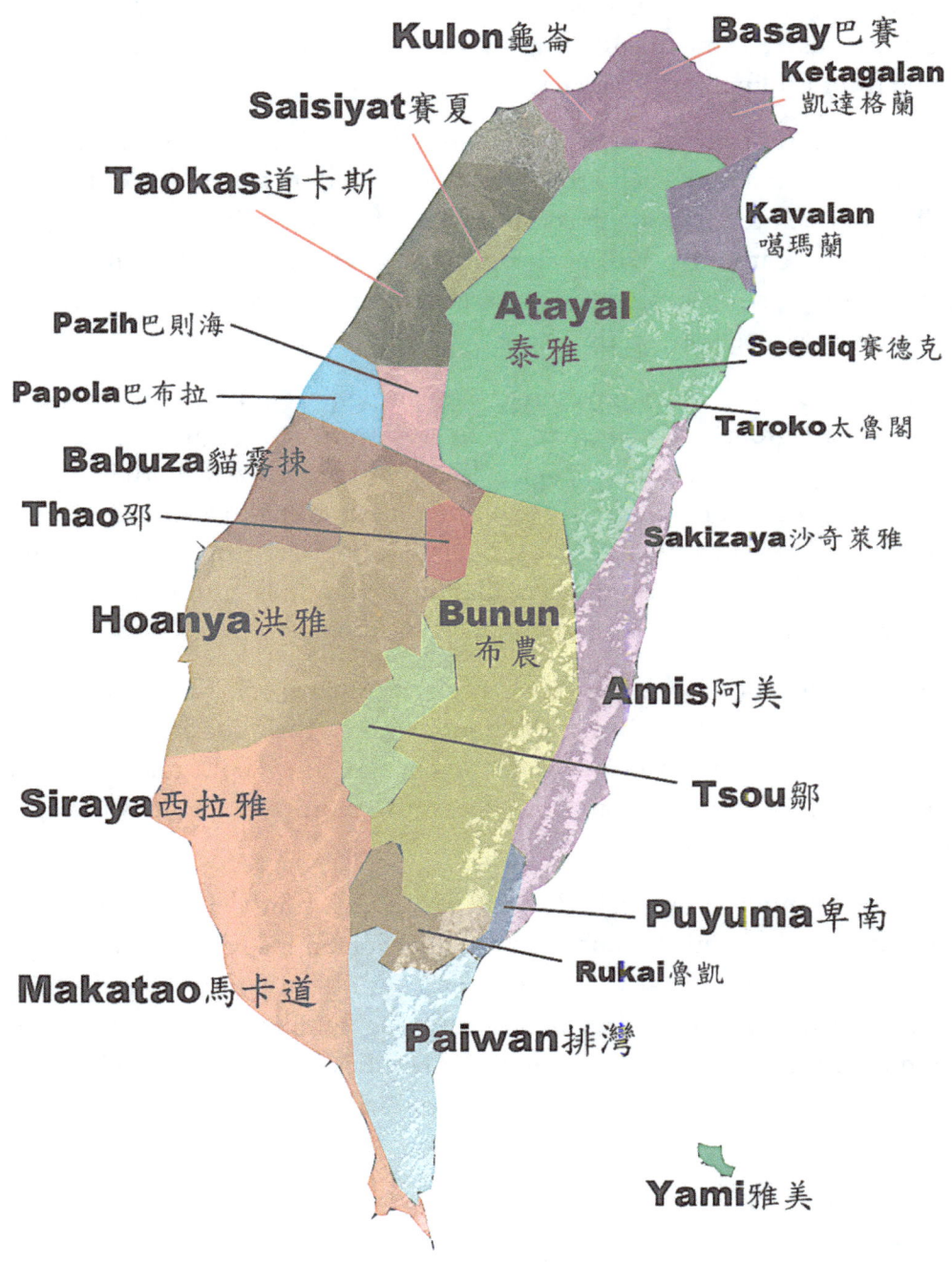

Indigenous People of Taiwan (Public Domain)

First inhabitants of Taiwan were Austronesians, the people originating across east Asia, who ventured to far reaches of land, which became islands at the end of the final Ice Age, when seas rose, and land bridges were inundated. People from islands continued migrating by rafts and later dugout canoes. People came from Philippines and Malaysia.

Malay migration story is relevant in Taiwan, as multiple peoples came to the island, independent of each other.[102] People settled on slopes of Mount Yu, in valleys of the interior or along coasts. Heaps of oyster shell near beaches tell of ancient food gathering. Diverse peoples of Taiwan, repeatedly dominated by foreign forces, never capitulated to intermittent periods of slavery. They held in common a rebellious spirit.

Today there are sixteen governmentally recognized groups of indigenous peoples, ten groups too small to merit government recognition, and three locally recognized aboriginal peoples. The largest recognized aboriginal people are Amis, ancient arrivals from the Philippines. Over thirty-thousand Amis, represent one-fourth of the total surviving aboriginal people, having official recognition. The total aboriginal population in Taiwan is miniscule today, after centuries of slavery and externally induced poverty.

Formerly animist in cosmology, today most Amis speak Mandarin and are Christian. Historically living in the interior valley, their cultural center, Amis survived by an ability to acclimate to change. They hold ancient harvest ceremonies, enjoyed by visitors, and record traditional chants on popular music formats.

Like the Amis, aboriginal Paiwan people of southcentral plains were matriarchies. Men hunted and fished, while women made decisions, unifying communities. Paiwan farms had concentric ring formation. Family homes occupied the inner-most ring. In the next ring, families maintained gardens. In the outer ring grew vegetable crops, for families and the market. Open areas held community agriculture. Until Japanese seized land, at the beginning of

---

[102] Read more on Malay migration in Cruise through History, Itinerary XIII Ports of West Africa to Southeast Asia - Malaysia, Peopling of the Pacific.

the twentieth century, for resale to arriving Chinese, Paiwan people were self-sufficient. Today, rare historic bamboo homes on stilts are empty.

Other formerly robust indigenous peoples have small populations, gathered into a few villages, meriting local recognition. Such is the fate of Siraya of the slopes, Makatao of the lowlands, and Taivoan of hills and basins. Siraya people farmed rice and sugarcane on mountain slopes. In the seventh century, Chinese warrior/pirates arrived and demanded tribute paid by Siraya for protection. Siraya refused payment. They were slaughtered and their villages burned. For protection, Siraya relocated further inland.

Prior to introduction of Confucianism and Taoism by Chinese arrivals, or Christianity brought by Spanish, French, British and Dutch missionaries, most Taiwanese were animists, believing in sea serpent gods. Gods made food available and kept flood waters in the bay. People of Taiwan were headhunters. They took heads of slain enemies, shrunken and worn around their necks to absorb the strength from enemies into themselves.

The exception to headhunters were Yami people of Orchid Island. Known today as governmentally recognized Tao people, Yami were Taoists, to whom all life is sacred. Their lives and cosmology are tied to the sea. Yami ancient roots are in the Philippines.

Regardless of unique language and lifeways, aboriginal people of Taiwan held in common a dislike of people from beyond their island enslaving them. They farmed and hunted antelope. Iron was mined from the fourth century BCE, smelted into weapons.

When seventh century Chinese visited Taiwan, their metal weapons and armor informed Taiwanese to improve smelting methods. Taiwanese iron became a trade staple, into the twentieth century. They minted coins, a novelty when there was no king or government.

Random Chinese arrived in Taiwan from the third century of the current era. Over a millennium, three regions of China were represented. Shu Han people left floods in the Yellow River region, Cao Wei came from north China, and Sun Wu were traders, lured by opportunities to trade in metals and salt.

Zheng Era Confucius Temple (Public Doman)

Chinese migrants had little to unite them. They joined disparate people of Taiwan, seeking life from land, without overlords.

Han Chinese introduced rules of Confucius and Taoism to Taiwan. Taoism is the way to immortality of the soul. Travels of the soul after death are unlike the concept of heaven in Christianity. Taoists seek simplicity and ways to contend with life's ying and yang.

In the seventeenth century, when more Chinese arrived, part of a diaspora fleeing war and famine, they introduced Buddhism to Taiwan. After the Dutch were expelled in the seventeenth century, Buddhism became the majority religion, replacing animism. Today, people of Taiwan are predominantly Buddhists, or Christian.

Turbulent Political History

By the late sixteenth century, no permanent Chinese settlements existed in Taiwan. Chinese migrants occupied coastal areas, living as fishermen and

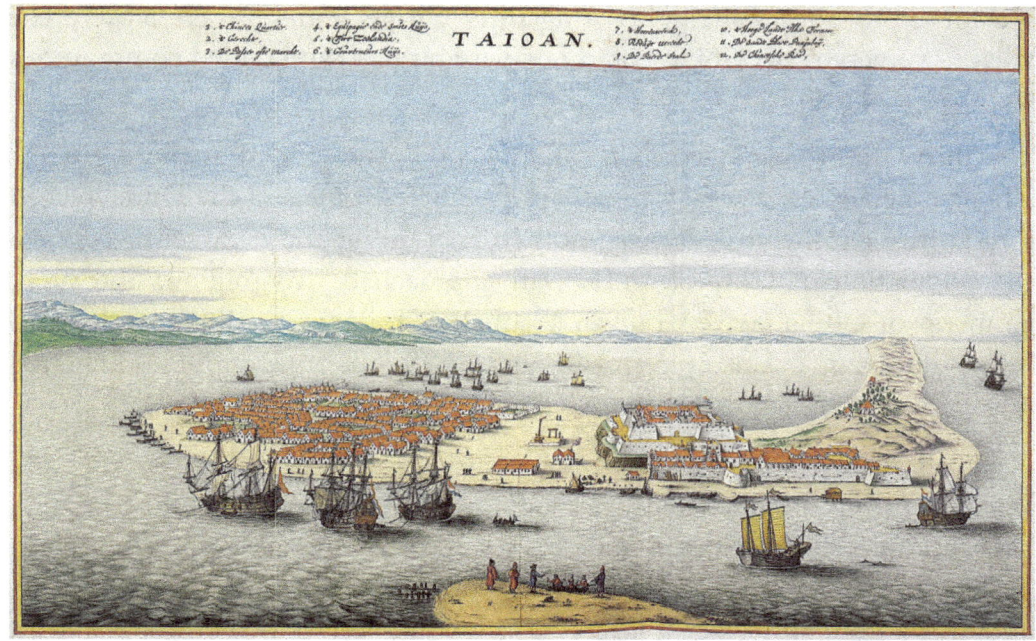

Dutch Fort Freelandia Formosa in 17th Century (Public Domain)

traders of metals and herbs. Aboriginal people lived inland, in communities of farmers and hunters.

When Portuguese explorers sailed by in the 1540s, they noted a beautiful island, recorded on maps as Formosa. The next off islanders were the Dutch, in commercial ventures of the Dutch East India Company. The Dutch were driven away by island people in 1622.

The DEIC returned in 1624 and began trade with coastal people. They made friends, enabling a peaceful landing. Over a decade, the Dutch built Fort Zeelandia. Walls of the fort still stand in Anping, on the south-west coast of Taiwan. When locals realized Dutch intended to remain, they fought skirmishes. Dutch had superior weapons and were well supplied. One by one, people of Taiwan entered into *Pax Hollandica*, agreements wherein locals offered peace for Dutch protection from pirates and other foreign arrivals.

Taiwan was never a valuable plantation enterprise for the DEIC, as was Jakarta, known to the Dutch as Batavia. Fort Zeelandia served as a port in politically stormy Far Eastern seas, to support trade between Manila and Japan, or with China. Within Formosa, DEIC obtained direct supplies of textiles and iron ore for export, destabilizing existing inter-village trade. Dutch activity left villages vulnerable to Chinese and Japanese pirates, who raided communities and captured people as slaves.

The thirty-eight-year reign of the Dutch in Taiwan ended at the urging of Zheng Chenggong, a great Chinese warrior, whose defeat of the Dutch placed him in the pantheon of Taiwanese heroes. During the eighteenth century, the population of Chinese in Taiwan approached two million. The Qing Emperor of China viewed Taiwan as a ball of mud, impossible to rule, with its conglomerate of unruly, disparate, and rebellious ethnic groups. He halted migration of mainland Chinese to Taiwan.

Next off-islanders looking for opportunities in Taiwan were Britain and France. During the nineteenth century, the nations were competitors for Far East resources. Britain forced trade with Taiwan, by engulfing ports in Opium Wars, which enabled British trade in China. In Opium Wars, the British obtained opium at no cost from its India colony, then traded opium for tea, a valuable commodity in England. Numbers of addicted Chinese in Taiwan is unknown. Lives were ruined. In Taiwan, Britain mined iron.

French forays in Taiwan were short-lived. In 1884, the French desired a trading station at Keelung, now known as Taipei. In the Keelung Campaign, known as the Sino-French War, French battled Qing Chinese troops at Fort Neuf, on eastern reaches of Taipei. The Qing Emperor sent reinforcements to Taiwan, until the French were overwhelmed. Both sides were inundated by disease. The war ended in a stalemate and truce. In the 1885 Treaty of Tientsin, the French agreed to forego claims to Taiwan, in exchange for Qing in China withholding resistance to French control of Viet Nam, known as French Indochina.

Keenly observing events in the Sino-French War, from a safe distance, was Japan. In 1894, China and Japan were at war. In a peace treaty, Taiwan, and its Penghu Islands, also known as Pescadores, were left out of agreements. Japan immediately attacked and took control of the Pescadores, then attacked Taiwan.

Under terms of the 1895 Treaty of Shimonoseki, China conceded Formosa to Japan. Since there was no Formosan government, people of the island had no say in any treaty. Treaty terms allowed Korea autonomy and opened Chinese mainland ports to Japan, allowing Japan most favored nation status in trade.

Although treatment of Formosans by Japan, in the period from 1894 to World War II, is best described as measured tolerance, slowly inducing Japanese culture, language and education, locals were never compliant subjects. Fifty years of Japanese control of Formosa was dotted by bloody uprisings and demonstrations in favor of independence. Culmination of disregard by Japan for aboriginals came in 1930, in the Musha Incident.

For sixty years, Japanese harbored memories of an 1871 incident, in which Paiwan people massacred fifty-four shipwrecked Japanese civilian sailors. When Japan took control of Formosa, aboriginal people were regarded as lesser beings. In the 1930 Musha Incident, Japan seized land of aboriginals and held aboriginal men as slaves. Women and children were sold as servants and induced laborers. The Association of Aboriginal People, formed to assert aboriginal rights, became militant and attacked Japanese soldiers, killing several. Internal war erupted. Headhunting resumed, perpetrated by both sides.

Chinese of the island were caught in the middle, when the Musha Incident erupted. Though they benefited from Japanese actions, they did not take part in violence. Most Chinese émigrés continued to live on the coasts of Taiwan, apart from native people.

By 1935, calm resumed. Former Keelung became New Taipei City, a showplace of modern development. There were free elections, in which the majority of elected representatives were Taiwanese nationalists. During World War II, Formosa aboriginals fought for Japan in the Takasago Volunteers unit.

During World War II, the Formosa Air Battle, from October 12 to 16, 1944, was devastating to the Japanese Airforce. Although Japan reported the battle as a victory, they emerged with a dearth of planes. Formosa was in ruins.

China assisted the Allies and assumed any treaty would resolve Formosa and Pescadores Islands to control of China. Instead, the 1951 Treaty of San Francisco, also known as the Treaty of Peace with Japan, required Japan to retreat from Korea, Northern China and Taiwan. Japan did so, leaving the national status of Taiwan ambiguous.

In an agreement between the Republic of China, led by Chiang Kai-shek and post-war Allied occupiers, the Republic assumed administration of Formosa. The result was a disaster. Corruption was uncontrolled. Japanese-speaking administrators, a legacy of fifty years of Japanese colonial control, were ousted. Aboriginal people were no better treated by Chiang than Japan. When Chiang's government nationalized mining and transportation, then taxed tobacco sales, to fund itself, people of Taiwan rebelled.

In February 1947, a woman selling contraband cigarettes was beaten to death by Republic of China officers. Resentment for Chinese and Republic emigrees by long-time residents, exploded into riots. By the time tempers cooled, from five to twenty-eight thousand people were left dead in the streets. Counts

US President Eisenhower Visit to Chiang in 1960 (Public Domain)

differ between reports. Like so much history of Taiwan, factual information is illusive.

Chiang Kai-shek, and his Chinese Nationalists, fled from mainland China to Formosa in 1949. In the last stand of the Republic of China, the island was renamed Taiwan. Two million Chinese relocated from mainland People's Republic of China, to the Republic of China on Taiwan. To control rioting, Chiang imposed martial law. Martial law remained in effect from 1949 to 1987.

In 1971, the United Nations refused recognition to the Republic of China in Taiwan, clarifying there are not two Chinas. *China* in the UN is the People's Republic of China, the successor government to Nationalist China on the mainland.[103] The UN Resolution did not resolve Taiwan; which the People's Republic assumed was part of China; the Chiang led Republic of China

Presidential Building Taiwan (Public Domain)

assumed was theirs to govern; and Taiwanese people assert is an independent country of Taiwan, irrespective of one or two Chinas. To Taiwanese, Chiang and his government were uninvited foreigners.

Chiang Kai-shek died in 1975. His son, Chiang Ching-kuo, assumed control in 1978. Chiang Ching-kuo organized Taiwan into a manufacturing center of transistor radios and textiles. Social quiet grew as corruption declined and the economy improved. Once martial law lifted and government was democratic, Taiwanese Nationalist candidates prevailed in elections.

---

[103] UN Resolution 2758, October 25, 1971.

In 1979, US President Carter signed the Taiwan Relations Act, which established US regard for Taiwan. National status of Taiwan is ambiguous in US law. In lieu of recognizing the Republic of China in Taiwan, the US established an American Institute in Taiwan, officed in the District of Columbia, through which the US maintains cultural and commercial Taiwan relations. The 1979 law replaced a Mutual Defense Treaty.

Taiwanization Movement continues in Taiwan, to establish identity of Taiwan, as an independent nation, of neither of the two Chinas. Whether Taiwan status remains ambiguous, or is resolved by China, or becomes a recognized nation, remains to be seen.

Warrior King of Tungtu, Liao's Ghost and Goto's Vision

In 1661, a great warrior appeared in Liaoluo Bay, on the coast of Taiwan at Anping. He led deliverance of Taiwanese from bondage of the DEIC. Under the helpless gaze of Dutch soldiers in Fort Zeelandia, Zhong Chenggong docked his fleet of hundreds of Chinese junks, carrying twenty-five thousand warriors, some in full body armor.

Zhong Chenggong, known in Taiwan as Koxinga, was a veteran warrior. Born a prince in China in 1624, during the Ming Dynasty, he and his family were loyal to the emperor. Koxinga received a royal education and was respected as a future leader. When he was twenty-two, he was thrust into leadership of an army, when Ming generals surrendered to Qing forces. Koxinga traveled through southeast China, battling Qing forces, village to village. When Koxinga was unable to remain in China, he directed his fleet to Taiwan.

Imagine the stunning appearance of Koxinga and his fleet of warriors as they arrived in port. Almost immediately, forces under Koxinga attacked the Dutch and placed a siege on Fort Zeelandia. The leader from China was hailed as delivering freedom to Taiwan.

Dutch overlords ran for safety, leaving slaves free. Locals and freed slaves joined Koxinga forces. The DEIC in Batavia sent a fleet to engage Koxinga. The land warrior proved his ability at sea in the Battle of Liaoluo Bay, a reprise of the 1633 Battle of Liaoluo Bay, led on behalf of the Ming Emperor, by his father Zheng Zhilong.[104] Dutch lost both battles.

Back at the Dutch fort, supplies ran low. In 1662, the last DEIC soldier fled the fort to a DEIC ship, sailing to Jakarta. Koxinga declared himself king of Tungtu, later known as Tungning. His reign lasted a few months, until he died of malaria at age thirty-seven.

The Koxinga Dynasty of rulers of Formosa lasted until 1683, when the grandson of Koxinga surrendered to Qing forces. In a turn of events, the next Qing emperor saw ethnic diversity in Taiwan as a seething ball of dissention and refused to acknowledge any relationship of the islands to China. Chinese were forbidden to migrate to Taiwan.

During the era of Japanese control, beginning in 1894, a new hero appeared to Taiwanese. Liao Tianding only lived to age twenty-six, although his ghost is immortal. Born in 1883, Liao was eleven when Japanese arrived. He was adept at living by theft from Japanese storehouses. He distributed his loot to poor Taiwanese, who cheered his actions.

In the course of a theft, a Japanese guard died. Liao was hunted as a murderer. He was chased into a cave near Taipei. Liao never emerged from the cave.

People see the ghost of Liao whenever wealth of oppressors is *redistributed*. Children's books recount selfless generosity of the little person, who challenged the evil giant. Liao lives in music and dance. His hometown erected a statue to honor him.

Despite distain for rule by off-islanders, Taiwanese highly regard visions of Goto Shinpei, the Japanese administrator, who saw Taipei as capital of civilian government in Taiwan.[105] He drafted the 1897 Bank Act of Taiwan,

---

[104] Elder Zheng changed loyalty from Ming to Qing; his wife and son remained loyal to the Ming emperor.
[105] Goto Shinpei was born in 1857 in Japan and died in Kyoto in 1929.

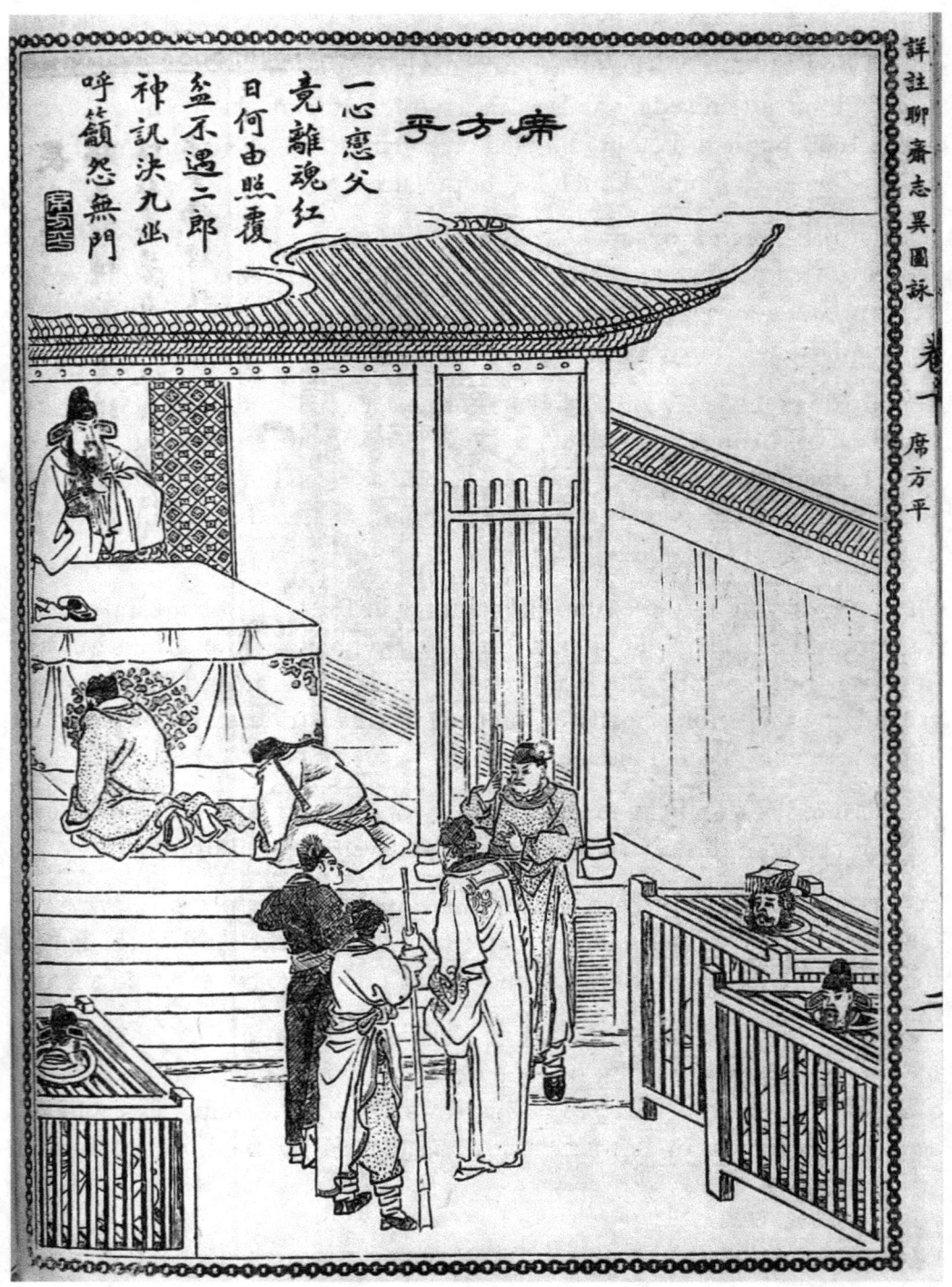

From Tales of Liao-Corrupt Officials Caged for Public Humiliation (Library of Congress)

enabling the first bank in Taiwan in 1899. He established Taiwanese currency and invited banks to Taiwan, which gave loans to small businesses. Railways, hospitals, roadways and infrastructure systems in Taiwan were begun by Goto. The Goto Vision is seen in New Taipei, Taiwan's first modern city.

Taipei Taiwan Skyline (Creative Commons by Heeheemalu)

Visiting Taipei Today

Today, cruise visitors come to port in Taipei, the cultural, commercial, population center of Taiwan. Densely populated, Taipei is a busy, expensive, modern metropolis of activity. For a view of culture and history, visit temples and museums. Highlights are the Taiwan Aboriginal Museum, Fine Arts

Museum and Taipei National Palace Museum.[106] A beautiful retreat in Taipei is the Lotus Pond in the Botanical Garden, adjacent to the National Museum of History.

Today Taipei is the leading city of Taiwan, not a national capital, as Taiwan is a geographical, not a national designation. Chinese Nationalists have a strong hold on Taiwan, where elected leaders have disparate views of the future. Views include retaining Chiang Kai-shek's Nationalist Chinese Republic of Taiwan; merging into China; or diverging from either China, into an independent nation. In a history of disparity, predicting the future is as elusive as catching Liao's ghost.[107]

---

[106] Some collection items are disputed; brought to Taiwan by Chiang Kai-shek from the Beijing Palace.

[107] As of 2020, China took an assertive position on Taiwan, Taiwanese officials call for independence, and the US agreed to sell arms to Taiwan. The voice of Chiang Kai-shek and his second China is fading.

PHILIPPINES
Steel Butterfly and Sainted Madonna

East of the South China Sea, between Taiwan to the north and Brunei on the south, spans the Philippine archipelago. More than seven thousand islands, some with no names and many with no occupants, comprise the nation of Philippines today.[108] A republic for seventy years, the country is leery of dominance by powerful nations, yet cognizant of a need to join world markets for economic opportunities. Largely Catholic, amid a sea of Muslim and Communists neighbors, three hundred years as a Spanish colony shaped the Spanish speaking, Latin culture, despite a desire of Muslim south islands for separation.

In US history, the Philippines was won in the Spanish American War in 1898, along with Cuba, Puerto Rico and Guam. Few realize the US part in turbulence in the Philippines, in which circumstances of the last Spanish possession in the Pacific were different from Caribbean cohorts in Spanish history. Filipinos prize independence, even more than democracy. US led democracy did not diminish corruption, the nemesis of progress for the Philippines. Knowing US/Philippine history leads to understanding Filipinos today.

Iconic of the wild ride though Philippine governance of the twentieth century are the lives and interaction of two women leaders, both wives of politicians, who rose to politics on legacies of their husbands. Imelda Marcos first came to the United States as the overwrought wife of President Ferdinand Marcos. She emerged from therapeutic treatment, as if from a cocoon, as the Steel Butterfly, who championed over Philippine strongmen and US courts.

---

[108] There are 7,107 islands in the Philippine archipelago and a population of ninety million. Part of the Pacific Ring of Fire, the Philippines has thirty-seven active volcanoes.

Corazon Aquino 1992 (Public Domain)

Corazon Aquino shared no traits with Imelda Marcos, other than political wife and mother. Aquino was the Sainted Madonna of the Philippines, in a country accustomed to male leaders and revered mothers. Her reticence to rule, lack of self-aggrandization or accumulation of personal wealth as president, drew Filipinos to trust Aquino. Marcos displayed flamboyant leadership, while Aquino offered lowkey, stable leadership.

This story is a glimpse into a nation as it went from Spanish colony, to US possession and into the twenty-first century. In that time, the Philippines had three female presidential candidates, and two female presidents. Of colorful Philippine elections, the contest between the Steel Butterfly and Sainted Madonna was most entertaining.

A War Not Taught in the United States

Intramuros & Spanish Cannon (Public Domain)

Spanish explorers arrived in the Philippines in 1556. They named their discovery for the crown prince, Filipe, hence the name Filipinos. The English-speaking world refers to the prince, who became king, as Philip II, hence the name Philippines for the islands.

When the Spanish arrived, the population massed on three main islands: Luzon, Visayas and Mindanao. The largest population was on Luzon, where the port of Cebu was a trade center from ancient times. The city of Manila is on Luzon.

St. Agustine Paoay Baroque Church WHS (Public Domain)

Spanish oppressed locals, who refused to be enslaved. Filipinos rebelled from the moment they realized the Spanish were not visitors, or merely interested in trade. Understanding Filipino response to political leaders today, begins with realizing Filipinos endured three hundred years of speaking Spanish and building Spanish Baroque churches and palaces, without accepting Spanish rule. Being Spanish and Catholic fused with historic culture.

Before the Spanish arrived, Filipinos lived in clan groups, with an informal leader, known as datu. Datu achieved authority through leadership skills. People paid tribute to datu.

Spanish employed an encomienda system of pressing people to labor for the landowner, given a bequest of land by the Spanish governor. Encomienda existed in all Spanish colonies in the New World. When Catholic friars arrived, they were given land by the church. Friars competed with lords for labor. People abandoned encomiendas for church lands, serving less onerous masters.

University of Santo Tomas founded 1611 (by Mark Joseph C. Olmedo)

Regardless of encomienda lords, people paid tribute to their datu. Datu power was never eliminated. Datu often acted as intermediaries between their people and the Spanish. Datu remained ready to fill a void in Spanish power and leadership.

While the Spanish were distracted in Europe by the Seven Years War of 1756 to 1763, also known as the War of Spanish succession, British forces took control of trade in Manila. Not wishing to trade one foreign overlord for another, datu revolted and imposed their governance on the islands. One datu, Francisco Dagohoy set up a government in interior islands, which defied Spanish rule until his death in 1829.[109] Muslim rajah in south islands pushed for autonomy until 2016, when they achieved status as an autonomous region.

When Spain acceded to Mexican independence in 1821, it was left with colonies of Cuba, Puerto Rico, the Marianas, known today as Guam, and the Philippines. Resistance to Spanish control in the Philippines increased over decades, sometimes becoming violent. By 1872, there were labor strikes in shipyards. In 1894, less than twenty thousand Spanish officials and military troops in the Philippines, faced seven million locals.

Events reached a crescendo in 1897, when warehouse worker and labor leader Andrés Bonifacio led rebellion with a people's militia. Despite Spanish presence, the country held elections. Emilio Aguinaldo won election and executed Bonifacio.

The Spanish governor made a treaty with Aguinaldo, in which he accepted $1 million and moved to Hong Kong. Spain resumed brief control. On February 15, 1898, the USS *Maine* exploded in Havana Harbor and the US rushed to war with Spain.[110]

Admiral Dewey led the US fleet to quick victory over the aging Spanish fleet in Havana Harbor. The one US casualty in the brief war was a man who died of heat stroke. Dewey took the fleet to the Philippines. In Manila, Spanish troops gave an appearance of resistance, then surrendered. In the Treaty of Paris of December 10, 1898, the US received all remaining Spanish possessions.[111] The first war was over.

Waiting to become the next Philippine overload, when Dewey arrived in Manila harbor, were ships from France, Germany, England and Japan. The US invited Aguinaldo back to Manila, where he promptly declared himself dictator of a united country. The US declared itself protector of the Philippines. Philippine flags flew in Manila.

---

[109] Luis H. Francia, A History of the Philippines, Overlook Press, New York, 2010 and 2014, p. 83.
[110] Cause of the explosion was a fuel-related accident within the ship.
[111] Guam and Puerto Rico are US possessions with non-voting representatives in Congress.

Disputes quickly arose between Aguinaldo, with his constitution, and groups with other plans. Another constitution called for a strong legislature in a Catholic state, in which Aguinaldo had no power. Muslim south islands did not accept a single Christian state.

The Philippine-American War began in 1899, when two US servicemen shot two Filipinos, who failed to halt when approaching a guard station. A bloody war ensued. President Theodore Roosevelt declared the war over in 1902, when Aguinaldo was captured, and Willian Howard Taft arrived as governor general of US held islands. Bloody battles continued until 1921.[112]

1899 US Soldiers and prisoners in Walled City of Manila (Public Domain)

---

[112] Various sources put casualties at four thousand US troops killed and three thousand wounded. Death of Filipinos from direct and indirect war involvement, alleged mass killings, hunger, and disease, at two hundred and fifty thousand to one million. US press reported statements of Mark Twain, Andrew Carnegie and Samuel Gompers of the Anti-Imperialist League to end US involvement in the Philippines. Cultural treasures of Philippines were looted by US military, including bells from Balangiga church, returned December 2018.

During US control, Filipinos were American citizens. Today, Filipinos comprise the second largest Asian-American population in the US after Chinese. Overseas Filipinos send home remittances, a significant portion of the Philippine economy today.

The US was negotiating independence for the Philippines in 1935, to occur in 1945, giving the US ten years of favored trade, when Japan invaded. General Douglas MacArthur left the Philippines vowing to return. At the time Japan invaded, there was a large Japanese population in the Philippines. Most iron ore produced in the Philippines went to Japan. US President Franklin Delano Roosevelt proclaimed that Filipinos serving in the US military were entitled to Veteran's Benefits. Over two hundred and fifty thousand Filipinos joined as US soldiers and bravely served.

Douglas MacArthur Lands in Leyte 1944 (Public Domain)

General MacArthur returned on October 20, 1944. The large naval battle of World War II, Battle of Leyte Gulf, occurred from October 23 to 26. There was hand-to-hand combat in Manila. Manila was devastated. Over one hundred thousand civilians died.

The Philippines was declared independent on July 4, 1946. The date was momentous in the US. For Filipinos, the landscape was filled by American and multi-national businesses. Trade favored the US. The US held a military base with a ninety-nine-year lease.

Emergence of the Steel Butterfly[113]

Imelda Marcos 1953 (Public Domain)

---

[113] See generally, Katherine Ellison, Imelda: Steel Butterfly of the Philippines, McGraw Hill, NY, 1988.

Little is known of early life of Imelda Romualdez. She preferred it that way. She favored her history as a beauty pageant contestant, who met Senator Ferdinand Marcos in the Manila Senate cafeteria, when she visited an uncle in the government in 1954. She was twenty-four. He was thirty-six. Ten days after meeting, they married in Manila Cathedral.

Their marriage was a bond that lasted to the death of Ferdinand in 1989. The one blemish was an affair of Ferdinand with an actress in 1969. When the affair became public, the actress so feared Imelda, that she sought shelter in the US embassy, from where she gave endless press interviews. The pair reconciled and the actress faded into oblivion.[114]

Despite poise and self-confidence, young Imelda was not a media hound. Her husband was her opposite. Born in 1917, Ferdinand Marcos loved the spotlight. An expert with a pistol, Ferdinand was convicted of shooting a political rival of his father in 1935. From his jail cell, Ferdinand graduated law school and wrote his successful appeal of the conviction. He led a guerilla unit during Japan's occupation of the Philippines, for which he touted receipt of twenty-seven medals, later exposed as fake.[115] As president in 1963, with Imelda at his side, Marcos imagined he was John F. Kennedy of the Philippines.

Imelda was constantly thrust in the spotlight with her husband. She was expected to be a model wife and mother, who effortlessly looked beautiful. The pressure was too much for her. She checked into a clinic in New York City to recoup.

Imelda's nightmare was life after the presidency. Philippine presidential terms were ten years. Imelda returned from New York as the Steel Butterfly, the same time her husband declared Martial Law, making his term indefinite. Their New Society Movement in the Philippines had no place for dissidents.

Leading opponent of the Marcos government was Benigno Aquino Jr. Like Marcos, Aquino was a political star. He was the youngest senator elected in the Philippines. Aquino exposed Marcos' fake medals. More important, Aquino questioned a need for martial law, when the only Communist threat was an event staged by Marcos.

---

[114] The actress was Dovie Beams, born 1932. Who? Mistress to Marcos was her best-known performance.
[115] Francia, at 256.

Lyndon B. Johnson and Imelda Marcos Dancing 1966 (Public Domain)

Aquino was sent to prison in 1972, where he spent eight years. He was released in 1980 for medical treatment in the United States for a heart condition. Meanwhile, Marcos used threats of communism as a basis to dismantle datu armies.

Marcos announced he was cleaning up corruption in government by privatizing services. Imelda garnered a seat in the national assembly and was made governor of the district which included Manila. The couple bought controlling interest in privatized Philippine corporations. Imelda returned several times to New York City, where she purchased commercial and residential property, with ostensibly private funds.

The power and glamour couple of the Philippines hosted US and other dignitaries, to assure them the Philippines was devoutly anti-communist. The pair appeared as authors on ghost written books, touting democratic government. The US increased foreign aid to the Philippines. Multi-national corporations increased investment. Imelda enlarged the Cultural Center to host the 1974 Miss Universe pageant.

During martial law, riots decreased. Bridges were built connecting major islands. A nuclear plant was built on fault lines, so it never opened. Meanwhile, there were thousands of unexplained deaths and disappearances. In 1980, when Aquino returned to the Philippines from heart surgery in the US, he was shot to death in the airport.

In 1986, Imelda's life unwound. Ferdinand needed treatment for kidney non-function. In the election that year, Aquino's widow, Corazon Aquino ran against Ferdinand. She had a massive outpouring of support. Both sides declared victory. US President Ronald Reagan encouraged Ferdinand to allow smooth transition in leadership.

Imelda hurriedly packed her crates. The couple left for New York. When curious folk entered the presidential palace, they found what Imelda had not had time to pack. She left behind three thousand pairs of shoes and thousands of garments. Receipts were found for $2 million in jewels from a New York jeweler.

Butterfly versus Madonna

Corazon Aquino Inauguration 1986 (Public Domain)

Corazon Aquino was not a politician. When drafted to run against Marcos, she initially declined, which endeared her to voters. Marcos ensured there was a dearth of able and experienced leaders to supplant him. Aquino was accepted as the reigning member of a talented team, that promised to rule under her spirit of reducing corruption and bringing government services to those in need. When elected president of the Philippines, she declined to live in the presidential palace. Instead she resided in the palace guest house.

Despite her calm and self-effacing manner, Corazon Aquino was an astute leader. Raised by Chinese-Filipino parents, who excelled in business through hard work, Aquino studied math and French in college in New York. Her credibility was her strongest asset. During the campaign, Ferdinand Marcos derided Corazon for being a housewife and mother. Motherhood is a precious status in Catholic Philippines. Marcos evoked the Madonna image for Corazon. Cardinal Sin of Manila fostered that image, when he absolved his flock for civil disobedience against Marcos.

Imelda attacked Corazon during the campaign as unattractive, even dowdy, and having a poor choice of wardrobe. Corazon was succeeded as president by a dashing movie star. For 1986, it was Imelda, who misjudged the mood of the public. Voters were tired of extravagance of the Marcos couple. It was Imelda who exhibited poor taste for the times.

Corazon was limited in what she could accomplish during one term. Her first project was human rights commission. Debt service was half of all government revenue, hampering further reforms. Marcos and friends owned privatized corporations, earning funds that previously supported government functions. The US Central Intelligence Agency aided the Philippines to track between $5 and $10 billion in national funds that disappeared during the reign of Marcos. The challenge was obtaining transfer of stolen funds to the Philippine treasury. Seizure of funds required court action.

In 1990, Imelda stood trial in New York City, under the US racketeering statute. The law recaptures proceeds of illegal activity, even if the person is not convicted of the underlying offense. Imelda also faced prosecution promising lengthy prison sentences.

There are limits to the reach of the law. An innocent spouse cannot be held accountable for acts of the complicit spouse, in which they did not participate or have knowledge. Property of the innocent spouse is not subject to seizure.

Ferdinand died in 1989, prior to the start of the trial. In the New York courtroom, Imelda's lawyers portrayed her as the poor, naïve, spouse, whose husband controlled all the transactions, unknown to her. This is known as the dead spouse defense. Amazingly, her expensive New York real estate was deemed personal property of the poor, unknowing Imelda. Ferdinand was her savior. She was acquitted and kept her assets.

In 1998, Imelda returned to the Philippines to run for president. She was outdone by a greater actor, the Philippine movie star, Joseph Estrada. Imelda was still the Steel Butterfly. She would not rest in defeat. Imelda let fly accusations of her husband's former associates for being ungrateful recipients of funds to purchase stock for themselves and the Marcos pair in major Philippine corporations. She declared ownership of most of Manila. It was a startling revelation from the woman, who less than a decade earlier walked from a criminal case portrayed as an innocent player in Philippine corruption.

Estrada was swept into the quest to reveal government corruption. He was exposed for receiving bribes for allowing illegal gambling and for siphoning funds from the national lottery, which caused him to step down two years into his presidency. It was well known that Estrada's mistress was high maintenance, although nothing comparable to Imelda. Imelda's funds were tucked safely away from the Philippines. Estrada was convicted of theft and sentenced to house arrest. He paid a fine totaling $15 million of the unaccounted for $2 billion in his account. The next Philippine president pardoned Estrada in 2007.

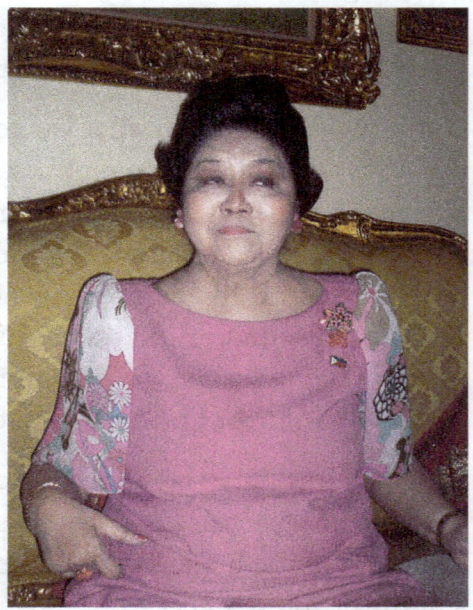

Imelda Romualdez Marcos in 2004 (Wikimedia by Object 404)

Philippines Today

Malacañang Palace (Public Domain)

Estrada's vice president, Gloria Arroyo enjoyed such high regard by the public, that she ran for a six-year term in 2004. Arroyo was an economics professor at Manila University, with an impressive resume in government. Early in her term she was tarnished by a phone call during the election, portrayed as vote tampering. The call was after-the-fact in the voting process and benign. A later charge for receiving kick-backs in a Chinese broadband contract was indefensible. Arroyo cancelled the contract. Regardless, she was indicted on corruption charges in 2012.

After the September 11, 2001 tragedy in the United States, the Philippine Muslim community complained of human rights abuses and receipt of military aid from the United States. Muslim autonomy groups in south islands of Mindanao maintained private armies of fifteen thousand soldiers. Arroyo was not effective in resolving tensions.

Elected president in 2016 was Rodrigo Duterte. He was the first president from Mindanao. His support in the south enabled negotiation with several armed Muslim groups, seeking an autonomous region. That goal became law, engendering peace in the region.

Lasting calm in the Philippines requires presidents emulating the Madonna and not the Steel Butterfly. In 2018, Imelda was convicted of corruption. Seizure efforts are ongoing. Prosecutors valued her worth at $30 billion, while the Steel Butterfly claimed her bank balance was $22 million. At ninety, she still looked like a beauty queen. Corazon Aquino passed away in 2009, prior to election of her son as president in 2010. Always the Sainted Madonna of the Philippines, her son's election was a tribute to a family of honor and national service.

Manila Galleons to Modern Tigress

Manila was founded by Spanish conquistadors, as a walled city in which only Spaniards could reside. Spanish arrivals landed in the midst of a centuries old trading network of Asia to Arabia, centered in coastal Cebu. First, the Spanish disrupted established successful networks, then rebuilt trade from Manila east across the Pacific to Spanish colonies in the Western Hemisphere. Manila grew from the ashes of Cebu.

Manila was a place of water lilies, known as Maynila to locals. Locals lived in tight clan-based communities, having long-standing trade with China. Clans had no use for the Spanish. They jabbed at the Spanish for centuries, while the Spanish imported Chinese workers for a colony on hostile turf. Spanish and locals lived parallel lives in Manila.

Ferdinand Magellan is credited as the first European to land in the Philippines, when in 1521 he sailed along the coast of Visayas, central of three major Philippine islands.[116] He was overwhelmed by sophistication of traders, who were not impressed by the Spaniard's offer to civilize them. The next Spaniard arrived forty-three years later, to colonize.

Miguel López de Legazpi arrived in Cebu from Mexico in 1564, for the purpose of siphoning trade from China and directing it to Acapulco. His effort resulted in Manila Galleons, a multi-century trade connection across the Pacific. Legazpi brought Manila and Mexico together in the sixteenth century, resulting prosperity for both.

---

[116] The other two major islands are Luzon in the north, home of Cebu and Manila, and Mindanao in the south.

Magellan

For Manila to prosper in the twentieth century, it needed to grow beyond its sixteenth century function to store goods from China for transport to Spanish colonies. It needed to capitalize on local talent and workforce, to produce goods for international commerce. Twentieth century Filipinos saw Manila as an Asian tigress, perhaps not quite the tiger economy of neighboring ports of China, Viet Nam, and Singapore.

This is a short story of five hundred years in the life of a city destined for largess. Manila is a popular cruise port today for its historic city, with a vibrant past. Far from sanguine, Manila is an apt model for negotiating economic waters in the South China Sea.

Pleasing A Pope with a Spanish Colony in the Pacific

Voyages of Magellan

Following voyages of Christopher Columbus in 1492 and 1494, doubling the known world and establishing extent of the Atlantic Ocean, the Pope issued a decree dividing the known and unknown world between Spain and Portugal. Pope Julius II cut the world in half, giving one-half to each of the Catholic countries most active in exploration. Battles with England and France followed. Immediate effect of the Treaty of Tordesillas was a race between Spain and Portugal to determine where the line around the sphere was drawn on the other side of the world, in Asia. This was land of valuable Spice Islands.

Key to reaching Spice Islands from Europe was discovery of a strait, facilitating transit around the southern continent of the New World from the Atlantic to the Pacific Ocean. Through force of an iron will, Ferdinand Magellan discovered the strait, mapped and traversed its length. The strait, now known as Magellan Strait, is as desolate and mysterious-looking today as it was in 1520. Cruise ship captains sail the strait today, aided by maps and charts, unavailable to seafarers until Magellan. By traversing the Pacific Ocean, Magellan completed knowledge of the actual size of the girth of the world.

Magellan was well educated in the known world before he sailed. As a young page for the Portuguese Queen, while living in Lisbon, he acquired knowledge of all things nautical. He worked in the king's India House, where ships' logs and maps were stored. He supplemented his reading by talking to sailors. Portugal was the well-font of explorers and Magellan sailed with some of them before he commanded his own ships.

In 1505, at age twenty-five, Magellan sailed to India, for the king of Portugal. The next year he captained a ship in the spice trade. At this time, Portugal had not captured a port in the Moluccas Islands, as the Spice Islands of Indonesia were then known.

Portuguese King Manuel I was infamous in the Age of Discovery for being stingy with rewards for exceptional service. Men of lesser talent than Magellan moved to Spain. When Magellan pressed the king for recognition, the king ignored him. Magellan asked his king, if not for you, then where shall I serve? The king told him to go where he liked, so he did. Magellan left Portugal for Seville. He received a warm welcome in Spain.

When Magellan launched for the Spice Islands, King Manuel I sent envoys to talk Magellan into returning to Portugal. Magellan declined. Once Magellan set sail, Manuel sent ships to follow him, policing the Treaty of Tordesillas. Manuel declared Magellan a traitor to his country, publicly disgraced his family and forced them into exile.

When he set sail into the unknown world, Magellan knew he was a man without a country. The fate of his pregnant wife and young child depended on his success. He knew that Portugal sent ships to sink him and Spain imbedded mutineers on his ship.

Magellan's Ship Nao Victoria in 1:1 model Punta Arenas

On November 1, 1520,[117] Magellan reached the channel known on maps from 1527, as the Strait of Magellan. He was too modest to give his name to the place. Magellan called the land Tierra del Fuego, Land of Fire, for lightening fires he saw across the landscape.

On March 6, 1521, after ninety-eight days at sea, and having traveled seven thousand miles since leaving the strait, the ships landed on Guam. The crew enjoyed liaisons with local women, while Magellan focused upon converting the natives to Christianity.

In the Philippines, the Europeans found sophisticated traders of the Kingdom of Cebu. The high-handed Spanish conquistadors assumed all non-European needed guidance. Magellan demanded tribute paid to his king. The Spanish model was dominance not enlightenment.

---

[117] October 18, 1520 is recorded also. Disparity in Julian and Gregorian calendars accounts for dual dates.

Magellan's downfall came when he involved himself in a dispute between local chieftains. Convinced of invincibility of Spanish armor and weapons, Magellan offered to avenge a slight on the tribal chieftain who pledged friendship to Magellan. The chieftain of Cebu, likely a Muslim, encouraged his village to convert, albeit facially, to Christianity. Magellan declined assistance from his new friends when he confronted their enemy.

Abandoning tactical knowledge, Magellan moored his ships off the coast, where tides carried ships' cannons out of range of attackers on shore. His army of sixty men waded ashore in full battle armor. As darkness approached, an overwhelming force of more than fifteen hundred natives attacked. They stayed beneath gunfire and aimed spears at unprotected knees of Spaniards. Quickly, Magellan was surrounded.

Magellan's Death

Dismemberment of Magellan distracted the natives, while the Europeans limped to boats. Magellan's scribe eulogized him as a man of talent, who almost circumnavigated the world. Baptized islanders quickly forgot Christianity. Still, the captain-general is recognized for locating the legendary strait and an accurate picture of the globe.

The first person to circumnavigate the globe was Magellan's Philippine guide Enrique. Enrique sailed west with Magellan to Portugal from Spice Islands in 1511. In 1521, the pair sailed west across the Pacific. Enrique completed the voyage to the Philippines.

Enrique convinced the rajah of Cebu to invite the Spanish to a banquet in thanks for Magellan fighting his battle. A dinner was held, after which Filipinos killed or captured Spanish sailors. The new Spanish captain, Joâo Carvalho, preferred the rajah keep captured Spanish as slaves, rather than return gifts Magellan collected in Cebu. Carvalho sailed for Spain in the remaining two of Magellan's original five ships.

One hundred and seven of the two hundred and sixty men who began the voyage with Magellan arrived in the Moluccas in November 1521. Awaiting them were clove trees, nutmeg, and ginger. Portuguese so alienated rajahs of the islands, that Spain could claim mastery of Spice Island trade, regardless of where the Tordesillas line lie.

The Greek pilot of the Spanish fleet drew maps placing the Philippines on the Spanish side of the pope's treaty.[118] Later maps disclosed the Tordesillas line put Spice Islands within Portuguese territory. Four surviving members of Magellan's crew told Spain of a fantastic voyage, heroism of Magellan and Spain's right to colonize the Philippines.

---

[118] See: Tim Joyner, Magellan, International Marine, McGraw Hill, Maine, 1992, p. 212; and Laurence Bergreen, Over the Edge of the World, Wm Morrow, New York, 2003.

Manila Galleons

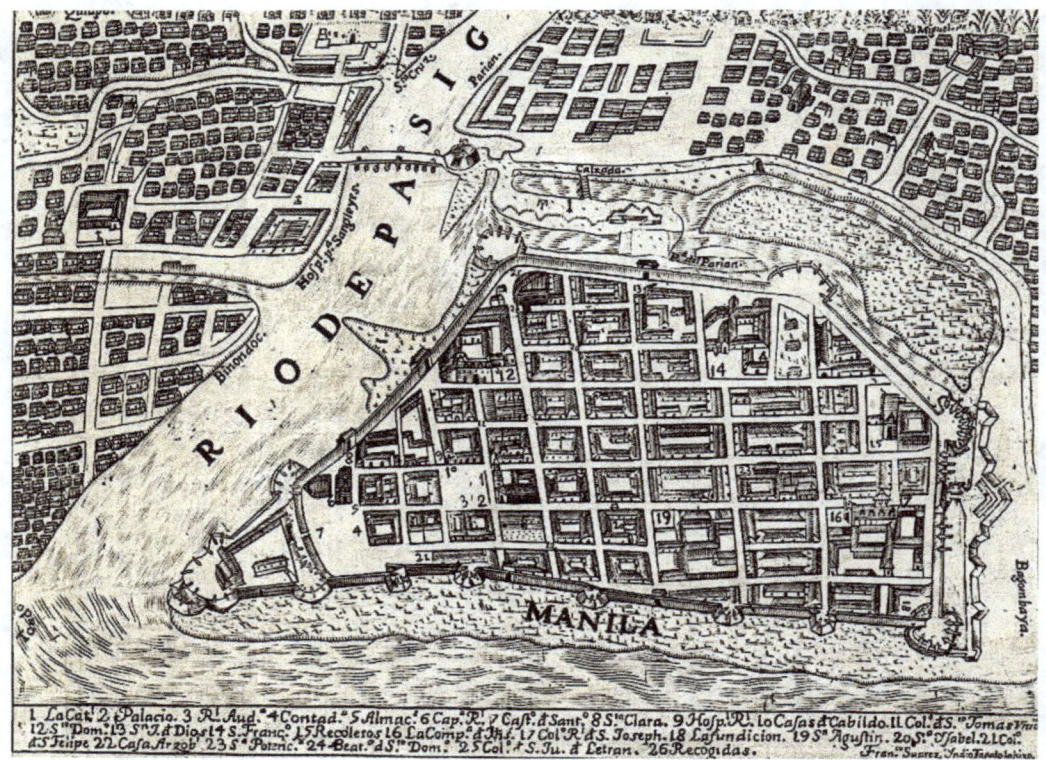

Walled City of Manila Detail from Carta Hydrographica 1734

From the seventh century, trade flourished from the Persian Gulf to the South China Sea. China sent cargo, including porcelain and lacquerware, to coastal cities of the Philippines by the ninth century. Cebu was a trans-shipping port, not a wealthy trade center. Chinese and Arab merchants kept warehouses in the city, where goods were stored and exchanged. Datu, clan leaders of Philippine communities, obtained goods in the process, although they did not capitalize on participating in commerce.[119]

---

[119] See generally Luis H. Francia, A History of the Philippines, Overlook Press, New York, 2010 & 2014. The author provides description of barangays, family communities forming defacto, not formal, political units.

Preceding the Spanish in Cebu, by more than a century, were Muslim rajah from the south, some related to rajah of Brunei. When Legazpi arrived in Cebu in 1564, to begin a Spanish-Catholic colony, he came into conflict with the rajah. Acrimonious relations escalated into armed conflict. In 1571, Rajah Suleiman of Maynila razed his city rather than cede to the Spanish. Seeds of Muslim desire for autonomous rule in southern Philippines, on Mindanao, relate to this time in history.

Undaunted by lack of a welcoming reception in Cebu, Legazpi built new Manila. In his city, only Spanish resided. The walled city followed the Spanish city grid decreed by King Philip II, with a main square on which sat a Catholic church. By 1603, six hundred homes were in Manila. To accommodate workers not entitled to live within Manila's walls, Spanish established Villa Fernandina, on land of Ilocanos people, now known as Vigan.

Spanish colonization in the Philippines was replicated in Mexico, where conquistadors landed in the Gulf of Mexico at Veracruze and fought west to the Pacific. Acapulco and ports along the Pacific housed Spanish troops, while locals led the newcomers to gold. Eventually, the Spanish had a string of forts, known as presidios, from Mexico to San Francisco, maintaining a Spanish presence in the New World.[120] Lacking gold, forts were ideal storage depots for world trade.

Andrés de Urdaneta sailed with Legazpi to the Philippines from Mexico. He returned in 1565, with a shipload of Chinese goods, including spices, ivory, porcelain and lacquerware. Cargo was loaded on carts headed east to Veracruz, ships sailed to Spain. Urdaneta did not find gold in Acapulco or Manila. He gained great wealth from trade between the ports, extending Asian commerce, across the oceans to Spain.

The four month voyage from Manila, or Vigan, to Acapulco, became a regular voyage, known as Manila Galleons. So successful were Manila Galleons, that the route competed with ships from Asia around the Cape of Good Hope of Africa to Cadiz. By 1593, the king of Spain decreed a limit on Manila Galleons to two each year.

---

[120] See Presidio, Pueblo and Parish in Cruise through History, Itinerary VII, Ports of the Pacific Coast of North America. Spanish garrison/presidios, town/pueblos and Catholic parishes in California mirrored Philippines.

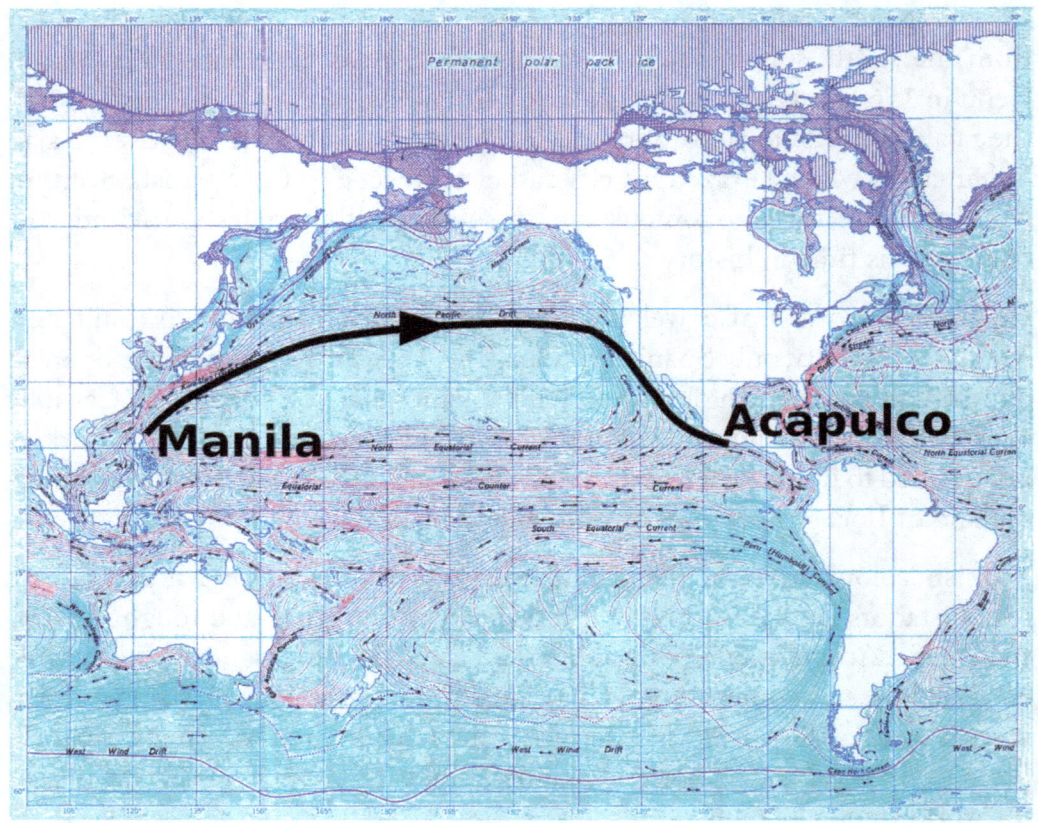

Ocean Currents Manila to Acapulco (Public Domain)

Over decades, Manila Galleons instigated cross polination of cultures. In exchange for Chinese goods transiting to Mexico, from Mexico to Manila came avacados, maize, tomatoes and sweet potatoes. Filipino sailors enamoured with Acapulco, jumped ship to stay in Mexico. In Manila, industrious Chinese opened retail trades, married locals and became Christian. Catholics persecuted in Japan sought asylum in Manila.

Manila Galleons traversed more than a trade route. Galleons established connections between points of the Spanish empire on both sides of the massive Pacific Ocean. By 1650, Manila had forty-two thousand residents, not including Filipinos outside the Spanish city.

Manila Galleons traversed the Pacific Ocean for three hundred years, until demise of the Spanish empire at the end of the nineteenth century. Ships brought spices to Mexico, enabling Mexican cuisine regarded as indigenous. Corns, beans and squash of Mexican natives was embelished with salsa, made possible by imports from Manila. The Acapulco-Manila Galleons Trade Route was designated a World Heritage Site in 2015.

Fuerte San Diego Acapulco Mexico

Visible vestages of Manila Galleons are seen in forts built to protect cargos from pirates. Fuerte San Diego in Aculpulco, detered rogues Henry Morgan and Sir Francis Drake. Built in 1616, then strengthened 1783, Fuerte San Diego is a museum today across from the cruise ship pier. In the Philippines, Fort Santiago, built in 1593, still stands.

An example of facinating lives made possible by Manila Galleons, is the story of Catarina de San Juan, a seventeenth century woman, who traveled the route of the galleons. Catarina was born in India, where she received a Christian education. As the story goes, Catarina was taken from home by Portuguese pirates and held in Cochin.

Catarina escaped her captors to a Jesuit mission. Her name suggests she was European or of European and Indian parents. A Jesuit mission was not a suitable place for a young girl.

Next stop for Caterina was Manila. Transit from Cochin to Manila was commonplace in the seventeenth century. Arriving with no financial means, she was purchased as a slave by a merchant, who sailed on a Manila galleon to Acupulco with Caterina.

Poblana Style

Caterina was notable to locals. She dressed in Asian fashion, the envy of local women. Living in Puebla, Catarina was considered exotic and inspired Poblana style. Wealthy locals had the ability to purchase silk screens and porcelain from China to decorate their homes. Asian style was the rage in Mexico and Caterina was apreciated as a style-setter.

Always a practicing Catholic, when Caterina's owner died, she had visions. Villagers, always in awe of Caterina, revered her as sainted. They reasoned she must be close to god to have persevered in life through so many challenges, particularly for a woman.

Catarina died in 1688, at the age of eighty-two. She instantly was a local saint. Her home in Puebla was a sacred site. Locals lit candles at her home, until 1691, when the Spanish Inquisition arrived and purified Catholicism by determining who was and was not saint.

Local saints, purged from the church, stayed in the minds of locals. With vases from China and spices from Asia, locals thought privately and fondly of Catarina. She exemplified beauty in the native, European, Asian population of Mexico and Manila.

Philippine Tiger Cub

Jones Bridge & Post Office 1930s, Rebuilt After War (Public Domain)

Jesuits in Manila fostered education for all classes of people, until they were expelled in 1768, for competing with other clergy. Jesuits returned in 1859, resuming their mission of education. The educated workforce was a valuable resource for the emerging nation.

By 1893, local governments supported secular education, not well funded by the emerging national government. Wealthy Filipinos sent their children to college in Spain. Educated Filipinos, foreclosed from positions in government and businesses, formed labor unions and agitated for independence.

Filipino, a name given by elite Spanish of Manila to locals, the Chinese, Japanese and in any event not Spanish, to marginalize the population, became a name of pride for all not of the oppressive Spanish regime. Filipinos no longer accepted work in lower service positions, watching trade pass from China to Mexico, with no resulting benefit to the Philippines. The Filipino mantra was - independence and nationalism.

The next century for the Philippines was a story of wars of independence from Spain and the United States. The story is punctuated by nationalist leaders, who marred growth of the economy by lack of skill, or overwhelmed positive ventures with corruption. The Philippines followed many twentieth century emerging nations by assuming excessive debt. Growth of Manila as an Asian Tiger economy was hampered by corruption.[121]

Emergence of Manila as an aspiring Asian Tiger began less than thirty years ago, with the election of Fidel Ramos in 1992. Ramos proposed an ambitious plan for Philippines-2000. Scoring Ramos success in fulfilling hopes for the country, must be considered in the context of his starting point and challenges faced.

Ramos candidacy is emblematic of modern Filipinos. A Protestant, Ramos went to school at West Point, despite anti-American sentiments in the Philippines. He was a veteran of the Korean War, in which many Filipinos served with American forces. He ran for president in a field of six candidates, where none achieved a majority of votes, on an election day, where eighty-thousand candidates vied for seventeen thousand seats. In the Philippines, the datu system still wields enormous power, despite national efforts.

Ramos sought to end corruption by privatizing businesses and dispersing land holdings. Entrenched corruption frustrated his efforts. Payments on debt

---

[121] Asian Tiger is a term used by business press and investment firms for explosive Asian economic growth.

absorbed income. Filipinos lacked safe water and reliable power, caused by years of deferred maintenance and a burgeoning population. The United States vacated military bases in the Philippines, a move popular with the people, resulting in loss of income connected to operating bases. Environmental degradation left by the military was a Philippine responsibility.

In 2016, Filipinos elected Rodrigo Duterte, the first president from Mindanao. Duterte fostered peace in southern Philippines by establishing an autonomous Muslim region. He pledged economic growth and upward opportunities. He planned to build infrastructure, to improve lives of all Filipinos and encourage economic growth. Jobs were created. Initial impact of Duterte was an increase in debt. Growing national income before debts are due, requires overcoming historic corruption that hampered well-intentioned predecessors.

Philippines is not yet an Asian Tiger. It is a Tiger Cub, in view of economic progress made. Forecasters predict, if the trajectory continues, by 2050 the Philippines will grow from thirty-sixth to fifteenth largest world economy. Capacity and desire exist. If leaders stay the course, and relegate corruption to history, Duarte will achieve his goals.

Visiting Manila Today

Fort Santiago welcomes visitors today, as a monument to history and home of memorials to heroes of the Philippines. Inside city walls are the 1607 San Agustin Church and Palacio del Gobernador, the original cityscape of Spanish Philippines. Foremost of heroes is José Rizal, a medical doctor, exiled from Manila by the Spanish for leading revolution.

Rizal returned to Manila in 1892 and was imprisoned in Fort Santiago. There he wrote *Mi Ultimo Adios*, My Last Farewell, smuggled from his cell to his sister and now a national sentiment of the Philippines. In Rizal Park are the remains of Rizal. Filipinos gathered there on July 4, 1946, to declare independence from the United States.

Binondo Plaza Manila

Manila today is a modern city, reflective of Spanish heritage. Beyond the walls are Chinatown, churches and historic milestones of the Tiger Cub seeking to be a Tiger.

Jose Rizal (Public Domain)

Borneo

BRUNEI
Sultans of Brunei and Rajah of Sarawak

Tiny Brunei, a nation of two thousand, two hundred and twenty-six square miles, much of which are sparsely populated equatorial rainforest, home to ancient tribes of headhunters, has in its history held off the mighty Majapahit Empire of Java in the fifteenth century, Spain in the nineteenth century and Britain and Malaysia in the twentieth century. Brunei Darussalam, the peaceful harbor, is home to the longest reigning monarchy in the world, from the fourteenth century sultan, to the world's wealthiest monarch today, who lives in the world's largest palace. Twenty-ninth ruler, Sultan Hassanal Bolkiah, reigns today as an absolute constitutional monarch, in a nation modern and traditional.

Brunei historically asserted control of the entire northern coast of Borneo, where tribes of Dayak headhunters controlled interior jungles of orangutans, and Arab, Malay and Chinese traders made inroads along the coasts. Early Brunei sultans of the tenth century, were at times vassals to Java or China. Life on the coast was sustained by trade. Interior tribes planted rice and hunted game.

Predecessor to Brunei, P'oni people of Buruneng, cast off Javanese overlords in the fourteenth century, while maintaining trade relations built on Muslim identity. As the sultan of Brunei coalesced power, in the eighteenth century, troublesome areas south along the coast, known as Sarawak, and north along the coast, future Sabah, were gifted or leased to Europeans. In the twentieth century, discovery of oil in Brunei, and off its coasts, enabled a small nation to thrive as a wealthy, sole source economy. An oil export economy sustains the nation today.

Beneath the sultan of Brunei in power were rajah, usually close family members. In 1839, Raja Muda Hashim, uncle to the sultan, befriended a swashbuckling adventurer, who was a military officer for the British East India Company. While a young man, James Brooke left British service, sailed to Brunei and aided Hashim to quell a revolt against the sultan by local tribes. In gratitude, the sultan made Brooke Rajah of Sarawak.

James Brooke founded a three-generation dynasty of Brooke Rajah of Sarawak. The second rajah expanded Sarawak territory, surrounding a reduced Brunei, to the border of Sabah. The third Rajah ceded Sarawak to Britain, joining British North Borneo in the east.

This story of Sultans of Brunei is interlaced of necessity with establishment of Sarawak and Sabah. In the twentieth century, the sultan of Brunei faced melding into one nation with neighbors, or joining the Malay Federation, as did his neighbors. Once again, the Sultan of Brunei stood alone against mighty nations. This is the story of sultans of Brunei and Rajah of Sarawak.

A Little History of Exotic Borneo

Dayak Headhunters

Three thousand years ago, rafts beached on north coasts of Borneo. Malay people of the sea, in their great migration, came across the South China Sea. Their new home had prior occupants, Dayak people of the interior. On southern coasts of Borneo, people arrived from the Straits of Malacca to the Java Sea, now the Indonesian archipelago.

Dayaks are the great headhunters of myth and mystery. Bands of Dayak people made homes throughout Borneo jungles. On the coasts, Dayak interaction with Malay, Chinese and British on the north, and Javanese and Dutch on the south, decimated their populations. Today, Dayak bands survive deep in Borneo's interior. Collecting heads of slain enemy, smoked to dry, painted and perched on rods, were testament to manhood, power and status within communities. Today, Dayak strive for survival.

Traditional knowledge of Brunei history is found in the epic poem of adventures of the strong and brave warrior Sya'ir Awang Simawn. When Simawn encountered the beautiful bay on which Bandar Seri, capital of Brunei, now sits, he cried out *baru'nah*, which means, now we have found it. From that time, the area was known as Buruneng, or Brunei.

Simawn was one of fourteen brothers, of a single father and fourteen mothers. Simawn was also the first sultan. His brothers were noble advisors, or wazir in Arabic. Early Brunei language borrows from Arabic and Sanskrit.

Brunei is an Islamic nation of shariah law. Its Islamic heritage dates to 1363, when religion came to Borneo with Arabic traders. Pigafetta, faithful scribe to ill-fated Magellan, arrived in Brunei in 1521, without his captain. He recorded two kings, one pagan and one Muslim. Pigafetta was greeted by the fifth sultan. Working back in time to the first sultan, brings Islamic historians to the fourteenth century. Sultan of today is the twenty-ninth.

In 1571, Spaniard Miguel Lopez de Legazpi claimed Manila for his king. Southern islands of Luzon and Sulu were controlled by the Sultan of Brunei. Spain competed with Brunei for trade with China. After wresting Luzon from Brunei and feeling no competition from Portugal, Spain decided trade with Brunei was preferable to conquest. Brunei gave the impression of a country of fierce warriors. Spain made no moves on lands of Brunei.

Brunei experienced a golden age during the reign of ninth sultan Hassan, from 1605 to 1619. The sultan's administration had four noble advisors, known as wazir. Several extended royals were lesser wazir. Below wazir were common officials, handling daily needs of government. Metal artisans and sword makers looked to the sultan as a patron. Even today, the garden of old Bandar Seri has a display of cannon crafted in Brunei. Old Bandar Seri was a capital of few stone palaces and many stilt houses over the water.

Late in the 1600s, the sultanate was split by civil war. The sultan was killed and his family briefly lost power. Nephew to the sultan, aided by Sulu Island warriors, retook control. In gratitude, the sultan granted Sulu Island independence from tribute to Brunei. Brunei, weakened by war, lost vassal tributes, diminishing income and power.[122]

Sultans and Rajah

In the eighteenth century, Britain made three attempts to establish a settlement on the north coast of Borneo. From the first attempt in 1761, warriors of the Brunei sultan frustrated British desires. In 1824, Britain and the Netherlands entered a treaty, in which Britain agreed to limit incursions to the north coast of Borneo and leave the south coast and most of the interior to the Dutch. The Dutch based operations on Java, as part of the Dutch East Indies. Neither nation consulted Borneo rajah or sultan of its intentions.

In 1839, acting as an individual adventurer, James Brooke accomplished what Britain could not. The charismatic former military officer of the British East India Company, headquartered in India, spent his inheritance on a yacht, the *Royalist*, and sailed for the South China Sea. In Brunei, Brooke befriended Rajah Muda Hashim, uncle to the Sultan.

At the time of Brooke's arrival, the unwieldy sultanate stretched along the north coast of Borneo. In the Sarawak area of west Brunei, Chinese and Malay traders resided in Kuching, without interference from the sultan. Inland, Dayak tribes, notably Iban people of the sea, fought either for or against the sultan.

---

[122] See generally, Evan Adams, Brunei: History and Monarchy, Sonit Education Academy, Abidjan, 2016.

Sir James Brooke (1847) by Francis Grant

By 1840, rebellious tribes sought independence. Brooke returned to Brunei in time to aid Rajah Hashim in quashing a revolt. In gratitude, in 1841, Hashim appointed Brooke governor of Sarawak, the western tail of the Brunei sultanate.

Brooke expanded his domain from the estuary of the Kuching River and small trading settlement of Kuching, to include interior domain of Iban tribes and east to Simanggang. He spoke Dayak and Malay. With assistance of the British Royal Navy, and his Iban warriors, Brooke ended slavery in his region and purged pirates from the coast. Britain gained a trade port in Kuching. Brooke gained fame in England. He was muse to novelist Joseph Conrad in *Lord Jim*, published in 1900.[123]

In 1846, Saifuddien II, the Sultan of Brunei, signed a treaty with Britain. In the Treaty of Labuan, Britain gained what it attempted for eighty years, an island base off the coast of Brunei. The British navy patrolled the bay for pirates, affording protection to commerce between China and Brunei. The sultan conferred on Brooke the title and lands of Rajah of Sarawak. James Brooke was known as the White Rajah of Sarawak, a hereditary title.

James Brooke truly loved a rowdy life. Although he felt compassion for his subjects, he did little to build infrastructure for a sustainable, independent Sarawak. He was a warrior, not a businessman. While in England, convalescing from jungle fever, Brooke sought financial backing. When Britain indulged him no further, Brooke secured his debts with a deed to Sarawak held by society maven Baroness Angela Burdett-Coutts.

Britain withdrew support for escapades of Brooke, when parliament balked at the cost of navy involvement on behalf of a man who slew natives, and sometimes Malays, under the guise of fighting pirates. Shortly after Brooke became Rajah of Sarawak, the Sultan of Brunei expanded reliance on aid from Europeans to control rebels in lands of North Borneo. A British charter company took ownership of the land, known as British East Borneo, future Sabah. Rajah Brooke had no friends of consequence remaining in Britain.

---

[123] Jozel Teodor Konrad Korzeniowski, Joseph Conrad, born in Russia in 1857, died in 1924 in England, deserves a story of his own for his exploits to the east and west fringes of the British Empire.

In England, Brooke told engaging tales of adventure in Sarawak with headhunters. Nephews and friends returned with him to the far-away land. Among his friends, were no capable administrators. Among his nephews, Charles Johnson Brooke, Brooke Brooke and Arthur Crookshank enlisted to the cause of Sarawak.[124]

Charles Johnson changed his name to Brooke, fought side by side with James, and repeatedly proved himself an able military leader. As heir to James, and second Rajah of Sarawak, Charles expanded territory across north Borneo, to the edge of British North Borneo, surrounded Brunei as its territory was consumed, then headed inland to homelands of Kayan people and the border of Dutch Borneo. As rajah, Charles built Sarawak to present-day borders, as he assumed debts of his uncle.

Fort Margherita Kuching (by Aron Paul 2004)

---

[124] James Brooke was not married. His sister married Francis Johnson. Johnson boys Brooke and Charles changed their name to Brooke at the request of Uncle James. Arthur was a cousin on the Johnson side.

When James died, Charles was Rajah of Sarawak, with debts to Baroness Coutts and an annual stipend due a son of James with a Sarawak woman, whom James acknowledged late in his life. James counseled Charles to marry a rich woman. In 1869, age forty, Charles went to England, where he courted twenty-year-old Margaret de Windt, a second cousin.

Margaret's marriage gift paid debts bequeathed by James. Her annual stipend, and eventual inheritance, enabled Charles to build a home for Margaret in Sarawak, buy boats for the small Sarawak navy and fund the Sarawak treasury. As Margaret grew older, and savvy to foreign relations, she returned to England, where she rejoined society, aided by caché as Ranee of Sarawak.[125] She wrote books as Queen of the Headhunters.[126]

Charles and Margaret lost three children to illness on a ship from Sarawak to England. The son of Charles with a Sarawak woman, a repeat of his uncle's history, survived.[127] The couple had three more sons, the eldest, Vyner, was born in England in 1874. That year, the child of Charles and his Sarawak wife was adopted by a clergyman, William Daykin.[128]

In 1883, Margaret left Sarawak for good. She lived to 1936 in Cornwall, long enough to see her son Vyner become the third Rajah of Sarawak in 1917, upon the death of Charles. Margaret used considerable political/social clout to arrange the title of baron for Charles, inherited by Vyner. Charles declined the title. He was knighted by Queen Victoria in 1888.

In 1888, Charles made Sarawak a British protectorate, removing the rajah's military expense. Margaret is credited with inserting a clause entitling

---

[125] Ranee is the title of a wife of a Rajah.
[126] Margaret wrote several books of her life in Sarawak, although she spent most of her time in England and Paris. Her exotic title served entrance to soirées of artists and writers, including Oscar Wilde, who dedicated a story to her, *The Young King*.
[127] Esca Brooke Daykin, born in 1867 to Charles and Dayang Mastiah. See, Cassandra Pybus, The White Rajah of Sarawak, Douglas and McIntyre, Vancouver, 1996, at 45. In birth and baptism documents, Charles acknowledged parentage of Esca. Esca lived to 1953 in Canada.
[128] Esca Brooke Daykin was raised in Canada, final home of the Daykins. Until the death of Charles, the Daykins received annual stipends. Late in life, Esca's wife sought recognition for Esca as a Sarawak heir.

Britain to choose the next rajah. Charles was disappointed in all three sons, who preferred society life with their mother in England, to time in Sarawak. Margaret projected Vyner into British society as prince and heir to the Rajah of Sarawak.

Last Rajah of Sarawak and Persevering Sultan of Brunei

British Highlanders in Brunei Jungle

The Sultan of Brunei signed a protectorate agreement with Britain in 1888. He turned down offers of Charles Brooke to buy Brunei, or its Limbang district, wholly surrounded by Sarawak lands in 1902. At the time, the Brunei palace was a hovel of rotting floorboards. For the sultan, poverty and British management of sultanate affairs was preferable to loss of identity.

When Britain entered into the agreement with Brunei, the sultanate had no roads and no public administration, such as a police force. There was no national income or treasury. Oil was discovered on lands of Brunei in 1909, though not profitable as an export resource until 1929. Britain created a structure, in which the Sultan built a nation.

Brunei, still a medieval sultanate in 1900, had three types of land: kerajaan, inalienable land of the sultan; kurigan, estates and income from land gifted to wazirs by the sultan for the term of their life; and tulin, individual land ownership, with rights of inheritance. British agents purchased all types of land and placed ownership and income in holdings of Brunei nation. Next, British agents sought export commodities for duty revenue.

Sultan Ahmad Tajuddin, twenty-seventh sultan of Brunei, presided over a thriving country at his coronation in 1940.[129] The next year, Japan invaded Borneo and took control of Brunei oil. Japan occupied Brunei and its neighbors, Sarawak and British North Borneo, until 1945 and liberation by Australian led Allied forces.

Once Japan surrendered Borneo, North Borneo returned to Britain as Sabah. The third and final Rajah of Sarawak, Vyner Brooke, ceded Sarawak in 1946, to Britain in exchange for payment of one million pounds.[130] Britain paid Esca Brooke Daykin an annual pension of five hundred pounds, in recognition of his rajah lineage.

Upon the death of Sultan Tajuddin in 1950, his younger brother, Omar Ali Saifuddien III became the twenty-eighth sultan of Brunei. The iconic Brunei mosque of golden domes was dedicated to Saifuddien III in 1958. It is a

---

[129] Sultan Ahmad Tajuddin was born in Bandar Seri, in the royal palace, in 1913 he was sultan under a regent until 1924. He was sultan to his death in 1950.

[130] Vyner's wife Sylvia Brett dressed in Malay costume and wrote a memoir, *Queen of the Headhunters*.

fitting tribute to the national leader faced with critical choices on the future of Brunei.

Sultan Saifuddien III faced the choice of melding with Sarawak and Sabah, as the nation of North Borneo, or joining Malaysia as individual provinces, the path chosen in 1963 by Sarawak and Sabah. The Sultan chose independence. Next, Sultan Ali Saifuddien III abdicated to his son, the twenty-ninth sultan Sir Hassanal Bolkiah, giving Brunei time to negotiate total independence from Britain, achieved in 1983.[131]

Visiting Bandar Seri, Brunei Darussalam Today

Panorama Bandar Seri (Creative Commons by Zulfadli51)

Sultan Hassanal Bolkiah leads the wealthiest per capita nation in the world today, in which ninety percent of revenue derives from oil. His goal is diversification of the sovereign portfolio. Brunei is a member of the Association of South East Asian Nations, a political and economic alliance. Brunei has a seat in the United Nations.

---

[131] Haji Hassanal Bolkiah Mu'izzaddin Waddaulah, Sultan Hassanal Bolkiah, was born in 1946 in Bandar Seri.

In Brunei, the Sultan is the chief of state, the foreign minister, and the finance minister. In a nation of half a million people, his family holds all but three cabinet positions. People accept governance, where there are no taxes, and many life needs are paid by the government.

Sultan of Brunei with President Rodrigo Duterte of Philippines & Indonesian President Joko Widodo 2017 (Public Domain)

Brunei is a stable force in the Muslim world. The Sultan adopted conservative, not radical, Islam. Shariah law applies to matters of inheritance, marriage and divorce. It is illegal to be gay or fail to fast during Ramadan. The sultanate received international reproach for attitudes toward Gay Rights. The Sultan builds mosques, schools, and sponsors hajj.

Today, Bandar Seri is a capital of tall, steel and glass buildings and gardens. Wedding of heir and eventual thirtieth sultan was a display of yellow umbrellas and a golden Rolls Royce. Sultan Bolkiah had seven thousand automobiles. Visitors enjoy Bandar Seri for glimpse of royalty of an exotic land, modern and accessible, yet independent.

INDONESIA
Java Ancient and Modern

Sitting in the middle of the Indonesia archipelago, home to over half the national population and the national capital, Jakarta, Java is the heart of the region. Java is the site of human population going back to Java Man, the one-million-year-old fellow discovered in 1891. Javanese were literate in Sanskrit before Greeks had literacy. Predominately Muslim, Javanese have a nuanced religious-moral observance, with unique cultural facets.

Java island is a six-hundred-mile-long mountain spine of volcanoes. It is one of the most fertile landscapes on the planet. People of Java had little reason to venture far. The world came to them. Java gave the world nutmeg and coffee. Trade brought oppression, which is a separate story.

Close to India's sphere of influence, Java's distance on the ocean allowed a unique Hindu-Buddhist culture. Java has its version of the Sanskrit classic book of legends, the *Mahabharata*, where adventures take place on Java. Java is the home of the *Righteous Prince,* who leads the people, blessed by the *Goddess of the Southern Sea.* In reverence to gods and ancestors, Javanese built the nine layered Borobudur Temple, one of the world's largest Buddhist monuments, now a World Heritage Site.

Any cynical idea that Javanese mythology is ancient history, is countered by the rise of King Senopati late in the sixteenth century, an aspirant to title of *Righteous Prince*. His dynasty battled European colonizers. Javanese identity references his kingdom.

Transformation of Java from Hindu-Buddhist to Muslim is attributed to the Nine Saints, the *Wali Songo* of Java. In their story, Sufi Muslim mysticism and tradition blend in beliefs of modern Javanese. In all ways, the past is present in Java. Javanese speak a dialect of Malay that has vocabulary from Sanskrit, Chinese, Portuguese, Arabic and even Dutch *lingua franca* of colonial times. Complexity of language is a tribute to depth of culture.

Vyasa Author Mahabharata

Modern Java, seen in high rise buildings of steel and glass, exits in few large cities. Most of the population of Java reside today in special districts of Jakarta, in West Java; Yogyakarta, in Central Java; or Surabaya, capital of East Java. Javanese people, sophisticated in the modern world, remain culturally attached to the ancient world. Cultural connectivity gave people strength to overthrow feudal Dutch rule.

This story is a little immersion in the Javanese cosmos of ancient legends.[132] Legends are expressed in batik and shadow puppets, the *wayang kulit,* an ancient art received from India. Stories told with puppets evolved, like forms of Hinduism, language and ritual, becoming uniquely Javanese. A port stop in Semarang, the visitor-inviting city of Hindu-Buddhist temples, is a perfect place to step into Java, ancient and modern.

Ancient Java and Kingdom of Majapahit

Mount Sumbing Java (Public Domain)

---

[132] Legends, based in fact, build over epochs of history. Myths as ethereal creations, help explain cosmos.

Wellspring of Indian Hinduism is mythical Mount Mahameru. Javanese revere Gunung Penanggungan, a volcanic peak in east Java, as Mount Mahameru with its peak broken away during transit from India to Java. The origination story recognizes heritage from India as cultural beginnings of Java.

In the time of dinosaurs, when supercontinents broke into Africa, India and Australia, the Java archipelago floated into existence. Ancient memories, in Javanese mythology, recall Java as a floating island, where god Shiva directed Brahma and Vishnu to fill with people.

Di Hyang in Indonesian means *Abode of the Gods*. Before Dutch, Muslim and Hindu Java, and possibly older than Sanskrit, people practiced ancestor worship on Java. Their volcanic landscape was filled with smoldering caldera. Little shrines on coastal northcentral Java date to the sixth century and early Hindu influence.[133] Throughout Java, Hindu replaced ancestor worship, although never in total.

In 732, King Sanjaya founded the Mataram empire on Java. His existence was recorded in Sanskrit on a rock in Central Java. Legacy of Mataram is seen in Hindu and Buddhist temples on the Java landscape. The name for Buddhist temple in ancient language is candi. Candi of Mataram in central Java include: eighth century Kalasan and Sewu, and ninth century Borobudur and Prambanan. All are visitor sights not far from Yogyakarta. Architecture of Mataram candi appears similar to sights in Southeast Asia. Mataram Empire extended into Cambodia, Thailand and Philippines.

Borobudur, the world's largest Buddhist temple, sits in the center of Java. It is iconic of uniquely Javanese ancestor worship, combined with Buddhist practice, in a Hindu temple. Stupa, the round, squat chambers, with a spire, seen throughout Southeast Asia, either as singular structures or in groups, are massed at Borobudur on nine levels, on platforms of reducing size. Borobudur has six square levels, then three round levels, ascending in diminishing area to the top. Each of five hundred and four Buddha sit within a stupa. Stupa of Borobudur are perforated around a bell shape. No other temple replicates this design and placement of numerous perforated stupa on nine levels.

---

[133] Dieng Plateau in north central Java had four hundred small shrines to ancestors, forerunners of Hindu temples, of which eight remain today.

Borobudur (Tropenmuseum)

Buddhist pilgrims to Borobudur walk around the temple and through passageways as they ascend, past fourteen hundred and sixty carved panels, narrative of life of the Buddha and the path to enlightenment. Twenty-seven hundred reliefs sit in temple walls. From the ninth to fourteenth century, until arrival of Islam to Java, Borobudur was a popular pilgrimage site. By the end of the fourteenth century Borobudur was abandoned.

Dutch of the East Indies Company, arriving in the eighteenth century, were intrigued by temples covered in jungle growth. Several Buddha were shipped to the Netherlands. In 1814, when British agents took control of Java, young Lieutenant Stamford Raffles made drawings of Borobudur, and other candi, which were helpful in later restoration. Raffles' official duties included conquest of local kings, even as he spent his personal time writing a history of Java. His book is credited with creating scholarly interest in Java candi.

Panoramic Views of Borobudur (Public Domain)

The Mataram dynasty flourished until civil war erupted between royal brothers, one Buddhist and the other Hindu-Shivaist. The brothers divided territory, with the Buddhist taking Sumatra and the Shivaist retaining Java. Distance did not abate hostility. Buddhists from Sumatra ended the Shivaist Mataram kingdom in 1006. Decades later, Mataram rose again in East Java and Bali, a bastion of Hinduism today.

Deep in annals of Javanese lore, so long ago no one knows whence it began, is the concept of *Ratu Adil*, literally meaning a *Just Queen*. In Javanese stories Ratu Adil often appears as a *Righteous Prince*. In times of chaos, deep calamity for people, a leadership void, or an unjust ruler, a *Righteous Prince* arises uniting and leading people to better times.

Legends of Mataram royals added to lore of Java superhumans. The last king of the Mataram Empire, Airlangga is often touted as a reference to the *Righteous Prince*. He rose in 1049, then soon died in an effort to free central Javanese people from Sumatra. His Javanese mother reincarnated as the witch Rangda.

14th Century Manuscript on Palm Leaf (Public Domain)

In legends of Rangda, upon death of the king, queen-mother and her son contested succession as ruler. The son banished his mother to a forest. She became a witch.

The Rangda story is similar to legends of India, written in Sanskrit in the *Mahendradatta*, where the king's mother is banished to a forest for practicing witchcraft. Recalling Airlangga's mother as a demon witch, may result from unfavorable stories perpetrated by contrary factions. In life, she favored Hindu goddess Kali, a beautiful consort to Shiva, known as a strong mother figure.

The *Righteous Prince* repeatedly rises in Javanese history. Ken Arok was a *Righteous Prince* who founded a dynasty, which began the colorful Majapahit Empire in 1222. He was the son of a poor woman, who left him in a basket, hoping he would be found by a wealthy woman. Instead, he was found by thieves, who raised him to be cunning. One day, while eluding capture, Arok encountered a Hindi rishi, an enlightened one of India.

Kris – Sword of Ken Arok (by Marc Chang Sing Pang)

Arok, as an avatar of Hindu god Vishnu, saw the beautiful wife of his employer, while she was bathing. He was smitten. Arok confided his feelings to his rishi. The rishi predicted the woman would be mother to a dynasty. Arok commissioned a special sword, which he gave as a gift to another man. The man was so proud of his new sword, he showed it to everyone. In the night, Arok took the weapon, killed his employer, a powerful lord, then left the sword to implicate the other man. Arok married the widow. Arok vanquished other kings and his sons led a large empire. Five centuries later, in an incarnation of the Mataram Empire, *Righteous Princes* tied authority to rule by descendance from Ken Arok.

The next *Righteous Prince* of Java was Raden Wijaya, who invited the navy of the great Mongol warlord Kublai Khan into Majapahit to aid conquest of a rival. Once firmly established as ruler, Wijaya, hearkening back to Arok, lured forces of Khan into a valley, and annihilated them. Wijaya died in 1309. In annals of Java, he is listed as the first great king of Majapahit.[134] Following Wijaya were more Righteous Princes and Queens.

---

[134] Majapahit Empire derives its name from the maja fruit enjoyed by temple priests and royals.

Queen Suhita of Majapahit reigned from 1429 to 1447. She appears in popular *wayang kulit*, shadow puppet theatre, depicting struggles between central and east Java kingdoms. Plays follow myths of the sun and moon, competing for day and night. Puppets enjoyed an encore of popularity three centuries later, during tenure of another queen of Majapahit, during Dutch control of Java.

Wayang Kulit (Collection Tropenmuseum)

Wayang kulit were initially created from bits of buffalo hide, cut into shapes, painted, and mounted on thin sticks, which operated as control rods. Puppets performed behind linen sheets, where an oil lamp cast a large shadow, and where puppet manipulators were hidden. *Wayang Wong* uses the same ancient stories in dances by humans.

Shadow puppets or dancers drew scripts from the *Mahabharata* or *Ramayana*, two great epic poems of ancient India. Like Shakespeare of the ancient era, themes of competition in war, illicit love and imperfect human emotions of jealously and greed play through actions of god-like characters. Part history lesson and part morality play, puppets and dancers perpetuate oral history of distant times, made fresh with facts from recent events.

Majapahit Empire of Java lasted from 1293 to 1527. Reference to glory days of the empire was popular in promotion of independent Indonesia in the twentieth century, as a united nation of diverse islands. Legitimacy to rule was the legacy of an empire united under Majapahit emperors, centuries before colonialism under the Dutch. At its height, Majapahit had ninety-eight vassal kings, from Sumatra to New Guinea, including the Malay peninsula, Brunei, East Timor, south Thailand and islands of the Philippines.

In the 1570s, enterprising King Senopati advanced his cause by straddling his Muslim and Hindu-Buddhist Javanese cultural inheritance. He announced he was related to kings of Majapahit, and that he was blessed by the *Queen of the Southern Ocean*. The queen took Senopati beneath the ocean waves to instruct him on love and war. Once back on land, he encountered an old *Wali Songo*, who said it was the will of Allah that he build a great kingdom. In fact Senopati built a prosperous kingdom. He died in 1601 and is remembered at his tomb outside of Yogyakarta. In 1613, his grandson, Sultan Agung, attempted control of all Java.

Wali Songo of Java[135]

Late in the reign of Majapahit rulers, Muslim traders came to Java from China and India. Central and East Java ports were part of an early fifteenth century trade network from Nanjing (Beijing) to Mecca. The great Chinese captain of the Emperor's Treasure Fleet, Zheng He arrived in Semarang and Jakarta in 1407. He noted presence of Muslim traders. Credit for transformation of Java to Muslim predominance is attributed to *Wali Songo*, the Nine Saints of

---

[135] Sometimes translated as Wali Sanga.

Javanese Islam. Ubiquitous in shops around the country are depictions of nine turban-wearing men. These are *Wali Songo*.

Wali Songo Poster (author unknown)

Wali in Javanese is trusted one, or friend of god, and songo, or sanga, is the number nine. The nine men of Allah traveled the length of Java, individually and not as a joined group, although they are connected by family. The nine did not all live at the same time. Reverence accumulated as recognition built and placed each within the lexicon of honored, that is *Sunan*. Graves of *Wali Songo* are pilgrimage sites in Java today.

Muslim religion came slowly to Java, displacing Hinduism, introduced by Arab, Persian (Iran), or Chinese traders to kings with whom they did business. Impact of new religion was localized at ports. Converted Muslim kings of Java did not travel to convert others. *Wali Songo* were devoted to religion. They traveled across the length of Java and left a swath of Muslim converts, beyond the coasts.

The first acknowledged *Wali Songo* was Malik Ibrahim, who came to coastal Gresik in East Java from Iran in 1404, as a trader. He preached of the Qur'an to all he met in the port. Unlike Hindu, Muslim acknowledges no castes, or pre-ordained classes of people. Ibrahim gave teachings to all, regardless of class.

Minangkabau Mosque Java (by Mamasamala)

When Ibrahim died in Gresik in 1419, his two sons lived with an aunt, who married a Majapahit king. Both sons received positions as religious leaders. One son of Ibrahim, Sunan Ampel, and a nephew of Ibrahim, Sunan Girl, were prophets of Islam. They are included as *Wali Songo*. The dynasty of Ibrahim continued in sons of Sunan Ampel, Sunan Bonang, born in 1465, and Sunan Drajat, born in 1470. They too, are *Wali Songo*.

The sister of Sunan Girl married Sunan Kalija, who is *Wali Songo*. Kalija is regarded for using shadow puppets to teach tenants of Islam. His son, Sunan Muria carried on the family work. Sunan Muria turned from life among royals bringing Islam to people in the fields and rural areas. He is honored by the naming of Mount Muria in Java.

Another of the *Wali Songo* was Sunan Kudus. He was a military commander for the Sultan of Demak, whose realm was a vassal of the Majapahit Empire and a coastal area of trade. The sultan was Muslim and Sunan Kudus, a grandson of Sunan Ampel, through his mother, who was a sister to Sunan Bonang, was a puppet master, who credited his teacher in puppetry, who was Sunan Kalija. Thus, the *Wali Songo* were connected and taught.

Kudus garnered attention of local Hindus by tying a cow to a stake in the courtyard of the mosque he founded. Curious about the fate of the cow, crowds gathered. Once the audience assembled, Kudus told a series of marvelous stories, including exciting tales of knights and heroes. Crowds so enthralled furthered conversion. The central Java city of Kudus, where he died in 1550, is named for this *Wali Songo*.

The ninth of the Wali Songo was Sunan Gunungjati,[136] the founder of the Sultanate of Bantam, another city of trade on the northwest coast of Java, and the only sultan among *Wali Songo*. Gunungjati was claimant to long-standing royal legacy, born in 1448, as the son of an Egyptian, descended from the royal house of what is Jordan today, and a mother of Hindu royalty in West Java. Earlier in his life, Gunungjati was a military commander, leading expeditions on behalf of the Sultan of Demak. Sunan Kudus is recorded having a father of Egyptian royalty, who joined the military in Demak.

Sunan Gunungjati traveled across northern Java, bringing converts to Islam. He may have died in the city of Cirebon, on the north coast of Java, where West Java meets Central Java. If the grave site, a place of pilgrimage, is that of Gunungjati, and if he died in 1568, as the person in the tomb certainly did, he lived to one hundred and twenty years old. If his birthdate came after 1448, and if he was the father of Sunan Kudus, reverence for both *Wali Songo* is unaffected. Key to reverence is proliferation of Muslim religion in Java.

Visiting Semarang of Central Java Today

Semarang is the capital of Central Java province, a favored port of the Dutch in the colonial period of the Dutch East Indies, and a popular tourist port today. Visitors enjoy Semarang for beauty of the area, with history of Hindu, Dutch and Muslim eras in Java. Semarang is an entry point in Java to sites of thousand-year-old Hindu-Buddhist temples.

---

[136] Sometimes the name is spelled as Gunung Jati.

Dutch East Indies Building Semarang (Tropenmuseum)

History in Semarang is iconic of Java through time. It was a coastal village, when Muslim traders visited early in the fifteenth century. Traders at port established further trade with locals in the interior. Some of the oldest temples in Java are inland of Semarang. People of the interior, practitioners of ancestor worship and later Hindu-Buddhists, were converted to Islam over two centuries of interaction with people at the port.

After the Treaty of Breda in 1667, between England and Holland, the Dutch East India Company strengthened its hold on Java. Local sultans were indebted to the Company, for luxury goods coming into Java, in exchange for spices exported to Europe. The Dutch put a low value on spice at the source, compared to exorbitant prices received in Europe. They tempted Javanese royalty with expensive luxury items, giving the Dutch high profits on both ends of the market. In 1678, Sultan of Semarang, transferred his town to the Dutch to pay his debts.

In Semarang, the Dutch built a city reminiscent of home in Holland. Characteristic of Dutch style is Blenduk Church in Old Town, built in 1753.

Locals were relegated to living outside the city. Semarang grew organically, as a central marketplace for locals, and in trade between port cities, connected first by a road along the coast and later by a railway. The Dutch railway terminal Lawang Sewu, begun in 1904, and built over fifteen years, is known as *the house of a thousand doors*, for its many arched doorways and windows. Temples ring the old town.

Today, the nineteenth century Dutch city and separate housing areas of locals are evident in historic Old Town Semarang. Adjacent to the old Dutch church is the 1953 monument to youth and independence of Indonesia, commissioned by then President Sukarno. The Great Mosque of Central Java, which can accommodate fifteen thousand worshipers, was begun in 2001 and punctuates skyline today. Semarang benefited from early Dutch city planning, as the population grew. Today the city is home to two million people.

Old Semarang is preserved, although surrounded by industrial growth of the post-World War II era. Semarang is representative of ancient and modern Java, in a compact city. It is enjoyable as a cruise destination and as a departure city for excursions to the interior and ancient Javanese temples.

Balinese Painting

BALI – ROSE OF THE WINDS

Bali Subak (drew-commonskiki)

The small green dot on the map, two miles east of Java, is the island of Bali. Situated close enough to feel impacts of powerful events in Java that shaped Indonesia, Bali is the only Hindu island in a sea of Islam. An area of two thousand square miles, Bali sits at the edge of the Asian continent, a demarcation line of all forms of life on the planet. On Bali, soil provides two rice crops each year. To the east, Lombok is arid.

Migrations to Bali are as old as human existence. Unlike other island people, who live from the sea, Balinese face inward to their land. Their cosmos emanates from ancestors. Hinduism from China, India and Java was melded with reverence for ancestors on Bali. Balinese Hinduism is unique from that of Javanese kings, fleeing to Bali in the sixteenth century when Java converted to Islam. Dutch came to Bali in the nineteenth century and Muslim and Christian residents arrived in the twentieth century. Later arrivals lack Balinese deep connection to ancestors, integral to belief systems and lifeways.

Dutchman Cornelis de Houtman landed on Bali in 1597. His crew wanted to stay forever. Naturalist Alfred Russel Wallace arrived at Buleleng in 1860, after traipsing through jungles of Indonesia, and found Bali incredibly beautiful. Wallace determined Bali was the eastern most point of the Asian continent, now known as sitting on the Wallace line. Artists and fun seekers of recent decades echo Dutch sentiments from Sanur, or bars, spas and surfing beaches of Kuta.

Compass Rose is the eight-pointed navigational star utilized by mariners from ancient times to today. To Balinese, Compass Rose is more than a tool; it is a map of cosmology, dictating all manner of existence from planting rice to building communities. A Balinese Compass Rose has nine points, including cardinal directions and upward to god, Siwa, ethereal creator of all beings. Bali sits at crossing winds of the Compass Rose. When Balinese people look into their land, they see the center of the world.

Today two Bali populations cohabit the tiny island: native Balinese and recent urbanites. Urbanites of capital city Denpasar are joined by fleeing urbanites from everywhere in the world, on holiday in Kuta and Legian. Duality of population is nothing new on Bali. When nine kings of Hindu Bali, represented in the national flag, arrived in the sixteenth century from Java, they were tolerated by locals, who incorporated new ideas into sophisticated ancient culture. Feudal kingdoms were parallel habitats to purely democratic village lives of Balinese, known today as Balinese Aga. Hindu recognizes a caste system, imported from India and abandoned in Bali. Caste has little meaning in Balinese Rose of the Winds.

Visitors to Bali today are instantly immersed in the same beauty of the island, from the beach to botanical gardens on the hills, that captivated de Houtman and Wallace. This story takes visitors deeper into Bali, to Bali of art, music and dance, as integral to self-identification of Balinese as is rice production and reverence for ancestors. This is the story of being Balinese in Bali, the people in the center of the Rose of the Winds.[137]

Setting for a Story of Bali

Mount Agung (USGS)

There are no tigers east of Bali. The island sits as a punctuation mark, at the end of creation of the planet, when supercontinents split the world as it is today. Bali is a small island, made smaller for humans, who occupy only a strip of area on the eastern slopes of Gunung (Mount) Agung, and a small area on the north, the historic port of Buleleng. Mount Agung, the island formative volcano, has several times exploded to depopulate Bali. Five times in 2017, Mount Agung reminded Balinese they exist at the pleasure of the god of fire. Landscape and tigers hold back population on three-fourths of the island.[138]

---

[137] Rose of the Winds and its importance to cosmology of Balinese is illustrated and deeply told by Miguel Covarrubias, a Mexican anthropologist who made repeated trips to Bali in the 1930s and wrote, Island of Bali, Periplus Publisher, 1946, republished Alfred A. Knopf, 1973, still a definitive work on Balinese culture.

[138] Resort developers pressing for land along the southern coast, tiger territory, threaten extinction of tigers.

Bali was populated during migration of humans across Malaysia to Indonesia, five thousand years ago. Indian Hinduism and Sanskrit, evident in Java, came across the two-mile separation of water to Bali. Javanese actively traded with China and Malaysia. In Bali, people were not seafarers nor traders. Early population lived in the central island, around the verdant mountains, not on coasts. The few fishing boats created by Balinese have carved prows with a mythical *gadja-mina*, the face of an elephant, with uplifted trunk, and mouth of a fish, with an eye to each side, to see at night.

Traditional Balinese gods live high in the mountains. The sea is full of demons. At ten thousand, five hundred feet in elevation, the highest mountain on Bali, Gunung Agung is the navel of the world. It is the center of life in the Balinese universe.

There are no elephants on Bali. Goa Gajah, Elephant Cave, is likely an early habitation site, or an early temple to the god Siwa, in the center of the Rose of the Winds. Name attribution of the temple, on the slope of Mount Agung, not far from Ubud, comes from an elephant motif carved in stone at the temple entrance. Outside the temple is a bathing pool, surrounded by seven pitcher bearers, representing seven holy rivers of India.[139]

Placement and design of Elephant Cave have much to tell of reverence of Balinese for their India-Hindu inheritance. Though the temple is dated to the eleventh century, the classic period of Java-Balinese culture, use of the site and designs, are far older. Balinese bathing rituals are ancient in origin. Carving stone and wood are ubiquitous in Bali, displayed in temples, community buildings and present-day arts.

Other notable temples in Bali are on the sides of Mount Agung and Mount Baturi, considered two halves of mythical Mount Meru. There are thousands of temples on Bali, known as pura, including family temples and house shrines. Most are decorated in stone or wood carving. Village temples are reserved for local use on festival occasions, while national temples, such as Pura Besakih, the temple of temples, a cluster of temples, one for each state within Bali, or the mountain temple Pura Batukan, are open to all.

---

[139] Elephant Cave was rediscovered by Dutch archaeologists in 1923, and the bathing pool in 1953.

Goa Gajah Elephant Cave Entrance (by Jack Merridew)

Balinese temples deviate from Hindu temples of India or Java, from whence religion originated. Bali temple carvings are not painted. In the mountain humidity, carvings age quickly. A riot of color is used in costumes and floral temple offerings. There are no idols in Balinese temples. Gods are ethereal, not represented in statues to which prayers are offered. Only ancestors are represented by stone effigies.

Essence of Balinese life is in the village. Villages grew from family/clan living, into sophisticated arrangements of village private, communal and ceremonial spaces arranged on a site-plan based upon Rose of the Winds.

Temple and village meeting places are in the middle of the village, where the temple is within a wall. Homes surround communal places. Beyond the homes are vegetable gardens and chicken coups. The cemetery is outside the residential area. Beyond the cemetery are fields of rice, ringing the mountainsides in terraces.

All adult men of the village sit on the village council. Society is democratic. The council assigns responsibilities to villagers. Everyone has a function in village life. To fail in purpose is a social crime.

The priest function is hereditary, yet not exalted as in typical Hindu caste societies, where the priest is above a royal and below god. Priests in Balinese villages, the pemangku, sweep the temple and care for shrine maintenance. When Javanese kings arrived in an exodus from Muslim rule in the sixteenth century, their feudal scheme of controlling land was tolerated in parallel lives to indigenous Balinese. Kings served no functional purpose.

Agents of the Dutch East India Company came to Bali in the seventeenth century. They lured Javanese royals with high priced luxury items, then put royal lands in hock for the benefit of the Dutch. Traditional Balinese villages, decentralized, independent and democratic, were harder for Dutch to control. When Balinese refused to pay reparations demanded by the Dutch for the cost of their conquest, or attempted conquest, the Dutch blockaded Bali harbors. Since traditional Balinese villages are not seafaring economies, the blockade failed without confrontation.

Until Dutch accomplished control of Bali in 1906, there was no poverty on the island. Food was abundant. People lived in village compounds. Transportation was walking. Cloth was woven at home. Crime in the sense of modern urban life, was little known in Bali. Society was highly sophisticated in local tribunals of governance and justice.

Dutch rule of Bali from 1906 forward destabilized a society, which endured successfully for several millennia. The Dutch put emphasis on export crops of coffee and tobacco over food. Imported goods desired by locals were held for sale at exorbitant cost, even as the Dutch paid miniscule prices for export items prized in Europe. Taxes were imposed on lands, to be paid in coin, a currency little used in Bali. Failure to pay tax resulted in Dutch confiscation of land.

Rose of the Winds in Rice and Ritual

Balinese Family (©CEphoto, Uwe Aranas)

Critical to sustaining life in Bali is the *subak* system of cooperative water management in canals and weirs, recognized as a World Heritage Site in 2012. *Subak* is the egalitarian, democratic method of managing the growth, harvest and shared benefits of rice within the village. Subak creates a cultural landscape manifesting historic *Tri Hita Karana* philosophy of spirit, human and nature realms in a unified existence.

Tri Hita Karana must be in balance to sustain life. Social rules are known, and compliance is required, enabling survival of the village. Slacking work is an offense against the village.

Drought evidences wrong doing of a villager, for which the whole village must participate in cleansing. Rice is a gift from the gods, so cleansing begins in the temple. Women create gifts to *nini pantun*, the rice mother. Even in times of poor harvest, no human eats rice left in temples for the gods.

Rice is planted twice a year. Rows are planted in a ritual, beginning with marking compass rose points on the landscape. Young men race buffalo, exhibiting prowess in furrowing fields. Only men plant. When weirs are open, and terraces are full of water, the land appears as mirrors to the gods, with green rice fields in the iconic Bali landscape.

Of numerous festivals in Bali, two are significant in the cycle of life. The spring equinox is the time of Nyepí, the new year festival. It signifies the end of the rainy season, a time of illness and evil. Nyepí is a time to sweep away evil. Galunggan is a new year in life, a time when ancestors visit. During Galunggan villagers celebrate the good in life. Galunggan is a time for family picnics, new clothes, and reverence to ancestors.

Nyepí is a two-day festival. The first day is lively, with cock fights, cooking for a feast and an evening of drumming and dance, ending with bursts of fireworks. The New Year's Day feast is eaten in quiet. Evil is allowed to slip away for another year.

Telling Ancient Stories in Art, Music and Dance

Legong Dancers (Collection Tropenmuseum)

Art, music, and dance are integral to Balinese community life. Each bandjar, the Balinese community, prizes its orchestra. Most villagers have some musical skill. Villages compete for musical preeminence.

Drums and bamboo instruments are as ancient as life on the island. The bronze drum of Pedjeng, with its elongated shape, is the ear plug of the moon. Decoration of the drum represents the moon on earth. Demon kings played such a drum. It lives in a temple.[140]

---

[140] The Moon of Pedjeng is the world's largest kettle drum at six feet high, with a cast bronze head. It is over twenty-three centuries old. It is kept in the Temple of Pedjeng, near Ubud, where it is sacred patrimony of local village people. People bring offerings to the drum.

Proficiency in carving wood and stone seem as natural to Balinese as growing rice. Few surfaces are left without decoration. Designs repeat characters from stories and forces of good and evil. Unbound by Muslim rules against idolatry, as in other islands of Indonesia, and reserving reverence for ancestors, represented in somber form, antics of mythical creatures, gods and demons are material for unique Balinese artistic expression.

New concepts creep into Balinese art. Temples have carved panels telling historic parables of good and evil, next to a panel of Dutch drinking beer, or people in a car, or pedaling a bicycle. All images, except evil characters, are adorned by flowers.

No visit to Bali is complete without attending a performance of *legong*, Balinese dance. More than a show for tourists, *legong* portrays several millennia of ancient stories of romance, kings, and heroes, repeated through interpretive movement, in costumes with meaning in each detail. In some forms of *legong*, dancers wear masks, which hold power of good and evil. Masks are village patrimony, requiring skill to create, and are preserved through generations. Though locals know stories well, they sit for hours watching performances. Experienced audiences appreciate skill of the performers.

Legong branched into several forms over the centuries. In Kawi, performers chant passages from Sanskrit texts, interpreted in Balinese. *Kris* dance is a display of ancient daggers, deftly maneuvered by male dancers in a trance. Early in the twentieth century, a well-known dancer in Bali, Mario, drew crowds for his seated form of *legong*. His dance became part of the lexicon of Balinese traditional dance. *Arelja* is a romantic Balinese opera, usually sung in falsetto.

In classic style of *legong*, a single dancer plays parts of males or females, old or young. Every outstretched arm and angular movement of arms, legs and fingers is pre-scripted in tradition. Though each dance is historically mandated in script and movement, acting of the dancer marks individual skill, much like a ballerina in classic ballet.

Popular in Bali are *wang kulit,* shadow puppets, seen through much of Southeast Asia, uniquely styled in Bali. *Wang kulit* are traditionally made from dried buffalo hide, painted and sometimes gilded. The puppet is attached to three sticks of bamboo, one for the body and another for each arm. Sometimes the lower jaw moves. The puppeteer sits behind a linen screen, backlit by a lamp to throw images against the screen, seen larger than life by the audience. Children are not the only audience enthralled by *wang kulit*. Puppets in traditional forms are popular collectors' items. Originals are held by villages.

Popular characters in puppetry and dance are heroes, nymphs, and clowns. Stories tell well-known history of Bali, parables of right and wrong, or funny mishaps of flawed characters. Clowns, who are servants of some prince, make frequent appearances in live performance and *wang kulit*. Twalén is the pot belly, long footed, magician, who uses intelligence and knowledge of the occult to make his hero look good. Counterpoint to Twalén are Délam and Sangut, comic villains, with little legs and big mouths. In their battles, Twalén always wins.

Stories of heroes and kings in Bali cross the same turf as stories told in Java, told from the other side of the strait. In real history, Java twice conquered Bali. Conquering kings or queens of Java are witches in Bali. The story told in Java of the princess *Mahendradatta*, mother of Airlangga, takes on poitent meaning, when the princess came from Java to wed a Balinese king. She contested rule of the Balinese kingdom upon death of the king and was banished to the forest. Unable to find a suitable marriage partner for her beautiful daughter, she sent a plague to Bali. King Airlangga vanquished her army of *leyaks*, witches of the forest.

Fall of the house of thirteenth century bandit king of Java, Ken Arok, is popular material for *legong* in Bali. Arok commissioned a magic kris, which he used to kill the king and set the scene in which his best friend answered for his wrongdoing. Before Arok killed the blacksmith, who made the kris, the smithy put a curse on the sword. Arok married the widow queen, who had a son with the deceased king. She and Arok had three more sons. Arok had additional sons with a second wife. In *legong*, the blacksmith's curse comes to fruition, when the kris is the instrument of death between sons, until all are dead. Through Balinese *legong*, evil is vanquished by righteousness.

Bali Muse for Art

Iseh at Dawn by Walter Spies (Collection Tropenmuseum)

Colorful, mystical Bali, with an indigenous population, that never lost its cultural essence through domination by Java, the Dutch, Japan, or twentieth century inducements, is muse to artists, indigenous and European, drawn to its warmth. Traditional skills in carving stone and wood are evident in craft stores, joined by silversmithing. Traditionally, silver was the medium of men. In Bali, where women have credibility, women artisans are frequently represented in galleries.[141]

In the post-World War I era, painters emerged from villages and cities, joined by Europeans, who arrived as tourists, then never left Bali. An artist community flourished in Sanur, along beaches where in 1906, Java-Balinese royals preferred ritual suicide rather than submit to Dutch rule. Today Sanur is a haven of beaches and art galleries.

Exemplary of the era was Adrien-Jean Le Mayeur de Merpres, who arrived from Belgium in 1932, married a *legong* dancer, Ni Pollok, and never left Bali.[142] Today Museum Le Mayeur celebrates his work. Mayeur preserved Balinese culture seen in *legong* through impressionist painting.

Anak Agung Gde Sobrat and Ida Bagus Made Poleng were indigenous painters from Ubud, whose work gained world attention.[143] Their work displays turbulent twentieth century emotions of domination, war, and independence, which they experienced. These artists credit Walter Spies with exposing their art to the world.

Walter Spies (Collection Tropenmuseum)

---

[141] Sanur Massacre, September 15, 1906, was a chilling episode in Balinese colonial history.

[142] Adrien-Jean Le Mayeur de Merpres was born in Belgium in 1880 and died in Bali in 1958.

[143] Gus Made, born in 1915 and lived to 1999 in Bali. Anak Agung Gde Sobrat, born in Ubud in 1912 and lived to 1992 in Bali.

Walter Spies was born in Russia in 1895, the son of a German diplomat to Russia. A multi-talented aesthete, he wrote music, painted and performed in Europe, until war disrupted his life. Spies came to Bali, when he was twenty-eight, and never left. Everything about the local culture fascinated him. He collected native music and art, becoming a cultural anthropologist of Balinese history. He was the creator and first curator of Bali's history museum. Fellow expatriate, Mexican artist, writer, and anthropologist, Miguel Covarrubias, hosted by Spies on several trips to Bali, found Spies the most influential sponsor of Balinese art.

Spies was captured during World War II on Japanese held Bali and was later imprisoned as a German national by the Allies. While being transported to a detention camp in Sri Lanka, his ship was struck by a Japanese bomb. German prisoners on the sinking ship were not evacuated. Spies drowned at sea. He was forty-six in 1942. The art of Walter Spies is prominent in the collection of the Museum Puri Lukisan in Ubud, where Spies fostered the Balinese Art Movement.[144]

Visiting Bali Today

Benoa cruise port for Bali sits a short equidistance from arts of historic Sanur to the east and beach and shopping havens of Kuta to the west. Denpasar is due north of the cruise port. Iconic rice terraces and temples of Ubud are further north. It is possible to see a wealth of Balinese beauty in a port stop on the Rose of the Winds.

Enjoying *legong* performance, or shadow puppets, is more than diversion for tourists. Traditional dance and puppets remain integral to Balinese social life. Performances are condensed for short-term visitors. Historic style performances often take place as all-night ritual. New forms of dance, adapted for tourists, are now historic.

---

144   In 1938, Spies, arrested as a homosexual, obtained release from jail with assistance of cultural anthropologist Margaret Mead.

Sanur Beach (by Dan arndt enwiki)

In 1963, Indonesian president Sukarno built a tourist hotel in Sanur, the long-time tourist favorite of Europeans. Sectarian violence, culminating in the bombing of a Buddhist temple in 2002, curbed tourism. In the next decade, popular books, movies, and photos of surfers, sailors and sunning tourists revived tourism in Bali.

Today parallel lives of transplants to Bali and Balinese Aga await visitors, who choose beaches and upscale shopping, or travel inland to experience lives of the indigenous culture of Bali. The Rose of the Winds inspires yoga in a garden, photographing World Heritage Site irrigation technology of rice terraces, or walking the beach of Sanur, where royals self-sacrificed rather than forfeit their lifestyle. The lure of Bali that entranced Javanese and European migrants, artists and anthropologists, draws visitors today.

Komodo Dragon (Varanus komodoensis)(sharpphotography Creative Commons)

GOING TO BATTLE WITH DRAGONS IN KOMODO

On a tiny island, in the string of Indonesian islands, dragons from an ancient world are the most numerous occupants. Largest of monitor lizards, largest lizard in the world, horribly unattractive, foul smelling, fatally venomous beasts draw thousands of tourists each year. Komodo dragons are the must-see adventure in exotic travel.

Relegated to tales of pirates and exiled criminals, Komodo Dragons were first observed by Dutch scientists in 1910. Three were caught, studied and named. Komodo, Dutch name for the beasts, is the name of the tiny island, actually a group of three islands, in the Indonesian archipelago, the only known habitat of the mysterious creature.

Komodo Dragons present commercial opportunities for impoverished eastern Indonesian islands, resulting in modern-age battles over ancient-age dragons for Indonesian politicians. Increased visitors promise greater income to the region, which draws more island residents hoping for work in a tourist economy. Increased human residents, on a previously depopulated island, threatens habitat of indigenous residents, the dragons.

Going to battle over dragons in Komodo is a twenty-first century battle of environmental preservation versus economic advantage. In this regard, dragons of Komodo are not unique in the world. Drawing on precedent in Galapagos and elsewhere, leaders of Indonesia are forearmed in battle.

This is a short story of the recent career of ancient Komodo Dragons, in their tiny, remote home, that is a battleground in a new era. It is also a story of Komodo Island, so often overlooked by humans, until recently. This story looks toward a happy ending.

Komodo Dragons

Monitor lizards are large lizards found across most of the African and Asian world, into Oceania, that is Australia, New Zealand and islands of the South Pacific. Most are a few feet long. Of the species, only the Komodo Dragon of the three islands in Indonesia grow ten feet long and weigh as much as one hundred and fifty pounds. Illegal importation of monitor lizards dispersed the species to most of the warm weather world.[145]

Monitor lizards have an aggressive nature in common. They are carnivorous, preying on small animals. Komodo Dragons have a larger appetite and feed on deer, or other mammals. Unique to monitor lizards among reptiles is a large heart, which enables breathing through long sprints when chasing prey. Like other lizards, Dragons reproduce by laying eggs.

Komodo Dragons look fierce and think smart. They cooperatively hunt in pairs, one as decoy drawing a protective parent crocodile from their young, and the other swooping for a feast. Sometimes Dragons play nicely together and share the feast. When held in zoos, zookeepers record a knowing recognition by their wards of the hands that feed them.[146]

Taking a Komodo Dragon as a pet is illegal. Few people would want one. Reptile skin is rough and dry. As the dragon ages, skin becomes tough and craggy, contributing to reduction in poaching, since old dragon skin looks awful on a handbag. Dragons have four squatty legs and an oblong body, doubled in length with a long, powerful tail.

Dragons have sixty sharp teeth and perpetual gingivitis. Scientists ponder whether victims of a Dragon attack are more likely to die from lacerations by sharp teeth, or venom dispatched into the wound by frontal fangs. For victims, distinction is academic.

---

[145] Monitor lizards on the loose proliferate in Florida.
[146] The Komodo Dragon exhibit at the Washington Zoo is a dark, hidden corner of the reptile compound. The Komodo Dragon in the small, cement cell, does not look happy. There is no room to run and no beach.

Komodo Dragons attack humans. They are by nature aggressive. Fortunately, for alert humans willing to accept a hint, dragons give warning before they attack. A dragon irritated or feeling cornered will hiss and swish their tail. This is a sign that walking away from the dragon is the better part of good judgement.

Dragons have poor hearing and very bad night vision. Non-moving objects are less likely seen at night. Dragons smell with long, yellow, forked tongues, which is why they walk with their tongues out, swaying in the breeze. They can smell food five miles away.

It is difficult to outrun a racing Komodo Dragon. They claw the ground for traction, as they propel forward with aide of their tail. When pursuing prey up a tree, dragons have been seen standing on hind legs, balanced by their tail. Docile puppies, they are not.

Komodo Dragons are cold-blooded lizards. They conserve body heat at night and spend hours in the sun during the day. They have a narrow comfort zone. A sure sign of Dragons nearby is a deep furrow, clawed from earth as a sleeping chamber. During the heat of the day, Dragons prefer shade.

Looking like creatures from a primeval world, it is logical to wonder whether Komodo Dragons are related to dinosaurs, which survived cataclysmic environmental change. In fact, they are. From eleven to two million years ago, in the Pleistocene, the age of dinosaurs, ancestors of Komodo Dragons roamed in Australia. In the movement of continents and formation of the Indonesian archipelago, giant lizards ended up in Australia and the few Indonesian islands of the Pacific group, that is, east of the Wallace Line. Of Australian cousins to Komodo Dragons, only remains exist.

Alfred Russel Wallace, the great naturalist, who arrived at the theory of adaptation to environment, otherwise known as evolution, through exhaustive study in jungles of Borneo and New Guinea, never came to Komodo. It is unfortunate not to have his insight on why Komodo has dragons, long after dinosaurs became extinct, or why Komodo Dragons, in their habitat are so much larger than other monitor lizards. Wallace placed the eastern islands of Indonesia, from Bali east, including Komodo, on the east side of the Wallace Line, which divides Asia from the Pacific, grouping Komodo with Australia.

The debate on size in adaptation to environment is ongoing. Some scientists conclude that other lizards survived in their habitats by growing smaller. Other scientists conclude the Komodo Dragon survived by growing larger, or sustained size in their unique environment. Scientists agree upon survival of Komodo Dragons being dependent upon isolation from humans.

On other islands of Indonesia, monitor lizards were harvested for medicines and their skins used in drums. Some lizards became extinct, while others are endangered. Ugly and dangerous, monitor lizards have a place in the food chain and are protected by law today.

On Komodo Islands, Dragons preserve their environment. Smaller lizards and animals are prey, not competitors.[147] Aggressive dragons keep their population in check by attacks on each other. Dragons attack humans, a fact that has not hindered migrants to the islands. Only humans present a danger to Komodo Dragons and threaten their existence.

There are three thousand Komodo dragons in the wild. Game wardens protect Dragons from poaching. A greater danger to populations comes from diminished prey. Human populations, hunting deer and small game, compete with Dragons for food.

Komodo Island Habitat Sanctuary to National Park

Komodo Dragons are found only on Komodo, Padar, Flores, Rinca and Gili Motang islands, all part of the Sunda Islands group of Indonesia. Komodo, Rinca, Padar and Gili Motang constitute Komodo National Park, where human habitation was almost non-existent until recently. Two million people live on Flores, which was a Portuguese bastion in Indonesia, prior to control by the Dutch.

---

[147] In World Heritage Site recognition for Komodo National Park, the World Heritage Commission noted an abundance of animal and bird species. Small animals are prey. WHC.unesco.org, last visited April 12, 2020.

Komodo Dragon at Komodo National Park (by Adhi Rachdian)

Early history of Komodo Island exists in legend. Sunda Islands were unnamed until recent history. Komodo Island, and nearby islands, were remote havens for pirates and a place for exiles from larger islands, or renegades from ships. Reference to Komodo Island as a convict camp infers organized action by kings of neighboring Bima maintaining a prison on the island. There is no history, or archaeology, to support stories of convict habitation.

Archaeology on Komodo Island is a rare event. An ancient population, now extinct, existed on the islands. Indigenous inhabitants numbered about thirty by the early twentieth century. Some current residents claim descendancy from indigenous Ata Modo people. In earlier centuries, most people were taken away by pirates. The Dutch recorded few Ata Modo people on Komodo Island in 1910. Later records indicate there were none.

Management of Komodo Dragon habitat by the Indonesian government dates to 1938, prior to national independence. In 1980, a National Park was created, increasing protection for Dragons. Laws strengthening government commitment to protection of dragon islands were enacted in 1990, precipitating disputes with people claiming connection to the island through ancient ancestors.

In Komodo National Park, Komodo Island has the largest population of Dragons, numbering around eighteen hundred. The park mandate requires maintaining the ecosystem for Dragons on land and aquatic life in the sea. A no negative impact management imperative contends with rising tourism and demands of Ata Modo descendants and extended family, to return to Komodo Island. Funding for Komodo National Park comes from the Indonesian government, supplemented with international contributions and dock fees. The park was designated a World Heritage Site in 1991.

Battle for Dragons on Komodo

Dutch scientists immediately knew in 1910, that beasts they studied were special. The island group was designated a preservation area, a unique concept in the early twentieth century. At that time, extinction of the human population was imminent.[148] Only dragons were an object of preservation.

The Indonesian government tallies the human population of Komodo Island from extinction at the beginning of the twentieth century, to several hundred residents by mid-century, to four thousand residents today. There were fewer than one thousand residents upon Komodo National Park designation. Residents demanded and received electricity, enabling permanency of homes. Park designation attracted new residents, contrary to park management objectives.

Residents of Komodo Island claim generations of connection to the island, as they resist relocation. Restricted from fishing, which has long been illegal around the islands, and from hunting, in competition with dragons for food, residents wage a media war of a people oppressed. Resident proponents cite government desire to remove subsistence residents in contrast with attracting wealthy foreign tourists to view dragons.

At the same time the Indonesian government is negotiating with residents on the ground, they are involved in a sea war with illegal fishermen, using environmentally destructive means. Bomb fishing employs beer bottles with

---

[148] Dutch recorded about five residents, over child-bearing age.

kerosene and fertilizer exploding in fish habitat. Fish are not caught, they are collected. Habitat is destroyed. Armed fishermen wage a fierce gun and bomb battle with government agents over access to Komodo.

As the world discovered Dragons, poaching began. Illegal taking of dragons for zoos and private collections so endangered populations, that the government put a closure order on park visits for all 2020. Komodo was removed from cruise ship itineraries. Controlling random visitor craft was difficult. Resolving issues of resident access to dragons was even more difficult.

Looking Forward to Komodo

Kanawa Island Tourist Area (by Jordy Meow)

Tourism on Komodo Island has an upside and downside for Komodo Dragons. On the upside, tourism necessitates government presence on the island, funded by port fees, which deters poachers and illegal fishermen. On the downside, resident populations are drawn to the island by economic opportunity of a tourist economy.

The Indonesian government looks to the Galapagos as a model, where tourism, under controlled circumstances, encourages and funds habitat preservation. Galapagos Islands are a government managed preservation area, which enjoys private funding for research, and has a permanent population in a contained urban center.

Increased port fees and charges for visitor access are coming to Komodo Island. There is no desire to build city on Komodo. Plans of the government for a resort have abated. For Komodo to operate on the scale of a Galapagos in Indonesia, would turn natural Komodo into zoo Komodo. The allure of Komodo for visitors is its exotic, natural environment. Environmentally responsible tourism is mutually beneficial for travelers and dragons. Ecosystem management is the course of the future.

Note: Kanawa Island is a resort community outside Komodo National Park on the island of Flores, which is served by an airport. Tourism and population on Flores are not in contention. Day trips from Flores take visitors to Komodo.

CREATING UNITY OUT OF DIVERSITY IN INDONESIA

Gunawan Kartapranata Creative Commons

Indonesia is a land of ancient culture and recent nation status. The population of more than two hundred and forty million people is comprised of over two hundred cultural and language groups. The country comprises nineteen hundred islands, spread across the equator at a distance as wide as Europe, or the United States. The population is ninety percent Muslim, with disparate views of Indonesia as a Muslim or secular state. Keeping modern Indonesia unified is a work of statesmanship.

Indonesia was formed under adverse circumstances as the Dutch East Indies. Once independent, the country retained geography under adversity. It ended the twentieth century stained by massacre and corruption. Organized in 1949 as a democracy, Indonesia experienced its first transition from one democratically elected president to another in 2014. In 2019, the president was given a second term, making democracy a decade deep.

It is fitting that the landscape of Indonesia is resplendent with volcanoes. The rich, black volcanic soil nurtured nutmeg, worth its weight in gold in eighteenth century Europe. Tin, tea and sugar produced wealth in the nineteenth century and oil in the twentieth century, benefits of which were held beyond the native population. Injustice erupted in twentieth to twenty-first century bloody revolts, until violence as a means of response to oppression was literally washed away by a tsunami. Peace is a treasured commodity.

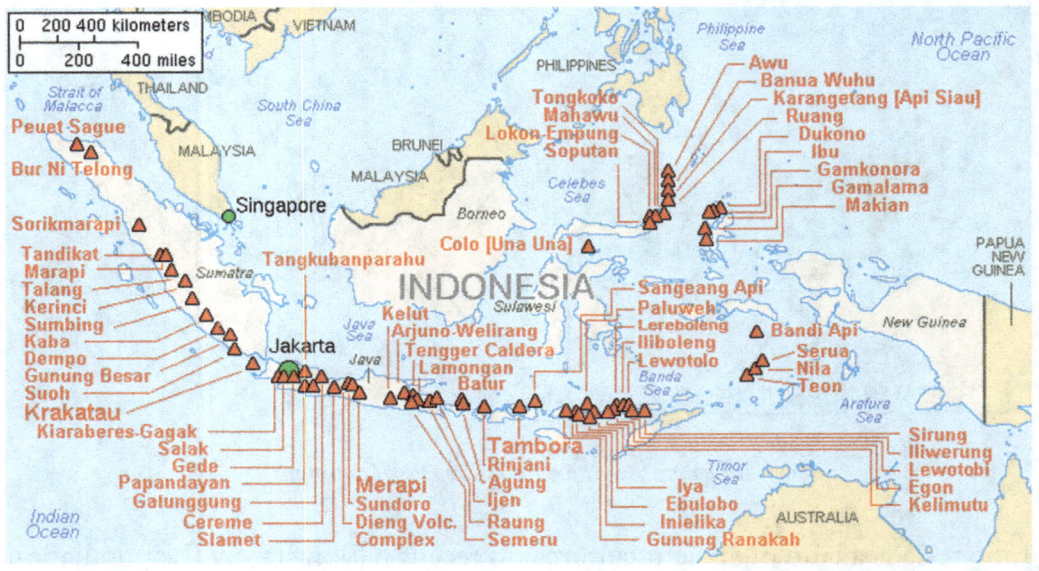

Map of Indonesia noting Volcanoes (Public Domain)

Melding vast and diverse islands into a national whole requires a vision of national identity. Most Indonesian political, religious and ideological faction group leaders agree on that goal. Factions diverge on accomplishing national identity against dreams of a mythological Righteous Prince and a reality of three centuries of Dutch domination. Developing identity borne of organic history, disregarding the feudal era, without criticism of contradiction, is a work in progress.

The making of modern Indonesia is a multi-faceted epic, reduced here to a few pages, to introduce this fascinating country to travelers. Modern Indonesia, experienced by visitors, was the product of world events, not under its control.

It was sought as a trading venue, colonized by fortuitous opportunity, then broken from feudalism by force of Japanese invasion in World War II. Talented, strong-willed Javanese wrested the Dutch East Indies from a return to feudalism by creating independent Indonesia at great human cost. This is a story of Indonesia, as it strives to remain unified, peaceful, and prosperous.

A Spice-Driven World

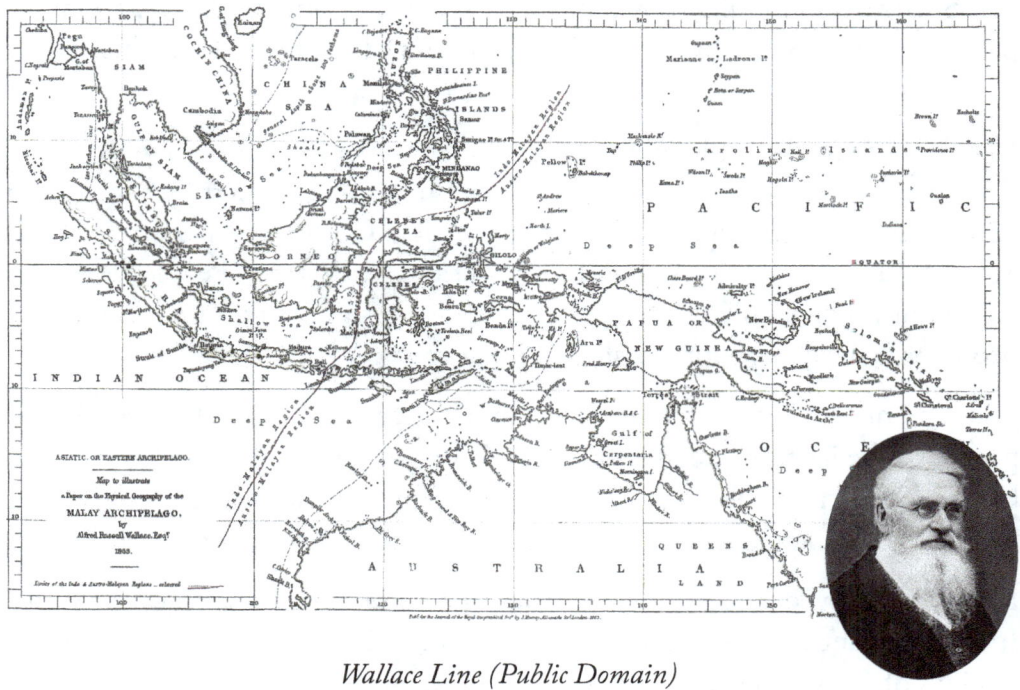

Wallace Line (Public Domain)

Indonesia stretches over three thousand, two hundred miles from Aceh, at the northern tip of Sumatra, east across Java and Bali, flanked by Borneo, Sulawesi, Maluku, and Halmahera Islands on the north and Timor on the south, ending at the line drawn across New Guinea, in which West New Guinea, now known as Papua New Guinea, forms the eastern national border. Over nineteen thousand islands are grouped into twenty-seven provinces of modern Indonesia. North Borneo island is home to a piece of Malaysia and the separate sultanate of Brunei. East New Guinea is in Oceania, not Indonesia.

Indonesia is an archipelago of volcanic peaks, ripped from two continents. The genius of the concept of adaptability of the species to environment, otherwise known as evolution, Alfred Russel Wallace, traipsed across Indonesian islands, until he was stricken by malaria in 1858. In addition to noticing that species adapted to different island environments, Wallace saw a point of divide between plants and animals of Asia and those of the South Pacific and Australia ecosystems. In tribute to Wallace, in 1859, an English biologist, Thomas Henry Huxley, named the division between Asian and Australian zones the Wallace Line. The Wallace Line runs north to south and cuts between Borneo and Sulawesi, continuing down between Bali and Lombok. Most Indonesian people live west of the line. The fabled spice islands lie to the east. There are no tigers east of the Wallace Line.

Remains of small people, with elongated feet, dated to ninety-five thousand years ago, were found in Indonesian islands. The modern population is descendant from the Malay dispersal, that left China seven thousand years ago, and arrived in the islands two thousand years later. People developed communities of family clans. Concepts of princes and kings are recent. Early people practiced ancestor worship, evident today.

In final centuries before the current era and into first centuries of the current era, people of the islands traded goods with China and India. Modern Indonesian language is heavily blended Malay, Chinese and early Indian. Early writing was Sanskrit, a language of India, that is older than Greek and Latin.

Religion received from India, Hindu, and Buddhist, was prevalent across Indonesia, until transformation to Muslim. Muslims of Indonesia retain vestiges of early belief systems, including reverence to ancestors.

Traders from the mainland were followed by armies. The concept of kings, sultans, and rajah in Indonesia adapted from India, as a response to external pressure, requiring organization of clans into larger, defensible social units.[149] In Sanskrit literature, a mythical Righteous Prince arises to lead his people. In Indonesian legend, the Righteous Prince receives blessings to rule from the Goddess of the Southern Ocean.

---

[149] See generally, Tim Hannigan, A Brief History of Indonesia, Tuttle, 2015.

Goddess of the Southern Ocean

General Gajah Mada of Majapahit Empire (Museum Jakarta by Taman Renyah)

Goddess of the Southern Ocean began in West Java myths of a princess banished by her father for refusing a chosen suitor. She remained a force over the oceans. Would-be kings sought her mandate to rule, before presenting themselves as the next Righteous Prince. Today in Java, politicians give offerings to the powerful Goddess, prior to elections.

In 1293, the great Kublai Kahn was duped into assisting a prince of Java defeat his enemy, only to have the prince lure Kahn's army into a fatal trap, once the enemy was vanquished. Thus began the pre-colonial empire of Majapahit. Harkening to the legendary Majapahit Empire, twentieth century Indonesians rekindled nationalism.

The Majapahit Empire golden age in music, dance, and batik art, was led by Elephant General Gajah Mada, who died in 1364, and his Righteous Prince Hayam Wuruk, who lived to 1389. Their great kingdom was less than a third of present-day Indonesia.

Consolidation of many islands into a national unit began in the sixteenth century. The harbinger of change was nutmeg. Indian and Chinese traders came for spice over the centuries. The great captain of Chinese Treasure Fleets, Zheng He arrived in 1407. Trade, not conquest, was the objective. Over the century, Muslim Arab traders favored trade with Muslim locals, which precipitated conversion among kings of port towns, who fostered conversion to Islam among their subjects. In 1527, an ambitious King Demak of Java consolidated his holdings on Java by supplanting Hindu priests. As sole Muslim king, Demak controlled spice trade.

Portuguese traders reached Melaka of the spice islands in 1511. Their cargoes of nutmeg were worth their weight in gold in European markets. Dutch sailors, already possessing great ability at sea, decided to obtain a share of spice trade profit by sailing to the source and supplanting the Portuguese. So many European ships came to Maluku harbors for nutmeg, that savvy locals raised prices. Regulation of Dutch trade by creation of a monopoly organization, established by the Dutch ruler, the Stadholder, began the Dutch East India Company, known by its initials VOC.[150]

---

[150] In Dutch the East India Company (DEIC) is Vereingde Oostindische Compagnie or VOC. For more on the DEIC, read Cruise through History Itinerary XII Port of Amsterdam.

The VOC was formed in 1602, as the first publicly held, foreign trade investment consortium. Anyone in the Netherlands had access to purchase shares of stock. By holding stock in a company of several ships, making numerous sailings in a year, investment at risk in a single venture was reduced. Successful sailings brought so much profit to the VOC, that the occasional ship lost at sea was not a financial catastrophe.

In a few years of numerous voyages, VOC established a local office in Ambon, in Maluku Islands. English merchants arrived in 1618 and operated from the west end of Java, named Jayakarta by its vassal prince Wijayakrama. Soon, Java's king, English, and VOC agents, viewed Jayakarta as the most attractive harbor in the area.

Thus began VOC forceful control of the islands. VOC forces battled Englishmen and the prince, in addition to remaining Portuguese, for control of ports. The Javanese king ruled the interior. Dutch supremacy in the spice trade was established by 1667, when the Dutch negotiated the Treaty of Breda with the English, resolving trade disputes across the globe.[151] In the treaty, the English received New Amsterdam from the Dutch. The Dutch kept their East Indies. They called their new port city Batavia. Profits from spices shipped from Batavia to Europe brought great wealth to the Netherlands.

An Accidental Colony

By the end of the eighteenth century, cost of operations in Batavia outstripped income derived by the VOC from spices. Protecting Dutch domain in Batavia required large armies in expensive forts. Directors of VOC reduced profits by self-dealing in cargo shipped on VOC vessels. Corruption and increased costs of operation resulted in deferred maintenance of canals and other Batavia infrastructure. VOC directors paid themselves with bank loans against future cargo.

---

[151] Treaty of Breda of 1667 goes beyond this story. Parties were England, the Dutch, France and Denmark, which controlled Norway. The treaty was one of four in ongoing trade conflicts, where parties staked claims to East and West Indies and north America. England protected claims to New York, New Jersey, Pennsylvania and Delaware. The Dutch kept Suriname. France claimed French Guiana and Acadia, known today as Quebec.

Submission of Prince to Dutch in Java War (Public Domain)

When Napoleon invaded Holland in 1799 and opened VOC books, he found records falsified profits.[152] The VOC was insolvent. Napoleon made his brother Luis Bonaparte prince of the Netherlands. Louis ended the VOC, ended its use of slaves, then impressed local laborers to build the Great Post Road across Java. The road was the first national infrastructure project.

French control was short lived. When Britain invaded Holland in 1811, British agent Thomas Stamford Raffles, a clerk in the British East India Company, was tasked with reorganizing Batavia. That he did. He was given orders to dislodge the Dutch and give Java back to the Javanese. At age thirty, Raffles decided to turn his assignment on its head and create a new economy in the islands, under control of British agents.

Raffles utilized British troops to storm Yogyakarta in central Java, usurp the sultan, and set up the sultan's son as a puppet ruler of a feudal workforce of peasant farmers, producing cash crops for export. Then Raffles replicated his actions in Borneo, Bali and Sumatra. Non-compliant royals were exiled to the old VOC fortress at Maluku. The islands of future Indonesia were a feudal colony of Britain.

---

[152] Hannigan, at 40.

On other islands, royals anticipated arrival of Raffles by leasing royal lands to European and Chinese absentee agents. Royals remained in place as feudal managers of former family lands. Food crops became cash crops of coffee, tea, and sugar. Peasants rented plots of land and were expected to pay rent in cash, a new concept in the islands. Income from exports and rents went to the British foreign office in Batavia

After the fall of Napoleon, for the second time in 1815, Britain negotiated with the Dutch for transfer of control of the expanded Dutch East Indies. The Java colony was lucrative for the Netherlands, more so than a VOC trading post. The Dutch placed higher expectations than Raffles on export production from farms. Severely oppressed peasants died in fields where they worked.

Royals did not submit to rule as a colony without dissent. A minor royal in Yogyakarta envisioned himself an incarnation of the Righteous Prince, blessed by the Goddess of the Southern Ocean in 1824, to rid Java of the Dutch. In a five-year war, the Dutch lost half their forces, while two hundred and fifty thousand Javanese died. The prince was exiled to Sulawesi.

For the remainder of the nineteenth century, retention of lands in the Dutch colony required military action. After rebellion in central Java, Dutch forces interceded in Bali and neighboring Lombok. Britain retained the lucrative pepper export town of Aceh, when the Netherlands assumed control of the colony in 1815. Aceh was in continual revolt. In 1871, Britain and the Netherlands met in the Hague and ceded Aceh to the Dutch. Britain received the gold coast of Ghana. Local rulers were not parties to the negotiation. One hundred thousand more people died in the Dutch taking of Aceh.

Artificial Economy of Feudal/Colonial Dutch Indies

In 1906, Dutch forces landed on the beach of Sanur, in southeast Bali. They were greeted by a ritual procession of royals and attendants in white robes, with flowers in their hair. The king stepped down from a sedan chair and performed ritual suicide. Dutch troops fired on unarmed attendants, until a pile of one thousand bodies lay in the road.

The Massacre of Bandung marked the end of a century of Dutch colonial feudal policy. In the Hague, Dutch leaders initiated an Ethical Policy for the Dutch East Indies. Having reaped substantial economic gain from the Indies, the policy required the Netherlands to invest in its colony. Schools, hospitals, and roads were built. Locals previously forbidden to use Dutch language, were now taught in Dutch, in Dutch schools, where former royal youth were learning to become proper Dutch civil servants.

The Netherlands, and its East Indies colony, was neutral during World War I. Tourism in Bali and Jakarta was a factor in the local economy by 1914. After the war, tourism blossomed. New hotels and beach resorts appeared. Although there was a clear demarcation by race of hotel guests, who were European, and workers, who were natives, a middle class of indigenous men and woman, plus Chinese, was growing in the Dutch East Indies. Among the natives was a growing, educated, group of intellectuals, who led the Dutch East Indies toward an independent Indonesia later in the twentieth century.

Indies or Indonesia – Defining Reality Post-World War II

Just as Napoleon dislodged entrenched nobles from thrones, ushering in modern Europe at the end of the eighteenth century, the Japanese invasion of South East Asia in the Second World War, disrupted colonial holds on the Asian continent in the twentieth century. The Dutch surrendered the East Indies colony to Japan on March 8, 1942. Japan turned Batavia into Djakarta. Dutch and other foreigners were imprisoned. Street signs and forms of colonial rule were stripped from the landscape. It

President Sukarno (Public Domain)

was the Dutch turn to starve, as they labored to build the Pekanburu Railroad, where tens of thousands died.

In 1945, upon surrender of Japan, British administrators came to Jakarta, leading a provisional government. Dutch emerged from prison, expecting to retake their homes and businesses. They assumed Britain would once again turn over the colony to them. Dutch citizens, who lived most of their lives in the Indies, and mixed people of locals and Europeans, dreamed of the rise of Batavia, just as freedom fighting royals and other rebels dreamed for centuries of Majapahit.

In reality, Indies was becoming Indonesia, even before the war. In the opening given to political parties, free press, and organized labor, a rising middle class of young intellectuals became political. Iconic of the movement was Sukarno, the single name, charismatic, orator, who knew how to organize a crowd. Born in Java in 1901, with a Muslim father and Balinese, Hindu mother, Sukarno exemplified the new Indonesia, Muslim, yet politically secular. The fez style cap was the Sukarno trademark of the man culturally Indonesian, yet modern and forward looking.

In 1930, Sukarno was arrested by the Dutch. Though he gave a stirring speech advocating anti-colonialism and freedom to govern, he was given a four-year jail sentence. Meanwhile, in another trial for leading unrest, this one at the Hague, Mohammad Hatta, a Javanese educated in Holland, also gave a brilliant speech about an end to colonialism. He was found not guilty.

The war with Japan ended so abruptly, there was little time to plan transition. Sukarno and Hatta were negotiating with the Japanese for independent rule in Indonesia. Militant youth came to the pair, forming a shield in moments of uncertainty. As the Japanese were packing, and Dutch emerged from incarceration, British administrators took the "D" from Djakarta. Dutch return to control was not an option.

In the morning of August 17, 1945, Sukarno went on radio, reading a proclamation of Indonesian independence. Flabbergasted Dutch took a last stand in West New Guinea. Hatta quickly prepared a constitution. By the time British administrators arrived, they found an Indonesian government organization taking shape through the islands. People cried, *merdeka*, freedom. A new flag flew.

Sukarno was the first president of independent Indonesia, a post he held until 1967. Often criticized for extending his rule in a democratic country, Sukarno was quick to recognize that challenges of diversity in Indonesia would dissolve unity unless government remained firm. Indonesia began as a republic of a cluster of local island identities. Forging unity meant fighting competing ideologies, including the rise of communism, in a nation where banks were owned by Dutch firms and a staggering war debt was claimed by Netherlands. Not until 1949, did the Dutch cede all territory, except West New Guinea.[153]

In 1962, the Dutch turned to the United Nations to resolve West New Guinea. The UN gave the territory to Indonesia. Papua New Guinea became the twenty-sixth province of Indonesia. In Jakarta, Sukarno commissioned a towering national monument to unity.

The initial Indonesian parliament was so divided on local identity and ideologies of socialism, political Islam and nationalism, that it could not deliver legislation. Sukarno declared martial law, made himself president for life, repudiated debt to the Dutch and repatriated one hundred thousand long-time resident Chinese to China. Despite his flamboyant lifestyle, his several wives and heavy hand in government, Sukarno, in his white suit and black fez, was a national treasure.

Early one morning in 1965, while people slept, six of Sukarno's generals were shot and tossed into a well. One general escaped. The so-called September Movement was attributed to communists. Across Indonesia there were violent reprisals against communists. The actual instigator of the purge has never been determined.

Emerging from the void in military leadership, in a time of waning support for Sukarno, was a quiet, understated General Suharto. In 1967, Sukarno was placed in house arrest in Jakarta, where he died in 1970. Suharto became acting president and later elected president of a tumultuous nation. Inflation was

---

[153] Also jailed by the Dutch for independence efforts was Pramoedya Ananta Toer, later jailed by Sukarno for supporting rights of Chinese. Toer's story of emerging from feudalism was written while incarcerated. *The Earth of Mankind*, first published in 1980, is an autobiographical account of the end of feudalism, Japanese occupation and beginning of Indonesia independence.

600%, areas of the country were in crumbling or non-existent infrastructure, and violence threatened unity.

Suharto, born in 1921, in a rural, modest community, spent his adult life in the military. In contrast to Sukarno, Suharto was a family man, of little apparent ambition and no skills as an orator. He brought to Indonesia economists from the University of California at Berkeley, invited foreign investment, including Standard Oil and Dutch Shell, and opened forests to timbering.

Suharto's tenure is known for an astounding reduction in inflation to single digits, high rise developments in Jakarta, and expansion of infrastructure, including freeways in west Java. He is also known for maintaining unity by using the military. In 1975, Indonesia invaded East Timor, the twenty-seventh Indonesian province. In 1991, the military fired on protestors in East Timor, Papua, and Aceh. In 1992, Suharto received a sixth term as president. Before 2000, UN Peacekeepers entered East Timor.

Balancing Diversity and Unity in Modern Indonesia

2014 Presidential Inauguration (Public Domain)

In 1999, ninety percent of eligible voters elected President Abdurrahman Wahid. Wahid had an international view of Indonesia in world commerce. He was Muslim, tolerant of other religions. He favored trade with Israel and designated Chinese New Year an optional worker holiday. His tolerant views led to impeachment two years into his term.

Wahid was succeeded by his deputy Megawati Sukamoputri, daughter of Sukarno. She connected with diverse peoples of the many islands. She oversaw prosecution and execution of terrorist bombers in Bali in 2002. She was unable to quell violence in Aceh. Megawati left office in October 2004 and in December violence in Aceh finally ended, when an earthquake off the coast of Sumatra, measuring 9.0 on the Richter scale, resulted in a tsunami that washed over Aceh and coastlines of the Indian Ocean.

In 2014, Indonesia experienced the first non-violent transition in power from one democratically elected president to another. Seventh president of Indonesia, Joko Widodo, known as Jokowi, received a second term in 2019. Adored by Indonesians as a reformist, in his second term he calmed political Islamists and continued infrastructure development, while maintaining responsible fiscal management.

Issues of cultural diversity, once threatening unity in Indonesia, are replaced by issues of religious ideology impacting efforts of a secular government. In a land of volcanoes, amid incursion of other nations in the seas, competing for food, and a desire for international commerce to support rising expectations of Indonesians, the goal of diversity within a democracy continues to be threatened by ethnic strife. The country can thrive in democracy without ending unity. Achieving peace in unity is a work in progress.[154]

---

[154] See also, Adrian Vickers, A History of Modern Indonesia, Cambridge University Press, 2013.

INDEX

A

Ainu, 115, 125-129
Aquino, Benigno Jr., 261
Aquino, Corazon, 252-253, 260, 262-263, 266
Architectural Style
    Five-Point Forts, 128-129
    Icon, 196, 197, 199, 233
    Imperial, 32, 34, 112, 121, 171, 185, 193
    Japanese Buddhist, 34, 36, 49, 64, 71
    Spanish Baroque, 210, 254
    Vernacular, 153
    Victorian, 210, 234
Arok, Ken, 303-304, 323
Arroyo, Gloria, 265

B

Bandung (Sanur) Massacre, 327, 346
Basho, Matsuo, 60
Battle
    Formosa (1944), 243
    Hakodate (1868), 129, 131
    Leyte Gulf (1944), 259
    Liaoluo Bay (1633 & 1661), 247-248
    Midway (1942), 85
    Tsushima (1905), 27, 173
    Veracruz (1846)
Bering, Vitus, 11, 16-28
Bolshevik Revolution, 210
Bonifacio, Andrés, 256
Bonsai, 11, 46-47, 61-62
Boxer Rebellion, 193-194, 228
Burdett-Coutts, Angela, 290

C

Chelyuskin, Semion, 22, 27
Chiang Kai-shek, 195, 212-216, 235, 244-245, 249-250
Chinese Dynasties
    Han, 146, 162-167, 181-182, 186, 188, 191, 240
    Ming, 63, 165, 168, 170, 180-185, 188, 198, 202, 204-205, 210, 212, 221, 246-247
    Qin, 165-167
    Qing, 132, 168, 180-184, 188, 191, 202, 213, 242, 246-247
    Song, 168, 201
    Tang, 168-170, 201
Chirikov, Aleksei, 20-22, 26
Chung Ju Ung, 178
Columbus, Christopher, 220, 269
Communist Chinese, 88, 176, 184, 195-196, 203, 214-217
Confucius, 47-48, 148, 159, 167, 169, 203-204, 221, 223-224, 240
Conrad, Joseph, 12, 123, 290
    Lord Jim, 123
Cook, James, 18, 25, 28
Cousins, Norman, 90
Covarrubias, Miguel, 315, 326
Cultural Revolution, 38, 184, 195, 216, 227

D

Dayak people, 285-290
Deng Xiaoping, 196
Doll Theater, 11, 97-98, 102-109
Duterte, Rodrigo, 265, 281, 296

E

East India Company, 172, 221-222, 241, 286, 310
Encomienda, 255

F

Forbidden City, 168, 179-198, 205

G

Geisha, 46, 50-60, 64
Gidayu, Takemoto, 102
Goryokaku Fort, 83, 125-132
Goto Shinpei, 246-247
Green Gang, 211

H

Habu, Junko, 115
Haenyeo, 148, 155
Haiku, 11, 46-47, 60-61
Haru, 149-151, 156
Hatta, Mohammad, 347
Hermit Kingdom, 151, 168
Hiragana, 169
Houtman, Cornelis de, 314

J

Jardine, William, 210, 222-225
Javanese Legend, 302-306
 Airlangga, 302-303, 323
 Rangda, 302-303
 Ratu Adil, Just Queen, 302
 Righteous Prince, 11, 297, 302-304, 323, 338, 340, 342, 345
Jomon, 11, 111-123

K

Kabuki, 11, 97-123
Kimono, 47, 50-57, 61, 64-65, 74, 83

Kings, Queens & Other Royals
Agung (Java), 306
Anna (Russia), 17, 21-26
Bolkiah, Hassanal (Brunei), 285, 295-296
Brooke, Sir Charles Johnson (Sarawak), 291-294
Brooke, James (Sarawak), 286-291
Brooke, Ranee Margaret de Windt (Sarawak), 292
Brooke, Sir Vyner (Sarawak), 294
Catherine I (Russia), 21
Cixi (Qing), 180, 189-195, 197
Go-Toba (Japan), 67
Go-Yosei (Japan), 34
Heizei (Japan), 67
Hongli (Qianlong) (Qing China), 180, 188-190
Khan, Genghis (Mongol), 168
Khan, Kublai (Mongol), 170, 181-183, 304
Lenin (Russia), 17, 28
Manuel I (Portugal), 270
Meiji (Japan), 31-43, 49-50, 61, 70, 79, 81, 92-93, 98, 131, 141, 160, 172
Nicholas II (Russia), 27
Peter I (Russia), 11, 17-21
Puyi (Xuantong) (Qing China), 180, 185, 194-195
Qin (China), 165-167
Saifuddien II (Brunei), 290
Saifuddien III (Brunei), 295
Sanjaya (Java), 300
Senopati (Java), 297, 306
Stalin (Russia), 27, 175-176
Suhita (Majapahit), 305
Tajuddin, Ahmad (Brunei), 294
Wijaya, Raden (Majapahit), 304
Yongle (Ming China), 179, 182-183, 198
Kojiki (Chronicles of Japan), 169
Koolhaas, Rem, 196

L

Laptev, Dmitri, 22
Legazpi, Miguel López, 267, 275, 287
Liao Tianding, 246-250

M

MacArthur, General Douglas, 86-88, 134, 176, 258-259
Magellan, Ferdinand, 267-273, 287
Mahabharata, 297-298, 306
Majapahit Empire, 285, 299, 303-308, 341
Mansion Hotel Shanghai, 212
Mao Zedong, 160, 166, 183-185, 195, 198, 214-216, 231
Marcos, Ferdinand, 251, 260-264
Marcos, Imelda, 251-253, 259-266
Mataram Empire, 300, 302-304
Matheson, James, 210, 222-225
Meiji Restoration, 31, 40, 61, 70, 79, 92, 98, 104, 112, 121, 131, 173
Minamoto, Yorimoto, 31, 34, 70
Museum
    Beijing History, 198
    Bering Discovery (Petropavlovsk), 16-17, 29
    Bomb (Nagasaki), 94
    Edo-Tokyo, 32, 103
    Imperial Collections (Tokyo), 41
    Jomon Culture (Aomori), 116, 120
    Le Mayeur (Denpasar), 325
    Meiji Restoration (Nagoya), 40
    Morikami (Delray Beach FL), 65
    National China (Beijing), 198
    National History (Taipei), 197
    Nebuta Matsuri (Aomori), 110, 112, 123
    Palace Museum (Forbidden City), 180, 186, 197
    Peace Memorial (Hiroshima), 90
    Puri Lukisan (Ubud), 326
    Shanghai History, 212
    Taipei National Palace, 250
    Taiwan Aboriginal, 249
    Tokyo National, 42, 63
Musha Incident, 243

N

Napier, Lord William, 172, 223-225
Nationalist Chinese, 184-185, 194-196, 201-203, 211-215, 243-245, 250
Noguchi, Isamu, 90
Noh, 11, 97, 98-109, 170

O

O'Kuni, Izumo, 104
Opium, 172, 207, 212, 219, 223-225, 242
Origami, 46-47, 61, 65

P

Peace Memorial, 89-94
Pedjeng Moon, 321
Pei Tsuyee, 211
Pekanburu Railroad, 347
Perry, Commodore Matthew C, 11, 36, 68-69, 79-81, 133-142, 172
Polo, Marco, 168
Polo, Niccolo & Matteo, 168
Potsdam Declaration, 85

R

Raffles, Thomas Stamford, 301, 344-345
Ramos, Fidel, 280
Renku, 60
Rice, 12, 36, 78, 117, 165, 168-169, 200, 202-205, 221, 239, 285, 314, 318-327

Righteous Prince, 11, 297, 302-304, 323, 338, 340-342, 345
Rizal, José, 281, 283
Roosevelt, Franklin, 86, 174-175, 258
Roosevelt, Theodore, 173, 257

S

Sakamoto Ryoma, 66, 74, 81
San Juan, Catarina, 277-279
Sanskrit, 287, 297, 200, 303, 316, 322, 340
Sassoon, Sir Ellice Victor Elias, 210
Sen no Riku, 56-57
September Movement, 348
Shadow Puppets (Wayang kulit), 98, 299, 305-309, 322-326
Shanghai Massacre, 215
Shakushain, 127
Shibusawa, Count Shibusawa Eiichi, 40
Shikibu, Murasaki, 169
 Tale of Genji, 169
Shinto, 34, 38-40, 46-50, 59, 61-62, 70, 74, 96, 98, 107, 123, 156, 170
Ships
 Chelyuskin, 22, 27
 USS *Fulton*, 136
 General Sherman, 173
 USS *Maine*, 256
 Mayflower, 134
 USS *Mississippi*, 139
 Royalist, 288
 St. Paul, 26
 St. Peter, 24-26
 Sibirakov, 27
 Sphinx- CSS Stonewall-Kotetsu-Azuma, 129-130
 USS *Susquehanna*, 139
Shodo, 46, 59
Shónagon, Sei, 169
 Pillow Book, 169
Simawn, Sya'ir Awang, 287, 290

Soong, Charles Jones, 212-213
Soong, (Kung) Ai-ling, 212-213
Soong, (Sun) Ching-ling, 212-215
Soong (Chiang) Mei-ling, 212-214
Spies, Walter, 324-326
Steller, Georg Wilhelm, 24-26
Suharto, 348-349
Sukarno, 311, 327, 346-350
Sun Yat Sun, 194-195, 212-214

T

Taiwan Relations Act (1979), 245
Takeda Ayasaburo, 128-129
Tea, 46-47, 50, 53-59, 62, 65, 71, 76, 100, 168, 170-172, 207, 224, 242, 338, 345
Temples
 Beisi Ta (Suzhou), 205
 Borobudur (Java), 297, 300-302
 Elephant Cave (Ubud), 316-317
 Itsukushima Shrine (Hiroshima), 96
 Kinkaku-ji (Golden Pavilion) (Kyoto), 71-72
 Man Mo (Hong Kong), 229
 Pak Tai (Hong Kong), 229
 Pedjeng (Ubud), 321
 Prambanan (Yogykarta), 300
 Pura Batukan (Bali), 316
 Pura Besakih (Bali), 316
 Ryoan-ji (Kyoto), 64
 Senso-ji (Tokyo), 33-34, 42, 50
 Shinto (Japan), 34, 48-50, 96
 Tenryu-ji (Kyoto), 64
 Wong Tai Sin (Hong Kong), 229
Terracotta Soldiers, 166-167
Tian Tan (Temple of Heaven), 197
Tiananmen Square, 180, 195, 197
Tokugawa, Ieyasu, 31—35, 70-72, 80-81, 91, 121
Tokugawa, Yoshinobu, 141
Tokyo Tower, 43

Treaty
    Breda (1667), 310, 343
    Harris (1858), 34
    Kanagawa (1854), 127, 140-141
    Labuan (1846), 290
    Paris (1898), 256
    San Francisco (1951), 88, 243
    Shimonoseki (1895), 242
    Tianjin (1860), 193
    Tientsin (1885), 242
    Tordesillas (1505), 269-270, 273

U

Urdaneta, Andrés, 275

V

Vancouver, George, 18, 28

W

Wali Songo, 297-309
    Malik Ibrahim, 307-308
    Sunan Ampel, 308
    Sunan Bonang, 308
    Sunan Drajat, 308
    Sunan Girl, 308
    Sunan Gunungjati, 309
    Sunan Kalija, 308-309
    Sunan Kudus, 308-309
    Sunan Muria, 308
Wallace, Alfred Russel, 11, 134, 314, 331, 339-340
War
    Boshin, 112, 129, 141
    Korean, 88, 143, 153, 160, 231
    Opium, 184, 193, 207, 219, 242
    Philippine-American (1899), 253, 257
    Sino-French, 242
    Spanish-American (1898), 251

World War II, 37-38, 42, 46, 85, 106, 141, 151, 154, 160, 173-175, 195, 201, 210, 243, 259, 326, 339
Warring States, 167
Widodo, Joko "Jokowi", 298, 350
World Heritage Sites
    Acapulco-Manila Galleons Trade Route, 277
    Atomic Bomb sites
        Peace Memorial (Japan), 95
    Baroque Churches (Philippines), 254
    Borobudur Temple Compounds (Java), 297
    Emperor Qin Mausoleum (Terracotta Soldiers) (China), 166
    Forbidden City (China), 197
    Grand Canal (China), 168
    Great Wall of China, 165-167
    Himeji Castle (Japan), 83
    Horyu-ji (tower)(Japan), 43
    Humble Administrators Garden (Suzhou), 207
    Jeju Island & Lava Tubes, 146
    Kinkaku-ji (Golden Palace) (Japan), 72
    Komodo National Park, 332-334
    Ming Dynasty Tombs (China), 165
    Mount Fuji (Japan), 123
    Nagasaki Christian Heritage, 91
    National Museum of Western Art (Japan), 63
    Nikko Shrine (Japan), 34
    Peking Man (China), 159
    Prambanan Temple Compounds (Java), 300
    Sannai-Maruyama (pending) (Japan), 116
    Senso-ji (Japan), 34, 42
    Subak System (Bali), 320
    Summer Palace (China), 183, 190
Wright, Frank Lloyd, 40

X

Xavier, St. Francis, 91

Y

Yanaka Cemetery, 35, 42
Yi Sun-Sin, 150

Z

Zen, 11, 46-50, 55-64, 97-102,
    107, 206
Zheng Chenggong (Koxinga), 246-247
Zheng He, 342
Zhou Enlai, 185, 195, 198, 214

www.ingramcontent.com/pod-product-compliance
Lightning Source LLC
Chambersburg PA
CBHW081739100526
44592CB00015B/2238